VOCATIONAL REHABILITATION
OF THE DISABLED:
AN OVERVIEW

Vocational Rehabilitation of The Disabled: *An Overview*

Edited by

David Malikin, New York University

Herbert Rusalem, Columbia University

New York • *NEW YORK UNIVERSITY PRESS*
London • *UNIVERSITY OF LONDON PRESS LIMITED*
1969

Seventh Printing, 1978

Copyright © 1969 by New York University
Library of Congress Catalog Card Number 69-19258
Manufactured in the United States of America

PREFACE

Modern rehabilitation places vast resources at the disposal of hundreds of thousands of disabled persons to assist them to assume functional and satisfying roles in society. This rehabilitation enterprise is growing at an increasing rate year by year, engaging increasingly large numbers of professional workers, institutions, facilities, and programs in services of growing complexity. Before our eyes a rehabilitation explosion is taking place in which voluntary groups in partnership with state and federal agencies are providing improved services for the disabled. In addition to these, over one hundred universities and colleges are training rehabilitation counselors, psychologists, social workers, physicians, occupational and physical therapists, and other specialists, who are better equipped than ever to meet the demands of a society that is increasingly aware of the need for their services.

This book, reflecting in part this massive development, resulted from an experimental lecture program conducted jointly by Hunter College, City University of New York, New York University, Seton Hall University, and Teachers College, Columbia University. The program was made available primarily to the combined student bodies of the four University Rehabilitation Counselor Training programs. Other interested rehabilitation professionals in the community were invited to attend the fifteen lectures as well, and audiences of more than 200 proved that they did.

The chapters of this text are based upon these lectures, which ranged widely over the entire field of vocational rehabilitation and were delivered by distinguished educators, psychologists, and government officials who have extensive competence in rehabilitation practice.

We are indebted to Dr. Elena Gall * of Hunter College, Dr. Patricia Livingston of New York University, Dr. Richard Acciavetti of Seton Hall University, and Dr. Henry Kavkowitz of Teachers College, who, as coordinators of their respective Rehabilitation Counselor Training programs, rendered invaluable assistance in the successful accomplishment of this lecture series. In addition, Dr. Marvin Wayne of Hunter College, Mr. James O'Connor of Seton Hall University, Dr. Jacob Jaffe of Teachers College, and Dr. Wilfred Haber and Dr. Patricia Dvonch of New York University planned and administered the experimental program. We are also indebted to Miss Charlotte Fischer, Shirley Alexander, Celia Gillen, Rae Malikin, and Rosalind Rusalem, who provided much editorial assistance in the preparation of the manuscript. Finally, this program could not have succeeded without the support and participation of the Social and Rehabilitation Service of the U.S. Department of Health, Education, and Welfare.

_____

* Deceased

CONTENTS

CONTRIBUTORS

Salvatore G. Di Michael is Executive Director of the Institute for Crippled and Disabled, New York City. He received his Ph.D. from Fordham University in 1942.

James F. Garrett is Assistant Administrator, Research, Demonstrations, and Training, Social and Rehabilitation Service, Department of Health, Education, and Welfare, Washington, D.C. He received his Ph.D. from New York University in 1941.

Lloyd H. Lofquist is Professor of Psychology and Associate Dean for the Social Sciences in the College of Liberal Arts at the University of Minnesota. He received his Ph.D. from the University of Minnesota in 1955.

John F. McGowan is Dean of the University Extension Division of the University of Missouri. He received his Ed.D. from the University of Missouri in 1954.

John E. Muthard is Head of the Regional Rehabilitation Research Institute and Professor of Rehabilitation Counseling and Education at the University of Florida at Gainesville. He received his Ph.D. from Ohio State University in 1952.

Cecil H. Patterson is Chairman of the Division of Counselor Education and Professor of Educational Psychology at the University of Illinois. He received his Ph.D. from the University of Minnesota in 1955.

Anne Roe is Professor Emerita at Harvard University, and currently a guest lecturer in Psychology at the University of Arizona. She received her Ph.D. from Columbia University in 1933.

Herbert Rusalem is Associate Professor of Education and Assistant Director of The Research and Demonstration Center for the Education of the Handicapped at Columbia University. He received his Ed.D. from Columbia University in 1951.

Milton Schwebel is Dean of the Graduate School of Education, Rutgers University. He received his Ph.D. from Columbia University in 1949.

Daniel Sinick is Director of Rehabilitation Counselor Education and Professor of Education at George Washington University. He received his Ph.D. from New York University in 1955.

Donald E. Super is Director of the Division of Psychology and Education, and Professor of Psychology and Education, Teachers College, Columbia University. He received his Ph.D. from Columbia University in 1940.

Mary Switzer is Administrator of the Social and Rehabilitation Service in the Department of Health, Education, and Welfare, Washington, D.C. In addition to earning a B.A. degree from Radcliffe College, she has received a number of Honorary Doctorates and awards from many private and governmental agencies.

Frederick A. Whitehouse is Coordinator of the Rehabilitation Counselor Training Program, and Professor of Education, Hofstra University. He received his Ed.D. from New York University in 1952.

Beatrice A. Wright is Professor of Psychology at the University of Kansas. She received her Ph.D. from the University of Iowa in 1942.

David Malikin is Associate Professor in the Vocational Rehabilitation Counseling Program at New York University. He received his Ph.D. from New York University in 1961.

PART ONE

VOCATIONAL REHABILITATION: PAST AND PRESENT

INTRODUCTION TO PART ONE

Much of modern vocational rehabilitation can be traced to the passage of the Vocational Rehabilitation Act of 1920. This landmark legislation is almost 50 years old. Yet, with its amendments, it retains the vitality and dynamic potential of a far younger program. By contrast, we have witnessed in the past 50 years the meteoric rise and deceleration of a number of social programs, disappearing or growing moribund in a slow but painful fadeout.

The distinguishing characteristic of American vocational rehabilitation, as reflected in the papers by Garrett, Switzer, and Di Michael in this section, is momentum. Despite its advanced age, as social welfare programs go, the vocational rehabilitation movement in the United States refuses to slow down and live on its past. On the contrary, the pace of change is accelerating. Hardly a year goes by without some substantial legislation being passed to enrich the program in some important way, and, almost weekly, one reads about exciting new program developments, in both the private and public sectors, that steer the movement into new and more challenging areas of service. At the moment, for instance, the horizon is crowded with ideas that are about to burst upon the scene, including new techniques for delivering service to "unmotivated" clients, short- and long-term rehabilitation residence programs, new patterns of meeting the needs of the homebound, and innovations in bringing services to where clients live.

An in-depth history of the vocational rehabilitation movement has yet to be written, but when it is, one of the areas which will merit investigation is that of the forces that keep vocational rehabilitation young. Some clues to rehabilitation's fountain of youth appear in the papers presented in this section. In part, at least, the remarkable vigor and momentum of American vocational

3

rehabilitation seems to derive from the fundamental soundness and incontestable logic of the rehabilitation concept, its unusually competent leadership, the sense of mission that characterizes some of its practitioners, and the well-balanced interplay between public and voluntary efforts. Out of this amalgam of influences has come a capacity for change that seems to overcome the status-quo forces that often permeate various professional fields, the "play-it-safe" attitudes of some public and private bureaucrats, and the lack of imagination of some administrators.

In this regard it is not coincidental that the papers in this section were contributed by individuals who, perhaps more than most others in vocational rehabilitation, not only accept change as inevitable but also take the initiative to bring it about. Some may say that a dynamic field creates its own leaders, but it is more likely that these vital leaders have created rehabilitation as we know it today. If the next generation of leaders also have the capacity to break through the inevitable inertia and retrogression that constantly threatens, the future of vocational rehabilitation is assured.

The history of rehabilitation in the United States reflects the developing attitudes of American society toward disabled individuals, providing a yardstick of our country's commitment to humanistic values. American rehabilitation has traveled a long road since the days when the unfit were ignored or even punished. Today, most Americans subscribe to a goal of enabling the disabled to realize their fullest potential, a goal that, while still unfulfilled in actual practice, is the target for the future.

I   THE CURRENT SCENE

Salvatore G. Di Michael

According to a United States Public Health Survey (1963), there were in that year approximately 81 million persons (45 per cent of the total population exclusive of people in institutions) who had at least one chronic health condition, ranging from comparatively minor ones, such as sinusitis or hay fever, to more severe ones, such as heart condition, diabetes, and other physical as well as mental illnesses. Of this total, an estimated 22,733,000 persons (about one in every nine Americans) had chronic conditions that resulted in limited activity. The members of this group lost about 370 million days of work, and 196 million lost working days were associated with chronic conditions of three months' duration or more. About 40 per cent had more than one condition causing a limitation of activity. The prevalence of chronic disabilities varies sharply with family income. The incidence of multiple conditions causing limitation was 60 per cent among families with yearly incomes less than $2,000, compared with 24 per cent among families of $7,000 or more yearly income.

THE NEED AND CURRENT PROGRAM

According to pre-1954 estimates of people with disabling chronic conditions and vocational handicaps—in other words, the people in need of vocational rehabilitation—the total was an estimated 2.5 million, with 250,000 additional persons becoming disabled each year. These are people of working age, about 15 years of age and over. The most recent estimates by the Vocational Rehabilitation Administration show a minimum of 3.7 million persons in need of and eligible for services, and 536,000 persons coming into need each year. If these disabled people were brought

5

together in one state, they would outnumber the total population of each of 39 states, be about the same as the population in Florida, Georgia, Tennessee, Virginia, or Wisconsin, and be lower than only seven other states.

If a typical cross section of 100 rehabilitation applicants were to be brought together, 95 of them would come from families with a yearly income of less than $3,000. There would be an age span from 15 to over 65, with 34 as the average. Eighteen of them already would be on public assistance. About half would have no dependents, 30 would have one to three dependents, and about 20 would have four or more dependents to clothe, feed, and care for. Almost all would bear the visible and unseen marks of poverty. (Vocational Rehabilitation Administration, Annual Report, 1964.) So much for a quick, sweeping picture of need.

How far has our society gone in restoring these people to productive employment? In the 1967 fiscal year, state-federal programs rehabilitated an all-time annual high of 173,594 persons. About three and a half times that number, or some 570,000 were on the active roles, being served. The average rehabilitation took about 13 months from acceptance to closure, and included a medical-social-vocational evaluation, with counseling, placement, and follow-up for all clients, various forms of training for about 40 per cent, physical restoration for about 35 per cent, living expenses for some 25 per cent, and, in lesser frequency but as needed, the provision of tools, job equipment, occupational licenses, and assistance in establishing small, independent businesses.

If 100 typical rehabilitants are examined, we find that 37 have skeletal impairments, ten are mentally ill, six mentally retarded, six visually impaired, six have hearing and speech disabilities, five have cardiac defects, five tuberculosis, four are blind, two are deaf, and the remaining 19 have a broad variety of other conditions.

When rehabilitated, their major job placements are distributed in almost the same proportions as in the general working population, from unskilled to professional employment. In addition, about 15 are in homemaking and three are in sheltered workshops. This is being done through a network of over 1,000 district and local offices, from which counselors travel everywhere in the United States and its territories. A substantial number of counselors and some medical consultants are located in schools, public employment and welfare offices, hospitals and institutions.

In 1968 the combined federal and state spending on services was about $250 million, as compared to about $35 million in 1954. The professional staff, including counselors, supervisors, consultants, and disability evaluation examiners numbered over 10,000, of whom about 5,000 were counselors.

The more complete picture should also include the resources, personnel, and services of private agencies, but no satisfactory estimate is available. Notions may be gathered from some known facts. Since 1954 the Hill-Burton law has helped in the construction of 35 new rehabilitation facilities, at a total cost of more than $200 million. Presently, there are about 1,000 workshops of various kinds over the country.

Rehabilitation facilities are an indispensable part of the expanding program, for they provide an unequaled means for evaluating, treating, and serving the severely disabled. There are many types: large rehabilitation centers; physical medicine units in hospitals; speech and hearing centers; optical aid clinics; adjustment centers for the blind; halfway houses for emotionally recovering and mentally retarded; and workshops for various purposes.

Adding significantly to the armamentarium are the programs of research and demonstration and of short- and long-term training. It should be noted that by the end of 1965, a total of about 1,000 research and demonstration projects were completed or in progress; in 1965 alone, federal grants for research support amounted to about $20 million. This figure is at least 50 per cent higher for 1968. Many counselors are included in the research projects.

In 1968, a training program was financed with about $34 million. It now encompasses some 450 long-term teaching programs in many disciplines, with over 4,000 persons receiving traineeships and fellowships. Rehabilitation counseling is being supported in about 60 institutions, with some 1,400 traineeships. There were about 800 graduates ready for employment in 1968, typically after two years of study, with a master's degree. The supply of M.A. counselors is hardly enough to keep up with nationwide attrition of staff through promotions, retirements, and job changes.

Turning to major goals, the U.S. Vocational Rehabilitation Administration, with active support from Congress and the executive branch of the government, set a goal of 200,000 rehabilitants annually by fiscal year 1968. This goal was surpassed in 1968 with 208,000 people successfully rehabilitated (Vocational Rehabilitation Act Amendments, 1965). With new legislative amendments in prospect of passage, it is expected that stepped-up financial support should make possible the target of 300,000 annual rehabilitations by 1975 or sooner. This will require a sharp increase in rehabilitation facilities, especially multiservice workshops.

It is expected that a doubling of counseling services, or as many as 3,000 more counseling units will be required. Since the estimated cost of each counseling unit is about $50,000 for case services, for salaries of the counselors and secretary, and for travel and office space, this would mean that the overall support will need to be increased about $150 million per year to attain projected goals. This cost is solely for counseling and rehabilitation services. Corresponding increases will be necessary in other areas, such as facilities, research, training, technical assistance, innovative projects, surveys of rehabilitation needs, and the like.

PHILOSOPHICAL BASIS OF VOCATIONAL REHABILITATION

A topic recommended for serious study is the philosophical basis of vocational rehabilitation. Such a study will make one understand why rehabilitation workers soon become not only professional enthusiasts but even "secular missionaries." Rehabilitation workers have something important to give along with skills —a set of values, principles, and attitudes, a message of hope to the disabled and their families, and a product of vast benefit to society. Rehabilitation personnel are, or should be, inspired by the purposes of the work, its humanitarian and even divinely blessed qualities. All who are interested in this field will have to cultivate these basic principles and become refreshed from time to time by newer, deeper insights into their meaning. Myriad facets of the strong motives that drive rehabilitation workers to work with handicapped people are observable to those who become involved.

Webster offers six definitions for the term "philosophy." A useful selection is "the general principles or laws for a field of knowledge, activity," that is, of vocational rehabilitation. Since we cannot cover the subject completely in one brief paper, three general points are proposed: first, to develop an appreciation of vocational rehabilitation's practical importance; second, to present the "basic dozen" principles; and third, to comment on major features in today's programs.

To cultivate more vividly the deeper meaning of a philosophy of rehabilitation, three illustrations are offered.

Until about 1950 the field of mental retardation was characterized predominantly by the philosophical conception that the retarded were better off in institutions. The retarded were, in the main, kept out of public awareness, seemingly consigned to oblivion or to a life of nonproductivity and artificial security through complete dependence. As the swell of indignation among the parents of the retarded began to stir the conscience of society, largely through the National Association for Retarded Children, the movement gravitated naturally toward vocational rehabilitation. Here was a philosophy that engendered hope, the promise of a return by the retarded and their families to the normal avenues of society.

These hopes were nurtured by a farsighted cadre of parents and friends of the retarded, of similarly disposed professional people, and by the fortuitous monumental support of presidents and influential legislators. Without a philosophy of rehabilitation there could have been just as much publicity and social awareness, but couched in the concept of larger, better institutions, of protection and charitable dependence. As one parent put it so well: "We don't want better laws to put the retarded out of sight; we want them to become a part of our everyday community life." The presence of a program of vocational rehabilitation and its philosophy served to give impetus to the restoration of the retarded and their families to a respected role in society, the benefits of which are being shown in dramatic fashion.

The treatment of the emotionally ill also has felt the impact of the basic concepts of rehabilitation. In 1955, Dr. Kenneth Appel (Babor, 1963), past president of the American Psychiatric

Association, said that very few psychiatrists had ever heard of the rehabilitation facilities available to mental patients since 1943. Because of better methods of treatment, such as chemotherapy, the efforts of preventive and social psychiatry and military psychiatry, and successful demonstrations, the hospital populations have decreased for the first time. As Irving Babor stated in 1963 in a paper before the Ninth International Congress of the International Society for the Rehabilitation of the Disabled:

> Experience demonstrated that short-term intensive measures with environmental supports could restore or improve social, psychological, and vocational functioning of large numbers of psychiatric patients with the objective, whenever possible, of getting them back on the job with little delay. . . . Behavioral scientists and clinicians . . . concluded that much of chronic disability of mental patients resulted not from the illness itself but from the inadequate care and the negative expectations.

The practical importance of a rehabilitation philosophy is to be seen again in the marked improvements of people with schizophrenia. In older textbooks on the subject (still to be found on bookshelves), schizophrenia was defined as a total lack of contact with reality. Now, with the principles and newer methods of rehabilitation, there has been a marked shift in thinking. No less an authority than the National Joint Commission on Mental Illness and Health (*The Modern Hospital,* 1961) states in its official report:

> Medical psychology has consistently observed and generally accepts the fact that functional psychosis involves only certain of the components of the personality. The patient is sick in some ways and healthy in others. Rational treatment directs itself toward salvaging the healthy and reducing the sick parts of the mind. The outlook for the schizophrenic . . . is not poor but good under optimum treatment conditions. He has a one-in-five chance of spontaneous recovery without systematic treatment. Through proper treatment, he has at least a three-in-five and perhaps as much as four-in-five chance of improving sufficiently to lead a useful life in his community.

Another illustration of the impact of the basic philosophy of rehabilitation is in the area of research. There are some people who ascribe to research such lofty values as to brush aside philosophy and seek to displace its meaning in life. However, research, too, must have its basic purposes, assumptions, and major directions for its products.

Can the philosophy of rehabilitation make a difference in research? Formerly there were research projects on the mentally retarded in institutions. By contrast, studies are being carried out today in the context of rehabilitation workshops with comparable populations. If we examine the fragmentary results of studies on manual abilities, IQ's, and social quotients in institutions or community workshops, the data may not differ perceptibly; it even could be shown that counseling of institutionalized persons would improve their personal adjustment for institutional life. Separate, isolated facts may not show much difference, but the overall picture of the style of institutional living compared with that in the community shows an enormous difference in the meaning of life to the retarded, their families, and the whole nation. (National Action to Combat Mental Retardation, 1962.)

Today there are some educators who contend that children with IQ's under 50 should not be trained in public schools, but they should be prepared for eventual adult living in institutions. The answer is not one of research but overridingly one of philosophy.

In the same vein, the following questions may be asked and answered:

Should the paraplegic in wheelchairs, either sitting up or in a more horizontal position, be employed in industry? Should the competitively submarginal be employed in sheltered workshops? Should the more severely handicapped marry, have children, join in community recreation, go to church? Should orphaned handicapped children and adults be placed in foster homes? These few questions are examples of many more that require discussion. Scientific research should develop better methods and techniques and hypotheses for improved treatment, but the context of use for the derived facts will depend upon the philosophy of professional workers, employers, fellow workers, family, and society in general.

Certain kinds of research—fragmentary, atomistic, nonhumanitarian, rigid—have been criticized afresh by persons in high places. At a convention of the American Psychological Association held several years ago, Dr. Gordon Allport, in a major address, raised grave questions about forms of stimulus-response research that claim to supersede philosophy and about the use of hypotheses and research designs that force data into artificial compartments.

Doctor Sam Kirk, in a paper dealing with the handicapped delivered at the White House Conference on Education in 1965, stated:

> There is no debate on the need for research and develop-
> ment in the education of handicapped children. There is,
> however, a definite need concerning the kinds of research
> that are most needed at the present time. Of the hundreds of
> studies on learning . . . , few have led to generalizations
> or theories about the retarded, or the deaf, or the blind.
> Reviews of research on learning conclude that the studies are
> heterogeneous and piecemeal, that no definitive generalization
> can be made. . . . Recent research has been criticized as
> unimaginative, sterile, and "methodology bound."

Neither professionals nor the esteemed scientists who have been quoted wish to downgrade the value of sound research. Nor is it meant to imply that the philosophy of rehabilitation is so wonderful as to engender complacency. There is a great need today for widespread acceptance of the philosophy of rehabilitation and the improvement of research. Each can enrich the other.

Early in 1958 a five-day institute of 66 persons of prominence and influence was held at Princeton, New Jersey. It was devoted to psychology and rehabilitation. The discussions were lively and, in the early portions, were devoted to the principles and assumptions of rehabilitation. In the proceedings so ably prepared by Beatrice Wright (Wright, 1959), she set down a set of statements derived from the conference that are as brief and clear as have been stated anywhere. These are now offered in propositions that are closely paraphrased from the publication in a "basic dozen" principles, all of which should be taken together if they are to have full meaning:

(1) Every human being has an inalienable value and is worthy of respect for his own sake.

(2) Every person has membership in society, and rehabilitation should cultivate his full acceptance.

(3) The assets of the person should be emphasized, supported, and developed.

(4) Reality factors should be stressed in helping the person to cope with his environment.

(5) Comprehensive treatment involves the "whole person," because life-areas are interdependent.

(6) Treatment should vary and be flexible to deal with the special characteristics of each person.

(7) Each person should assume as much initiative and participation as possible in the rehabilitation plan and its execution.

(8) Society should be responsible, through all possible public and private agencies, for the providing of services and opportunities to the disabled.

(9) Rehabilitation programs must be conducted with interdisciplinary and interagency integration.

(10) Rehabilitation is a continuous process that applies as long as help is needed.

(11) Psychological and personal reactions of the individual are everpresent and often crucial.

(12) The rehabilitation process is complex and must be subject to constant reexamination—for each individual and for the program as a whole.

A few important extensions to these propositions are offered, as they impinge on the current scene. These added remarks are not in the nature of qualifications, rather they are amplifications related specifically to vocational rehabilitation.

The meeting at Princeton was set in the context of general rehabilitation. The intention was to consider all persons with chronic impairments: whether they had potentialities for eventual productive work or were likely to need independent-living services.

In vocational rehabilitation a very prominent place has been devoted to the goal of suitable employment. The public federal-state program was first established in 1920 under such a requirement, and it has not changed its major thrust. While maintaining the primary goal of employment, the concept has been broadened in a most liberal way, both by administrative regulations and the consent of legislators and executive administrators. The concept of treating the whole man has not been subverted, for it has been clear that successful employment at a maximum level depends upon comprehensive rehabilitation. The concept of employment has been broadened to include homemaker, sheltered employment, and home industries.

Seemingly, there should be no conflict over the compatibility of the philosophy of rehabilitation either in the context of productive employment or of independent-living, as suited to the individual. However, from time to time sharp differences in viewpoints have arisen. One contention has been that the public agencies have placed undue emphasis on acceptance of clients with high odds for eventual employment. Another contention has been that the reality factors of available employment have been so strong as to give superficial attention to comprehensive treatment. Still another contention has arisen from efforts to obtain public support for an integrated program for independent living and vocational rehabilitation. Others contend that strategically, at this time, it is better to use the increasing popularity of vocational rehabilitation to spearhead an impetus for greater support.

Undoubtedly, the most potent argument, and the most successful, for increasing support for vocational rehabilitation has been its social and economic justification. In the public arena of competition for public funds (and for private donations, as well), this justification has been necessary.

The economic values of rehabilitation to society are tangible and identifiable. Rehabilitation is an investment that repays society for its effort. For example, the average cost of a rehabilitation is returned fivefold in income taxes by the employed handicapped worker; the average rate of income after rehabilitation is seven to ten times greater for the average person than before he was accepted. The rehabilitation of disabled persons on public assistance can be effected at a one-time cost comparable to that it took to support them on relief during a one-year period. These kinds of data have been used as a solid backdrop for the economic validity of the programs. Their appeal, added to humanitarian values, has been convincing, particularly to legislators.

From time to time protagonists have felt impelled to decry a seeming overemphasis on social and economic arguments. Such persons have appealed to the first proposition mentioned in the "basic dozen" principles—namely the value and dignity of the individual. Observation has revealed that the appeal to "personal dignity" is most often mentioned by those in charge of the most severely handicapped, such as those in institutions, and by professional workers who are responsible for treatment of the individual. The degree and direction of emphasis of rehabilitation principles depends upon the context of use and upon the person or groups to which convincing appeals must be made.

In vocational rehabilitation remunerative employment is one of the primary goals, but not the exclusive one. To some people it is like waving a red flag before a bull to speak of remunerative employment as a goal of special importance. Before beginning to look like the charging bull to such matadors and receiving the verbal *coup de grace,* we should hasten to add that by this time it must be clear that there is no personal antipathy to the complete desirability of "comprehensive rehabilitation," "independent-living rehabilitation," the basic unassailable value of "human dignity" and all the other precepts. We must, however, give serious thought to such a goal in keeping with the nature of man, the value of work, and the vitality of the vocational rehabilitation program today.

On the international scene, the president of the International Society for Rehabilitation of the Disabled in 1963 said: "The ultimate goal of all rehabilitation is to enable the handicapped individual to work . . . . A job is essential not only to enable the individual to be economically self-supporting but also to assure him his rightful place in his home and community." (Introductory remarks by chairman, 1963.)

At the same 1963 meeting in Denmark, Mr. Aarno Ranta (Ranta, 1963) said it a little differently but in perhaps more extreme form: "[Job] placement is the last but important—perhaps the most important—link in the process called vocational rehabilitation. It is said that rehabilitation cannot be considered successful until the rehabilitee is placed in remunerative and satisfying employment. This is recognized as the ultimate goal of rehabilitation."

Work is one of the prime reality arenas of life. Sigmund Freud, the founder of psychoanalysis, so alluded to it in his monumental studies on modern psychotherapy. Work is a most important focus on human motivations. For man's good, his nature demands activity in a harnessed direction that permits him to unfold his being, and realize his best potentials for himself, his family, and society. The dignity of the individual has no real meaning unless the person with potentiality for work is given opportunity to so engage himself.

As those in rehabilitation know, work has a therapeutic quality, which is released through work evaluation, work conditioning, and personal adjustment in centers and workshops.

Work is a stabilizing force in the life of man in that it opens goals for achievement, attainment, self-dependence, and self-esteem.

Work has a social value in that the welfare of family, friends, and society in general is advanced. Work brings acceptance, status, and other fruits of a full life, with culture, better health, recreation, and human comforts. It makes possible a life of full citizenship for each man.

Work has religious significance in that the brotherhood of man may be advanced, and the Fatherhood of God may be earned and nourished. Religion even offers man the solace of regarding his work as an offering to God.

All of these values of work and employment have been intensively nurtured in the philosophy and programs of vocational rehabilitation. We often hear how rehabilitation has graduated man from a second-class role to one of full participation as a family supporter, family member, trusted worker, productive citizen, and active church member.

In fact, it was the fundamental conviction that the returning servicemen and civilian disabled workers should be assisted toward employment that established the veterans and federal-state programs of rehabilitation. The sustained effort to help the sick, aged, and infirm has not suffered as a result of the programs of vocational rehabilitation. Rather, it is more correct to say that vocational rehabilitation has been an ally for such other programs, achieving growing influence and support as the program gained in its own vitality and strength. An interesting illustration of this alliance is the effort to find a method of preventing retrolental fibroplasia, as well as to assist the blind disabled by it. More recently, the application of the philosophy and treatment of "thalidomide babies" born with skeletal abnormalities attests again to the pervasive wholesome influence of vocational rehabilitation. ("Congenital Defects," Ninth World Congress, 1963.)

CURRENT ISSUES

Now that the needs, scope, and philosophy of rehabilitation have been examined, major current issues will be considered. In so short a space, some matters of primary concern to counselors and to university educators can only be dealt with briefly and pointedly. The vocational rehabilitation program is replete with issues. Recent national and state conferences have spotlighted the need for change, for increased vitality, and for increases in services, personnel, and facilities. Rehabilitation seeks to establish not more of the same but continued improvements. May it always be that way. However, the improvements that are sought are not easily accomplished, and the ways to bring them into being are ever open to constructive scrutiny.

ISSUE: Should greater emphasis be given to quality or quantity?

This issue is usually couched in terms of extremes, as though there were a head-on-clash of irreconcilable viewpoints, like the specious riddle of the irresistible force and the immovable object. In theory, everyone would like all services to be of the highest quality and applied to all the disabled with vocational handicaps. Practically speaking, rehabilitation is far, far from that goal. If each counselor were to spend twice as much time on his client as he now does, his output would be cut in half. This means fewer people served. There is, then, a sense of obligation to reach the three million or so who desperately need vocational rehabilitation. Who should be neglected? Priorities, when tried, have not worked.

At present, there are some people who contend that counselors do not give full assistance to clients because of a heavy burden of caseloads. Among those who voice this criticism are university teachers. On the other hand, administrators have noticed that some of their highest producers are more apt to be their better counselors, in that they can evaluate more effectively, sense the client's needs, and come to the critical points quickly. We might even say that experienced counselors have a more characteristic viewpoint on

the issue of quality or quantity; they express it in the form of concern about the definition of responsibilities for their job and
usually complain about paperwork and records. This will be dealt
with more fully in the next major issue. Just now, it is best to get
out of one issue so as not to become hopelessly entangled in the
jungle.

It can be stated that a good part of the apparently clashing
viewpoints is due to each group's view of the varying aspects of a
total reality. The university educator has a student in preparation
and wants to train him as fully as possible. The student has lots to
learn, needs time to do it, does not have the benefit of experience,
and so both teacher and student want more time than usual to do
a good job. In training, quality is sought in highest possible measure while quantity is necessarily limited.

On the other hand, the administrator has the force of community groups on his professional neck. He knows the many, many
disabled people who need the services. He is painfully aware that
there is not one community group interested in a particular disability that does not complain about the large number of unserved
people. Furthermore, the administrator must ever search for more
efficient methods; counselors are as perfect or imperfect as any
other professional group, and can improve their quality and output.

The experienced couselor sees all too clearly the imperfections
of the community; the harsh realities that form the daily life of
clients and families. If the counselor is to keep his soul and spirit
intact, he must try to help his clients make the very best of a host
of practical matters in their daily lives. So he wants to give his
best but is mature enough to gain satisfaction from the visible
victories and few defeats among his clients. He sees the clients who
are in the waiting room to be helped as people, not statistics; and
hopes that society will soon furnish the personnel and resources
to tackle the really big job ahead.

That is part of the answer. There are many other challenges
to be met before the apparent issue is solved. For one thing, there
are three million people to be served. At least twice the personnel
and resources now at hand will be needed before vocational rehabilitation can come close to serving the newly disabled each
year, let alone the backlog. What an opportunity lies ahead for
those who are training to be counselors! Vocational rehabilitation

desperately needs a lifetime of service from all future counselors. The jobs ahead will be legion.

Rehabilitation needs the future counselors or, better, the handicapped need them: the blind, deaf, mentally disabled, tuberculars, cerebral palsied, epileptic, speech and hearing impaired, the skeletally impaired. Rehabilitation has hardly touched the possibilities with heart, stroke, and cancer victims, the alcoholics, narcotic addicts, and so many of the multiply handicapped. Recently, Congress urged vocational rehabilitation to help society in coming to grips with the rehabilitation potentialities of public offenders.

Exciting partial victories are almost within grasp. For example, vocational rehabilitation is on the threshold of a saturation of services for one group—the blind. With the new legislation passed, it soon may be possible to say that all blind people in need of vocational rehabilitation will have services available to them. Perhaps the counselors of the future will have the deep satisfaction of being there when barriers are broken—when the comprehensive needs of all the blind, and later other disability groups, will be met through a saturation of services.

ISSUE: How should counselor jobs be redesigned: with or without counselor-levels and with or without the assistance of aides?

Since the enactment of the 1954 amendments concerning vocational rehabilitation, training sequences have been established for counselors (and other professionals) in about 60 settings, each leading to a master's degree. Rehabilitation leaders and university educators have been in the forefront of a movement to upgrade the level, status, and proficiency of new counselors. This gain took no small effort.

As the training efforts proceeded, serious questions were raised about the aim of training; that is, the types of responsibilities to be assumed by these new graduates. One of the central issues was whether the counselor should be primarily engaged in counseling or in the coordination of services for his clients. Here again, the issues were portrayed as irreconcilable. There seems to have been little said about the need to have coordination in the counseling; that is, in letting the client know what is planned for him to do in agreement with the agency, what steps are to be taken, and when they are to be effected.

In addition, the issue served as a focus for other real matters of job responsibility. Should the trained counselor look for and make job placements and make arrangements for agreed-upon services to be furnished by other professional people and agencies? Should counseling be pitched strongly toward psychotherapeutic aims or lean more toward the solution of environmental blocks to acceptance of the handicapped? (This, as one may now surmise, is an encapsulated version of hundreds of papers and thousands of speeches on the subject.)

As was shown earlier in this study, many more counselors are needed, and the supply—with M.A. degrees—is not available, nor will it be for as far ahead as can be seen. Accordingly, vocational rehabilitation may have to set up counseling positions on various levels, with the more highly trained and longer experienced taking the most difficult cases requiring all their counseling skills, and the counselors with less training and experience taking on people whose reality-orientation is more intact. Salaries would be commensurate (at any rate, it is hoped that civil service commissions and boards of directors of private agencies could be logical about this).

Personnel must be hired below the M.A. level, with college degrees and major electives in the humanities. They will have to be given liberal doses of training, so that they can handle the less critical parts of the counselor's job. This is preferable to a rigid adherence to initial requirements for an M.A. degree. As financial support for expansion becomes available, legislators and society must be convinced that increasing numbers of people are being served. The doors of rehabilitation agencies cannot be locked with a sign that reads: "Handicapped Keep Out—Caseloads Closed."

As for "rehabilitation aides"—they are needed too. Many other professional fields are taking a similar step. The counselor's time spent on necessary paperwork and records should be decreased (although he will have to continue to do case recording unless invisible secretaries are invented), and he should be helped to train rehabilitation aides. These jobs could be filled by highly motivated persons who can derive a deep sense of satisfaction from their contributions to the rehabilitation of handicapped people and who have the ability to make arrangements for services by hospitals, physicians, schools, rehabilitation centers, and workshops.

Finally, vocational rehabilitation should admit that in the recent past one counselor was needed to look after each client's progress in rehabilitation from referral to placement and follow-up. Now other patterns must be sought. Specialists will be needed in initial interviewing and intake, others in placement and follow-up. The coordinating counselor will be a specialist in individual, and perhaps group, counseling and will help each of his clients to develop a clear plan of action and stimulate his inner resources to see himself through.

If rehabilitation counselors pride themselves on their ability to work in interprofessional teams and interagency coordination, it should not prove difficult to evolve ways to work with fellow specialists and rehabilitation aides in the same agency.

ISSUE: When is a disabled person rehabilitated?

It has become customary practice to count most cases as "Rehabilitated" one month after job placement, although there are no federal requirements for such a definition. Sometimes, agencies have stipulated that a period of three months of employment must ensue for specified groups of disabled people before they can be counted as "Rehabilitated." (Agreements in profusion and papers aplenty have been spun around this issue, but there is always more. The attention comes in cycles. Just now, the front is quiet but the peace is temporary; not even a statement can be claimed.)

Some opponents to customary practice say: "How, indeed, can you say a person is 'Rehabilitated' just because you stamped a paper while your conscience pricks you with uncertainty? And who, indeed, is ever completely rehabilitated?"

The prospects of counseling and rehabilitation must, indeed, be reexamined. There is no absolute certainty of continuous adjustment to life for any person. Individuals with disability and vocational handicaps need special help to establish themselves in society and in productive jobs. The challenges, frustrations, and successes of life are part and parcel of the human destiny—disabled or not. Counselors can overprotect their clients as surely as they can underserve or fail to serve.

The basic purpose of rehabilitation is to help the individual to aspire, not to a theoretically ideal way of life but to a set of practical goals where opportunities for self-dependence, personal satisfaction, and social contributions are made possible. To encourage him to strive for the improbable, or impossible, is to do him a disservice. If he chooses to seek the improbable, the counselor must make it as clear as he can, and as the client is able at times to accept, without real danger to his body or his mind. Man grows, not as he is fed with donations of success but with the cultivation of wisdom, courage, and understanding that issues from his own abilities to make and capitalize upon opportunities.

When, then, may one say a person is "rehabilitated"? According to the way some experts use the word, one fears it may be only when the person has returned to his Creator. Nor can one condone the subversion of the word when it stands for a "quickie," that is, when the counselor realizes that the job placement is imminently insecure, or that it is already a matter of history in the person's life.

Counselors should seek to prepare the handicapped person so that he will retain the job and establish his reputation as an efficient worker, thereby opening up other suitable opportunities consistent with his abilities and motivations. Perhaps he may stumble again; if he does, he should have the confidence to return to the counselor for assistance. Perhaps the business firm may fail him for reasons beyond his control, and the counselor will be ready to serve again.

In brief, the administrative requirements of closing a rehabilitation program after one or three months of employment is a practical device, not a guarantee. The practical device must be used with prudence. In some small percentage of cases a form of continuing supervision is needed, especially for the more severely mentally retarded and emotionally ill. Sheltered workshops may be in the best position to exercise such supervision. Yet the public agencies may be better advised to adopt a posture of "ready to serve when needed."

In 1959 the author had occasion to prepare a paper as the outgoing president of the American Catholic Psychological Association (Di Michael, 1960). After much searching, I decided upon the topic, the "Emotional Effects of Physical Disability Upon Religious Attitudes," as a subject for study. In the course of making the study, it became apparent that adjustment to the incurrence of disability could be conceived in horizontal and also in vertical dimensions.

Rehabilitation has dealt almost entirely with horizontal dimensions, that is, psychological defenses such as "denial," "distortion," "withdrawal," "compensatory," and the like. Vertical dimensions were hardly mentioned or studied, and were seen as progressively higher stages of adjustment. It also became very clear that present rehabilitation thinking and literature were almost totally "problem-centered," and they seldom mentioned the higher forms of psychological acceptance of disability.

The situation today is no different. Use of the term "adjustment" is singular and it should be plural. Adjustment is used globally to cover much and explain little, and is obscure in its meaning when read by an American, and even more devoid of meaning when translated into a foreign language. The counselor must keep in mind that "adjustment" is multifaceted, not a unitary concept. There are many adjustments in various areas of life, and the level of success or failure in each area is usually uneven. For example, a person may be high in knowledge, low in skill, make a good father but an unsatisfactory husband, do little in the community, yet be a good immediate neighbor, and so on.

In this study an outline of descriptive stages in the person's level of abilitiy to cope psychologically with his handicap was proposed.

The first stage is "regression," in which some people are overly dependent and emotionally defensive and use their disability as a self-centered lever in interpersonal relations. The second stage is "accommodation," in which some people use their disability to play the role of martyr: they regard life as barely tolerable; the role gives them a partial crutch on which to maintain self-dependence. The third stage is a kind of "practical compromise" with their handicap: they manifest their feelings in self-perceptions of moderate inferiorities with the nondisabled; they have self-esteem and self-worth, but it is tinged more or less by competitive feelings with people on the basis of disability. The highest stage is "integration of disability," in which the person has developed a deeper, more lofty set of values; the disability has served to draw out of him great inner strength, unusual personal courage, and maturity. He now sees himself as a much better human being than he might have been if he had not learned to cope with his disability. He is not glad that he has the disability, but he cherishes the great values of life that he struggled for and found. Few people go so far.

The discussions of the concepts of "acceptance of disability," and "adjustment," and "rehabilitated," and employment now will permit me to make several pertinent points.

There is no perfect correspondence between the various concepts. For example, one man may have so severe a condition of arthritis that he cannot be employed, but he is a responsible husband and loving father. Another person has mild arthritis, stays at home much of the time, believes she cannot work, tries to keep her parents from worrying over her, and warmly receives family and friends. Another is a recluse, depends upon his housekeeper at the boarding home to bring him meals, but works faithfully at his job from Monday to Friday. Still another is doing a very creditable job, has a prosthetic arm, is seldom at home, and both his wife and children are the worse for it, but he is active in community affairs.

How far should the rehabilitation counselor go with his client? At the present time rehabilitation programs cannot provide continuous counseling to the time when "integration of disability" takes place. Nor is it advisable to do so. People who reach the lofty heights of mature acceptance of disability are those who do it on their own. They need some help, professional or friendly, to see the possibilities. Then they make the continuing, upper spiral journey in their own uneven way.

Can counselors be expected to devote the necessary time not only to help the person to obtain employment but also to stimulate a high level of personal, family, social, and civic adjustments? It seems doubtful that this could be done in the present context of the rehabilitation program, with so large a number of people in need of multiple services. Probably these issues form the crux of the argument as to when counselors should say a person is rehabilitated.

It was stated earlier that one of the bench marks of a rehabilitation is that the person has been prepared to capitalize upon employment opportunities. This concept can be broadened beyond employment. The person should be counseled so that he has the opportunity to seek higher levels of effectiveness in his personal, family, social, and civic life. Counseling, then, from a practical point of view, has to try to take away the major roadblocks. In a positive sense it should stimulate the natural tendencies of the person toward levels of maturity and growth that were not possible before. This viewpoint does not deem it desirable for rehabilitation counseling to aim to remake the personalities of clients. Such ambitious undertakings are for the severely psychologically distressed, and they require the ministrations of psychotherapy, with a capital "P."

Although this viewpoint attests to the difficulties in nurturing acceptance of disability and adjustments during the counseling process, it certainly does not stop there. This whole area must be explored as intensively as possible, with imaginative, even daring research. There is need to find out how better to liberate the natural tendencies of better psychological growth and maturity. Group counseling methods may have to be discovered that would make it feasible. If this is done, a key may be found that would benefit not only the handicapped but mankind in general. This whole area is admittedly complex. It is better to admit it than to try to perpetuate rehabilitation's refuge in the superficial simplicities of terms, as now used, such as "adjustment," "acceptance," "rehabilitated."

ISSUE: What will automation do to employment of the handicapped?

It seems that the issues become increasingly difficult as this paper proceeds. The whole business of automation is itself hard to penetrate, and it has many subsidiary and related issues. The problem of the handicapped merely adds to the complexities created by automation. Perhaps a more realistic approach is to see what can be done today, and not to get lost in spurious convictions on prophesies for the future. The future cannot be predicted for sure; but we can and must speculate, think, and grapple with possibilities or probabilities. However, no one can be sure what will be the lot of rehabilitation ten, twenty, or thirty years or more from now. We can make studies and get glimpses of what happens in some places today and probably will happen more and more frequently with passing time.

Today it is known that more work can be done by fewer people, with machines more efficient than have ever been seen before. We know that some jobs are closed forever, and that others open up. It is harder indeed to find the new ones. The loss of jobs through obsolescence is jarring.

The painful displacements of workers and their families are observed, while shifts in employment seem to be more frequent. We read about automation in books and magazines, but so much of what is written is emotional and confusing. Yet, total employment is higher than ever, and newspapers inform us that the rate of unemployment has been decreasing.

On the other hand, committees and individuals who have given some time to observe the effects of automation upon the handicapped have agreed on a few important facts. New automated machines require less physical output, a point in favor of the handicapped. It has also been observed that more jobs are being created in the service occupations, and the mentally retarded have benefited. Counselors give accounts of many new jobs into which the handicapped have been placed—the blind in computer programming, the orthopedically impaired in electronics, others in television repair; some find employment in the new agencies for space voyages, intercontinental missiles, research in government and industry, and so on.

Any serious study of the effects of automation upon the handicapped will soon show that the economic welfare of all society is of critical importance. For this reason we must take a special role as citizens to see that the hope of full employment is realized. It is inconceivable that mass unemployment will be permitted when the level of productivity is the highest in America's history and in the world. Ways must be found to have the economic methods work for man, rather than for him to become slave to a system of his own making.

A review of America's pattern of employment discloses that the high point of this country's predominantly agricultural economy came in 1910. Before that, over 50 per cent of the workers had to produce the food that was needed; today only 7 per cent can furnish the nation with as much food as is needed. In the middle 1950's, industrial workers were in the majority; today less than 45 per cent of all workers can furnish all the material goods needed. According to a study of the National Bureau of Economic Research (reported on the first page of the New York *Times* of June 28, 1965), there has been a shift into a "service-to-people" economy; the majority of workers are in such jobs as trade, finance, insurance, real estate, general government, and in personal, business, repair, and professional services. Seen in this context, society will have the ability to support programs such as vocational rehabilitation, education, training, anti-poverty, and health, as never before. Why not? People live not by bread and material goods alone. There is a way to make the economy man's handmaid, not his master. It will take some time before society realizes the shift that has taken place, and the beneficial significance of a "services-to-people" economy.

Undoubtedly, the best possible posture to be taken in the present situation is to seek out relentlessly every possible job for handicapped clients in newly automated industry and in new and established jobs that are not vulnerable to automation. As a matter of fact, every such job found is a kind of insurance, a premium payment on a paid-off policy of full employment tomorrow. As members of society we must do everything possible to foster full employment; as rehabilitation workers, we must seize every present opportunity to give the handicapped a full share too. In this study much more has been said about the problems of disabled persons than of the obstacles unwittingly set in their path by their fellowmen. In the future, counselors also will have to undertake the vast work of educating society.

II   HISTORICAL BACKGROUND

James F. Garrett

Before we examine historical precedents, it may be best to consider the philosophical concepts that guide present-day vocational rehabilitation. Out of the many concepts that might be suggested, there are six that appear to be of particular importance:

> The first concept is that the principle of equality of opportunity for all citizens imposes an obligation on the American people to provide specialized services for persons who are disabled, in order that they may be physically and vocationally prepared for employment and participation in the privileges and responsibilities of American citizenship.
>
> Second, in order to discharge this responsibility, it is required that a public program of vocational rehabilitation be established in which all disabled adults, regardless of disability, geographical location, or other factors beyond their control, have an equal opportunity to receive rehabilitation services.
>
> Third, that a public program of rehabilitation services can best be conducted as a joint effort of the federal, state, and local governments. In such a joint venture, the federal government would participate in sharing the costs and provide national leadership and technical assistance while the state and local governments would, in addition to sharing in the costs, direct the actual operation of the various services.
>
> Fourth, that it is the proper role, in this federal-state program, to include voluntary, nonprofit organizations engaged in rehabilitation by means of financial aid and other cooperative assistance.
>
> Fifth, that the most constructive approach to problems of public dependency created by physical, emotional, and

social disabilities is through an expanded program of vocational rehabilitation that will involve all disabled persons in gainful occupational activity in both industrial and sheltered facilities.

The sixth philosophical concept, which in essence sums up our entire approach, is that rehabilitation is a practical expression of the American ideal of the human dignity and worth of the individual.

The purpose of restating these philosophical concepts is to remind us that consideration of human worth, or the dignity of the individual, or of societal responsibility, is not common to many parts of the world, nor was it common for America in the recent past. Though the current rehabilitation program has its roots deep in the American past, and is consistent with the statement appearing on the Archives Building in Washington, D.C.—"The Past Is Prologue"—it will be discovered that the past has been full of detours, uncertainties, and false starts and a reflection of "man's inhumanity to man."

Attitudes toward illness, medicine, and disability reach far back into man's history and vary considerably with different cultural milieus. In early times, long before Christ, a king of Judea was strongly condemned because he sought the help of physicians rather than the Lord during a serious illness. It was common at that time to ascribe disease and illness to divine and supernatural intervention and to associate healing with religious practice (Obermann, 1965).* By the year 2000 B.C., although the Law of Hammurabi still attributed disease to supernatural causes, legal aspects of medical practice had already been established, including fees and punishment to be inflicted in case of failure, which gave the physician a recognized and acclaimed status in society.

It was only much later that the Hippocratic Oath—still taken solemnly by new physicians in the United States—attributed a moral role to the physician. Hippocrates, who practiced medicine during the fourth century B.C., was among the first to depart from the idea that a part of medical practice required the exorcising of the evil spirits roaming the earth through prayer and propitiation.

---

* Most of the early historical references were obtained from *A History of Vocational Rehabilitation in America*, by C. Esco Obermann.

He took the position that disease was a product of an earthly process and should be treated by rational and scientific means. His urgent belief that medicine could be a science and a profession has earned him a special place in medical history.

Other examples of ancient attitudes toward disability and illness were found in Sparta, where deformed and disabled children were systematically eliminated, this action being justified on the basis of a need to keep the human race pure—shades of Hitler! Even in enlightened Rome, centuries later, some deformed and unwanted children were disposed of in sewers, located, ironically, outside the Temple of Mercy. To dispel the notion that these were only ancient attitudes, we leap to the twentieth century and find the following quote attributed to Karl Pearson, well known to all students for the product-moment correlation:

> You are enabling the deformed to live, the blind to see, the weakling to survive—and it is partly due to the social provision made for these weaklings—the feebleminded woman goes to the workhouse for her fourth or fifth illegitimate child, while the insane man, overcome by the strain of modern life, is fed and restored for a time to his family and paternity. In our institutions we provide for the deaf-mute, the blind, the cripple and render it relatively easy for the degenerate to mate and leave their like.
>
> In the old days, without these medical benefits, and without these special provisions, the hand of nature fell heavily on the unfit. Such were numbered as they are largely numbered now, among the unemployables; but there were no doctors to enable them to limp through life; no charities to take their offspring or provide for their necessities. A petty theft meant the gallows, unemployment meant starvation, feeblemindedness meant persecution and social expulsion; insanity meant confinement with no attempt at treatment. To the honor of the medical profession, to the credit of our social instincts we have largely stopped all this, but at the same time we have to a large extent suspended the automatic action whereby a race progressed physically and mentally. . . . What will happen, if, by increased medical skill and by increased state support and private charity, we enable the weaklings to survive and propagate their kind? Why, undoubtedly, we shall have a weaker race (Obermann, 1965).

The demonology concept of illness prevailed over the centuries. In 1564, Dr. Johann Weyer of Cleves estimated that 7.5 million demons were roaming the earth, contributing to human illness. Martin Luther did not deviate from demonology, but instead attributed serious illness and disease to the work of Satan. However, he acknowledged that those who were possessed of evil spirits were susceptible to treatment and should be helped.

A turning point in the care of the ill occurred during the reign of Elizabeth I of England, when the first poor laws were passed. At that time institutions for the orthopedically disabled were established that, while acceptable in spirit, were cruel and unjust in their actual treatment of human beings. Another example of inhuman treatment of the ill is found in the following quote from a public health service publication:

> The earliest asylums for the insane appeared in Europe in the late 16th century. Typical of these was Bethlehem Hospital in London, which came to be known as "Bedlam." It was notorious for its deplorable conditions and practices. Violent patients were exhibited to the public for an admission fee, while the harmless were sent into the streets to beg. Stripped of all human dignity, the patients were subjected to beatings, chains, and other means of physical force. The more fortunate were given antidotes of such materials as crabs' eyes, frogs' spawn, dog lice, human perspiration and saliva, earthworms, and vipers' flesh. Their quarters were unspeakable (Public Health Service Bulletin #1345, 1965).

In reaction to this unfavorable level of patient care, humanists such as Locke, Rousseau, Blake, and Thomas Paine called for greater humanity in man's treatment of man. Aware of the need for greater humanitarianism, particularly in relation to the physically disabled, they opposed the use of physical force and withdrawal of food and drink for disabled individuals who declined to work.

In America we find the first hospitals for the mentally ill little different from their European counterparts. Deutsch describes patient care as follows:

> Patients' scalps were shaved and blistered: they were bled to the point of syncope; purged until the alimentary canal failed

to yield anything but mucus; and in the intervals, they were chained by the waist or ankle to the cell wall (Deutsch, 1949).

Later, America followed the example of Pinel in France and Tuke in England and brought about widespread reforms in many institutions. However, again this did not apply to the poor:

> The aged, orphaned, and insane poor were grouped together under the brand "pauper" and treated as criminals or wild beasts. Some community aid for their support was available. But more often towns auctioned them off, ran them out of town, or packed them off to the almshouses, which soon became as miserable as the old mental hospitals. Many were simply jailed (Public Health Service Bulletin 1345).

It was not until the late nineteenth century that a system of public mental institutions was created that was importantly different from past practices.

Although in early days the goal for the disabled was a return to a work status, the manner in which it was conducted was cruel and inhuman. Those who were not kept in institutions were driven either to become beggars or to perform the most menial tasks available, especially since no assistance was given them by the community. Today, the concept of a vocational goal is a respected one, not because of a lack of support for the disabled but rather because it is considered therapeutic and a necessary step in the rehabilitation of an individual. In fact, workmen's compensation and social security programs contain provisions for assisting the disabled to return to work, but without coercion and only with the full cooperation of the individuals involved.

Demonology was finally laid to rest with the coming of the Industrial Revolution, which imposed its own oppression upon the weak and disabled—that of technology. The factories established in the early nineteenth century employed large numbers of women and children who, because of poverty, were forced to work under the most oppressive conditions in order to survive. As a result of the working conditions of that time, the life expectancy of industrial workers was most unfavorable. Indeed, many of the young people who were employed by these plants became disabled as a result of fatigue, inadequate protection, and other industrial malpractices. Thus, a body of individuals lived in society who suffered simultaneously from poverty and disability with few resources available to help them to make the most of their residual capacity. It was these conditions that ultimately aroused the anger and concern of sensitive people in the Western world and led to various social welfare and labor laws designed to correct the worst of these abuses.

Many centuries ago there were people who recognized that education could be a valuable tool in improving the status of the disabled. The earliest reported efforts to educate handicapped children involved the deaf and the blind. In 685, St. John of Beverly was believed to have taught a deaf-mute to speak, a claim that was challenged. At other times, in the fifteenth and sixteenth centuries, reports were made of deaf individuals being taught to read and write. However it was difficult to achieve acceptance of the idea that the deaf could be educated, because Aristotle had much earlier stated that this was not possible. Finally, in the sixteenth century, Pedro Ponce de Leon, a Benedictine monk, was successful in teaching a number of deaf pupils to speak, read, write, and understand arithmetic. After he died, in 1584, his work was continued by Juan Paulo Bonet, another Benedictine monk, who developed and taught a one-handed manual alphabet to be used by deaf persons in communication.

Early in the seventeenth century, Charles I, who was then the Prince of Wales, became familiar with Bonet's work while on a trip to Spain, and helped introduce education for the deaf in England. The teaching of the deaf took hold in England in the seventeenth century with the perfection of a two-handed means of communication. At that time we already find disagreement among teachers of the deaf as to the comparative merits of the manual or oral methods. While the English technicians were quarreling among themselves, progress was continuing on the mainland of Europe with schools in Switzerland, Spain, and Holland all claiming success in the education of the deaf.

In 1760 the first "public" school for deaf children was founded in Paris by Charles Michel, abbe de l'Epee. One of the unusual features of this school was that it included the children of the poor, who formerly had been excluded from most schools. The abbe attempted to use the oral methods of Bonet, but was forced to change to a group manual method when the numbers of children at the institution became too large for individual instruction. He concluded that speech was not necessary in the education of the deaf.

In 1778, Samuel Heinicke disputed Michel after he had taught a number of deaf children to speak. His practice of teaching deaf children to speak at his Leipzig school became known as the German method, while the manual approach at the Paris Institute became known as the French method. Following a protracted debate between Heinicke and Michel, the Zurich Academy was asked to decide which was the better method for teaching the deaf. Heinicke, however, refused to supply the academy with details of his method, so it recommended the manual "French" method as the better of the two. This decision was unfortunate, because it was based on inadequate information, and it did not settle the bitter argument between the "oralists" and "manualists." The argument persists even to this day.

Thomas Gallaudet, an American, was sent overseas in 1850 to study methods of teaching speech to the deaf. In his first stopover in England, he made contact with John Braidwood, whose academy used the oral method. The Braidwood family, which operated a number of schools for the deaf throughout England, set such severe terms for Gallaudet regarding their teaching methods that he could not accept them. He proceeded to Paris where he was readily taught the manual method. This in turn led to its introduction into American schools, where for many decades it remained the dominant educational approach for the deaf.

Almost from the very start, the blind were regarded as special subjects. Then, as today, the blind were regarded with special sympathy and concern and, what was more important, as objects of great pity. Among the earliest known organized institutions to care for the blind were special hospices created by St. Basil, in the Roman capital of Palestine in the fourth century and one in Syria in the fifth century. In the mid-thirteenth century, Louis IX established a national hospice in Paris to serve soldiers blinded in the Crusades. It still stands as an institution serving blind people. However, these early institutions served the basic purpose of providing a home for the blind and did very little either educationally or in any other way to help them adjust to a sighted world.

The search for an efficient reading and writing technique for blind persons continued for centuries.

In 1651 wax tablets were produced in Germany that permitted the blind to write. Later, in the 1780's in Paris, embossed alphabetical letters were used as a means of instruction. However, it was not until Louis Braille in the nineteenth century developed an embossed dot system that the turning point occurred and a formal communication method for the blind came into being. It is interesting to note that the Braille method was not immediately accepted, even at the National Institute in Paris, because prejudice and tradition were too strongly entrenched among the teachers of the blind. It was over forty years before British and American schools adopted the Braille Code.

At about the same time that the Braille Code was developed, vocational training for the blind was introduced in Britain and elsewhere featuring, as might be expected, music instruction and manual arts. The program of remunerative work for the blind in eighteenth century Britain served as a forerunner of American sheltered workshops, which offered similar kinds of vocational activity. Early British workshops produced baskets, rope, thread, clotheslines, and hearth mats—products similar to those in existence in some American workshops even today.

The mentally retarded were among the last to be assisted in achieving a social and economic adjustment. Saint Vincent de Paul in the early seventeenth century provided custodial care for mentally retarded adults in an asylum for the mentally ill. It was not until a century later that attention was paid to the learning problems of mentally retarded children and efforts were directly applied to their education. By the 1840's we find institutions for the mentally retarded operating in Germany, Switzerland, Britain, and the United States. In addition to the fact that facilities for handicapped children developed late in Europe and throughout the rest of the world, the emphasis almost from the beginning was on vocational training rather than on developing each child according to his fullest potential: the goal of modern rehabilitation.

It has already been noted that in the beginning the United States borrowed freely from European countries in developing facilities for the handicapped. This was natural, considering that the American colonists were mostly Europeans, who brought with them European customs, superstitions, and human values. Also, America was a new continent, largely undeveloped and with few medical or educational institutions for the training of professionals. Because there was such a profound shortage of physicians, medicine was practiced in many cases by barbers, clergymen, landowners and other untrained persons willing to take the risk of ministering to the sick. The following was one of the remedies used by Governor John Winthrop of Connecticut, a well-known amateur physician, who practiced in the mid-seventeenth century:

> Pare the patient's nails when the fever is coming on; and put the parings into a little bag of fine linen or sorenet; and tie that above a live eel's neck, in a tub of water. The eel will die and the patient will recover (Obermann, 1965).

The first medical school in the United States was founded in 1765 at Philadelphia College, thirteen years after the first hospital was established. This should conjure up an image of what early medical practice must have been like in the Colonies.

In the United States, as elsewhere, the early attitude toward illness was a moral rather than a medical one. The concept that disability represented punishment for sinful behavior was prevalent and shaped the kind of treatment given the ill and disabled in early times. Further, the cause of illness was often attributed to an individual suspected of being a witch, and an unfortunate association was frequently made between physical malformation and witchcraft. Thus we find many disabled among the hundreds of persons arrested throughout the Colonies for witchcraft in the late seventeenth and early eighteenth centuries.

In general, the colonists were actively hostile toward all persons who came upon difficult times for any reason, including those who were disabled. This has frequently been attributed to the Protestant ethic, which connected health and illness with one's "goodness" or "virtue." Following the European tradition, we find many of the disabled in early America reduced to begging as their only form of occupational pursuit and being viewed with contempt —the prevailing public attitude of that time.

More than contempt, the poor and disabled were treated most inhumanly by people who regarded them as public nuisances and social dangers. When a town felt that it had too many beggars, it tried through various means to have these beggars transferred to other communities. Failing this, the townspeople would sometimes drive the beggars away without any concern for their future welfare. We even find remnants of these practices in current American life, in the various vagrancy laws and welfare provisions in different parts of the country. Another Colonial practice was to house the poor, the vagrant, the disabled, and the mentally ill in almshouses and poorhouses. Not until the late eighteenth century do we find the poor being separated from the physically and mentally ill.

It was not until the middle of the nineteenth century that, through the efforts of such humanitarians as Harriet Beecher Stowe, we find an important change occurring in the medical climate. For the first time the federal government took an active role in helping to provide for the mentally and physically ill. Another group that was influential in initiating many reforms in the care and treatment of disabled people was the Quakers. Not only did they establish the first general hospital in the Colonies in 1752, but throughout and up to the present time have remained a compassionate segment of our population, campaigning for social reforms and improvements.

Since other papers in this text dealing with legislation, theory, and practice cover the story of modern American rehabilitation, this seems an appropriate point at which to stop. It is important to know the many historical streams that contributed to our current attitudes toward disability and to the rehabilitation movement that has developed to assist the disabled. This knowledge is important in at least two ways: first, as a reminder of our past inhumanity, which still persists in some ways to this day, and, secondly, to impress upon us the strength and rigidity of public attitudes toward disability, which still have to be overcome. To know the present is to know the past, and if the future is to be a reflection of both, it holds many challenges for the field of rehabilitation.

III   LEGISLATIVE CONTRIBUTIONS

Mary E. Switzer

It is an interesting exercise to examine the legislative history of vocational rehabilitation over the past 40 years. It is a story of growth and development and of change in attitude toward the disabled, resulting from the ever-increasing education of the public. It is also a tribute to the special character of vocational rehabilitation as a service program, which, over the years, has earned it a cherished place in the hearts of those whom it has served.

If we go back about a hundred years to the time Dorothea Dix founded St. Elizabeths Hospital, we develop some insight into the way the United States organizes itself and brings about social change. Calling St. Elizabeths a *hospital* for the mentally ill, and not an *asylum* for the insane, was but one of the innovations introduced by this pioneering author. She succeeded in persuading President Millard Fillmore to provide for federal cooperation in the building of St. Elizabeths and further proposed legislation for a network of state-sponsored mental hospitals throughout the country. Although this proposal eventually was adopted by both houses of Congress, it was vetoed by then President Franklin Pierce as a violation of the principle of states' rights. This example serves as a reminder of the difficulties encountered in bringing about changes in social mores. It also suggests why, in many instances, it is necessary for certain legislation to be introduced over and over again before it is adopted.

In 1917 Congress created a Federal Board for Vocational Education under the terms of the Vocational Education Act, thereby establishing a precedent for future legislation that would create programs to assist disabled workers to develop new skills for new jobs. Shortly afterward, in 1918, Massachusetts passed the first state vocational rehabilitation law. This was followed closely by similar actions in Minnesota, Nevada, Rhode Island,

39

North Dakota, California, New Jersey, Virginia, Pennsylvania, Illinois, New York, and Oregon. At about the same time, Public Law 178 was adopted by Congress in June, 1918 to assist the wounded veterans of World War I in becoming rehabilitated. During hearings on this bill, an attempt was made to widen its provisions to cover disabled civilians as well, but this was resisted successfully by influential lawmakers of that era. One Middle Western Senator, for example, said that he could not support the "coddling" of the disabled.

For the next two years there was a continuing congressional debate about the provisions of the proposed Vocational Rehabilitation Act, and proposals were placed before Congress that included all of the elements of what we have come to think of as a modern rehabilitation program. These included such features as medical and surgical services, compensation for the disabled, assistance for the family, retraining when necessary, and job placement. However, the comprehensiveness of these proposals was rejected as unrealistic even by federal officials who would have been concerned with their administration. Finally, in 1920, Rep. Simeon Fess of Ohio, then chairman of the Committee on Education, presented the bill that, when adopted almost a year later, became the first Vocational Rehabilitation Act. The program created by this legislation, small as it was, contained many sound elements that have endured to the present day.

Initially the program was administered under state departments of education along with vocational education and was, in a way, an extension of the vocational education program. This led to development of a premise that the rationale for vocational rehabilitation was the saving of trained manpower that otherwise would be lost. Thus, unlike vocational education itself, rehabilitation came to be recognized as a direct service to people. Vocational rehabilitation gained an identity of its own. It was not confused with teacher training or with educational administration. Rather, it served the disabled through staff members analogous to the rehabilitation counselors of today.

A major shortcoming of this early legislation was that it did not provide for medical and certain other services vitally necessary for rehabilitation, but offered little more than vocational training. Since the rehabilitation process did not include medical correction of disabling conditions, the number of disabled people who could be served effectively was unduly limited. One of the rehabilitation bulletins of that time put it this way: "Physical rehabilitation is that part of rehabilitation with which the State Board of Vocational Education is vitally concerned, but not lawfully involved."

For the first four years the vocational rehabilitation program received very small appropriations: $796,000 the first year and $1 million for each of the next three years. As might be expected, the number of individuals served was also small, with 532 being rehabilitated the first year and 5,600 by 1924. There was as much pride in these accomplishments as exists today in rehabilitating 150,000 in a single year.

There always have been sharp differences of opinion among those concerned with rehabilitation as to whether the needs of the disabled are being sufficiently met at any given time. Some of these differences related to the question of whether one considered only the industrially injured or included nonindustrial victims and the congenitally disabled. Doctor R. F. Little, the first director of vocational rehabilitation in New York State and a dynamic voice in the councils of rehabilitation in those early days, was constantly combatting complacency. At the first National Conference on Vocational Rehabilitation in Milwaukee in 1928, he said: "We are not measuring up to the needs at all. We can possibly double the amount of work we do in New York and still not do all that should be done." His contention was supported by the Federal Board for Vocational Education, which issued the first national estimates of the size of the rehabilitation problem in 1928. The board reported that "annually, 180,000 persons become disabled through industrial and other accidents alone. From all causes, over 200,000 persons become permanently disabled. For every work accident, there are two other accidents. Every community has its handicapped, and each year finds the number growing."

In defending the need for, and breaking down the costs of, vocational rehabilitation, the approach taken by state directors in the 1920's was very much like that of the 1960's. For example, it was shown statistically that the cost of maintaining a person in idleness or in a poorhouse or other custodial institution was far greater than the cost of rehabilitating him. This was of course long before our modern concepts of public welfare had evolved.

Through the 1920's and until 1932, the level of federal support remained low, and there was no substantial increase in the $1 million-a-year federal authorization mentioned earlier. This federal money was matched by the states on a 50/50 basis. The only exception to this was in the early 1930's, when some of the emergency relief money was made available to the disabled for relief and rehabilitation services.

In glancing back, we might speculate on what would have happened if Congress had then recognized how a rehabilitation philosophy could be applied to the public assistance and aid to dependent children programs. We might imagine what a different course could have been charted from the one that has led us to our present-day problems of welfare costs. While the initial Social Security Act (adopted in 1935) led to an increase in appropriations up to $2 million, it did not take special cognizance of rehabilitation philosophy.

Another important addition to the 1935 legislation was the passage in 1936 of the Randolph-Sheppard Act, which created primary rights for the establishment of vending stands in public buildings for the blind. This has been one of the most successful specialized approaches to the rehabilitation of a single category of disabled that we have had.

An interesting fact about the efforts to obtain new legislation has been that most of the push for improvement has come from within the vocational rehabilitation movement itself. Until fairly recently, most of the legislative interpretations, drafting of new proposals, and efforts to obtain passage of improved legislation were initiated by state departments of vocational rehabilitation. Only in the last five or six years have we seen a broad spectrum of citizens and professional groups band together to use their special knowledge and experience in the interest of influencing congressional action.

When we consider the kind of public support that has been accorded the National Institutes of Health of the Public Health Service from the first, the difference in the vocational rehabilitation legislative experience is brought into perspective. For example, the recently expanded cancer, heart, and mental illness services were established only because thousands of interested individuals urged Congress and the executive branch of the government to come up with new programs and legislation dealing with these major health problems. Until recently the blind were virtually the only group of disabled persons that had organized to initiate special services for themselves. It is an interesting question as to why other groups have not organized to do similar things for various disability populations until only recently.

Vocational rehabilitation programs remained a part of state departments of vocational education until 1939. In most states these agencies were sections of the state departments of education. The agencies that administered vocational education had a profound effect on the traditions, the methods of operation, and the kinds of people that came into rehabilitation. In many states the confusion resulting from the lumping together of educational and rehabilitation goals led to a number of negative experiences that held back the growth of vocational rehabilitation.

Finally, in 1939, President Franklin D. Roosevelt brought together under one umbrella a whole group of federal agencies that served people. These included the Office of Education with its Federal Board for Vocational Education from the Department of Interior, the Public Health Service from the Treasury Department, the Social Security Board, the National Youth Administration, the Civilian Conservation Corps, and others. For the first time, and under one roof, all of the service programs within the federal government were joined in one organization—the Federal Security Agency. This facilitated efforts by those interested in vocational rehabilitation to influence future legislation to a larger degree than before. For example, it enabled Dr. Henry Kessler, an early leader in rehabilitation, to put across his concept of medical care as a way of lessening a vocational disability instead of working around it.

With the advent of World War II dramatizing the need for manpower, the Barden-LaFollette Act of 1943 was passed for the primary purpose of conserving and training those men who had been rejected by Selective Service as physically unfit. This bill really represented the first big push forward that had taken place since the first rehabilitation legislation in 1920, and it was accomplished only after many stormy congressional sessions and the hurdling of many obstacles. The assistance of state leaders such as Mark Walter of Pennsylvania and Paul Barrett of Georgia was instrumental in persuading Congress to adopt the measure.

At that time, as today, one of the major problems in serving the disabled was the lack of money needed for staffing and setting up new services. By this time it had become clear that the rehabilitation counselor was the anchor man of the program, and that the need to increase and expand rehabilitation counseling was of the greatest urgency. In response to this need, the new law included a provision making it easier to increase state rehabilitation staffs and, at the same time, withdrawing them from the control of state personnel commissions and budget offices.

The way in which this was accomplished was ingenious, especially in view of the nature of the financing provided for the 1943 Act. The act provided that the federal government would bear the entire expense of rehabilitation of the war disabled, half the expense of the rehabilitation of other disabled persons, and the entire expense of guidance and placement services.

The 1943 Act achieved several other very important results. It underscored the importance of medical services in rehabilitation and included them in the administration of the act. The additional medical components included a physical examination for every client, planned treatment of acute conditions, and comprehensive rehabilitation measures as necessary. It spelled out in detail the items to be included, such as corrective surgery, therapeutic treatments to reduce or eliminate a disability, hospitalization, education, equipment, licenses, and tools.

Of far-reaching importance, the act provided federal support for the rehabilitation of the blind for the first time. While formerly certain individuals with visual handicaps had been served and other services for the blind had been provided, it now was specified that every state was to serve blind persons who could benefit from rehabilitation services. This led either to the creation of separate state commissions for the blind or to arrangements under which departments of public welfare provided rehabilitation services to blind persons. There are about thirty states with separate agencies or commissions for the blind.

A final important feature of the 1943 Act was a provision for services to the mentally ill in the public rehabilitation program. Doctor Winfred Overholzer, who was at that time head of the rehabilitation committee of the American Legion and superintendent of St. Elizabeths Hospital, played a major part in presenting the case for the rehabilitation of the mentally ill and their inclusion in this program. However, many years were to pass before substantial numbers of mentally ill persons became the beneficiaries of vocational rehabilitation. The foundation was laid, however, and this feature of the Rehabilitation Act was farseeing and, for those days, revolutionary. Public Law 113 was to be the first large column supporting the rehabilitation temple that we know today, and this was the law in effect when I became commissioner in 1950.

By that year the disadvantages of insufficient financing for vocational rehabilitation were highlighted and dramatized, and it became far more clear as to what could not be done than what could be accomplished by rehabilitation. Although the federal appropriation had reached $23 million annually, it could not seem to rise beyond that plateau, and it was clear that some new approaches would have to be developed.

Soon after World War II, several national committees were created to explore means for returning our veterans to their previous social role. These efforts involved plans concerning the reconversion of defense jobs, guidance, training, and many other procedures necessary in the wake of a world war. One product of this effort was establishment by law of the President's Committee on the Employment of the Handicapped. This committee, still a vital force in rehabilitation, quickly became influential in the development of new rehabilitation legislation and in supporting the funding necessary to implement this legislation. In addition to performing functions in public education, the president's committee serves as a medium through which organized labor and business come together and work for common goals. Under the active leadership of Harold Russell, the committee works effectively with its state and community counterparts on behalf of rehabilitation.

During the 1940's a series of significant events bearing on future legislation transpired. Extensive hearings, conducted in the House of Representatives under Congressman A. B. Kelley of Pennsylvania and in the Senate under Sen. Paul Douglas of Illinois, developed a wealth of impressive information about the record achieved by rehabilitation. Doctor Howard Rusk, recently returned from active military service, focused public attention on the spectacular story of rehabilitation in the Air Force. Similarly, Dr. Henry Kessler had returned from service in the Navy with reports of rehabilitation successes at Mare Island. Thus, cumulatively, an aura of success was developing around rehabilitation, as colorful and well-known public leaders came forth to suggest how experiences gained under wartime conditions might be applicable to civilians in rehabilitation programs. They also pointed up the need for more money to broaden and improve activities already underway.

In late 1950 Senator Douglas held extensive hearings and drew up a bill that, when adopted, resembled Public Law 565. In fact it was because the Douglas bill contained most of the features needed to improve the program, such as the provisions affecting research, training, and counseling, that it was possible for Public Law 565 to be adopted easily in 1954.

Public Law 565—the Vocational Rehabilitation Act of 1954 —was so monumental that it might be useful to pause and examine some of the circumstances surrounding its passage by Congress. This is of particular interest because the story involves personalities as well as political maneuvering, and it is encouraging to note that sometimes human considerations prevail over political expediency.

In 1953, the Federal Security Agency was redesigned as the Department of Health, Education, and Welfare. Its first secretary was Oveta Culp Hobby, former commander of the Women's Army Corps, with Nelson Rockefeller as undersecretary. For the previous four years an international debate had been raging over the rise of socialized medicine and Medicare. Every suggestion proposed by the Federal Security Agency, *and* every health or welfare measure that was sent to Congress during the second Truman administration, was colored by the bitter fight over Medicare, with the result that anything remotely resembling a Medicare program had to be avoided at all costs.

The prevailing climate placed vocational rehabilitation in a very difficult situation with respect to increased financing and the broadening of its program. In consultation with Secretary Hobby, it was agreed that something had to be done, but what? This led to an examination of the Douglas bill, which had been supported by Sen. Robert A. Taft, Republican leader in the Senate. Senator Taft, with assistance from some of Mr. Rockefeller's expert advisers, drafted a policy that proved farreaching in its eventual effects. This policy was based on the concept that the vocational rehabilitation of civilians was lagging far behind what was being done for the military. When President Dwight D. Eisenhower first heard of the new policy proposal, he was skeptical. However, after speaking with Dr. Rusk and other knowledgeable individuals, he agreed that something had to be done to implement this policy. Thus, it was not difficult to win the president's support for the establishment of a broad public vocational rehabilitation program.

President Eisenhower was not interested in the technicalities of formulas, but rather in actual progress. He favored legislation that would meet the needs of all segments of the population. The crucial question was specifically what should be suggested. An increase in benefits usually is widely acceptable, but in this instance more was needed. As a first step in what later developed into a program for paying cash benefits to the disabled, it was decided that a disabled worker would have his Social Security earnings account "frozen." Under this provision, the period during which a worker's earnings are stopped or lowered as a result of his disability will not be counted either in determining his eligibility for future benefits or in computing his benefit amounts. Thus, income credit is maintained so that when a disabled worker reaches retirement age he has not lost his entitlement to his Social Security benefits.

Protecting the Social Security retirement income of the disabled worker represented a tremendous gain. In addition to overcoming political opposition, it also was necessary to win over organized medicine, which was strongly resisting any proposal that might be equated with "socialized medicine." The Social Security Administration agreed to include in proposed legislation a provision that the state rehabilitation agencies, where possible, would be responsible for making the determinations of disability. This is how it came about that the disability payment plan forms an important part of the total rehabilitation program, and why in the 1965 amendments to the Social Security Act the Vocational Rehabilitation Administration was granted the authority to support the rehabilitation of selected Social Security disability beneficiaries, with the costs paid out of trust fund monies.

It may be useful to trace the progress made during the first decade of the disability insurance program. The first step was the provision for establishing the freeze in earnings. Then cash benefits were added by the 1956 provisions, followed by removal of the age 50 requirement for receipt of disability insurance payments. Finally, there was authorization to use trust funds for the payment of rehabilitation costs to selected disabled beneficiaries of disability insurance. Considering the development of the disability insurance program before the advent of Medicare or any provision for hospital payments for the aged, it can be seen how revolutionary an approach this actually was. It also is apparent that establishment of this program encouraged the establishment of Medicare and Medicaid.

The present vocational rehabilitation law, as amended, goes much further, with the establishment of comprehensive rehabilitation facilities; the creation of specialized clinics for speech, hearing, cardiac, and other disorders; and the development of a variety of services that at one time would have seemed unattainable.

Public Law 565 contained a new financial formula for state and federal sharing of costs that was contributed by Undersecretary Rockefeller. This grew out of his efforts to obtain grants for special youth programs in which he was interested, and also out of a desire to create a simpler approach to the financing of vocational rehabilitation grants. However, what did emerge was little different from the basic elements of financing established by the Hill-Burton legislation for joint state and federal support of hospital construction. This was a formula involving the granting of money in proportion to the size of the population to be served and property income available to this population. At any rate, the financial base for funding rehabilitation did increase phenomenally, so that from $23 million in federal money in 1955 it reached $121 million in 1965.

In addition to the basic financial support, there is Section III of the act, which provides for what we call the "Extension and Improvement Program." This section arranged for the federal government to provide 75 per cent of the funds, with the state paying the balance, in order to improve existing rehabilitation programs and experiment with new ones. This special funding initially was for a three-year period. As a result, considerable experimentation was encouraged, such as the development of special programs for the mentally retarded, the addition of specialized counselors for certain disability groups, the improvement of administration, and sometimes the creation of new facilities.

The two most exciting new features of Public Law 565 were those providing for research and training activities. These had been added to the new legislation along with provisions for supporting rehabilitation facilities and personnel, and they relate to functions that form the very foundation of a modern rehabilitation program. Essentially, the act authorized the creation of a research program patterned in large measure after those of the Public Health Service and National Science Foundation. While these organizations were selected as models because they had achieved great success in medical research and were well known to vocational rehabilitation agencies, it is not implied that there might not have been other equally good models for establishing the means to conduct research.

The same was true of the training program, since the offering of grants and fellowships in the various rehabilitation specialties followed the example of the Public Health Service and, as it turned out, is proving one of the best elements of our program. We now have a large number—probably 1,000—of comprehensive and far-flung research programs in operation investigating various aspects of rehabilitation ranging from the simple to the most complex of designs. Our training programs, in addition to supporting the basic disciplines that comprise rehabilitation services, are also providing training for medical and paramedical specialists in various rehabilitation centers and hospitals. These include specialists in such fields as speech and hearing, nursing, physical and occupational therapy, and special education.

Other legislation closely allied to rehabilitation developed simultaneously with the 1954 amendments to the Vocational Rehabilitation Act. The Captioned Films for the Deaf bill, which provided special services for the deaf, was sponsored by Sen. William Purtell of Connecticut, who also was the manager of the vocational rehabilitation bill in the Senate. The Republicans had organized the Congress that year, and several influential Connecticut citizens were members of the board of directors of the

American School for the Deaf, where a small captioned film service had been begun and maintained on a voluntary basis. Consequently, Senator Purtell was familiar with the objectives of the bill, and it was fortunate that he could guide it through Congress.

Another new bill provided for the first time for the special training of teachers of the mentally retarded. As the educational needs of the mentally retarded became a dramatic part of our increasing social awareness, it was clear that there were not enough teachers or specialists working in this field, and that a priority need in special education was for the creation of programs to train these teachers. This was quickly followed by programs for training special teachers for the deaf, the blind, and other disability groups.

When President John F. Kennedy took office and established major priorities for education, Medicare, new medical programs, and civil rights, it represented a continuation of the expansion in social and welfare services already in existence. Two of the new programs establishing centers for the mentally retarded and the mentally ill, as part of comprehensive community mental health programs, had far-reaching implications for vocational rehabilitation. For one thing, they decentralized rehabilitation services so that every program activity was not dependent on the state agencies. Secondly, they stimulated much new research and service innovations with the promise that future rehabilitation efforts would be even more effective than in the past.

A significant achievement of the Kennedy administration was the amending of the welfare provisions of the Department of Health, Education, and Welfare's legislative program. These amendments placed great emphasis on vocational rehabilitation as an integral function of the administration of welfare, authorizing the expenditure of $75 of federal money for each $25 to be provided by the states. Although the potential of such programs has not been fully realized, they are dramatizing the growing acceptance of rehabilitation philosophy in our society today.

Thus, in the early days of the Kennedy administration, the strengthening of rehabilitation services through the Social Security Act and through the administration of welfare funds was accomplished. This was a prelude to the great expansion that began with the introduction of the antipoverty program. The Civil Rights Act, the Economic Opportunity Act, and other antipoverty legislation dramatized the condition of urban America. Inevitably, the nation turned toward vocational rehabilitation techniques as a possible means of resolving the problems of people in trouble. It is overwhelming to think of serving millions of people on a person-to-person basis. And the need for spectacular innovation has become urgent. However, the idea of a goal-oriented program, of a "patient"-oriented program, instead of an agency-oriented program, is an indispensable characteristic of vocational rehabilitation, and seems particularly applicable to the antipoverty effort.

The congressional committees that were responsible for bringing about the Area Redevelopment Program, the Economic Opportunity Program, the Manpower Defense Program, and the Manpower Retraining Program, were the same committees that also considered vocational rehabilitation. As the members of these committees listened to the testimony at committee hearings, they became convinced that vocational rehabilitation was not getting the full recognition that it merited in relation to the vast social problems. Consequently, they felt that a far more comprehensive financial structure was needed to enable vocational rehabilitation to demonstrate its effectiveness in coping with social disability.

At first the administration proposed a conservative bill, which did not provide financing commensurate with the ambitious plans underway. It became necessary for advocates of rehabilitation to take a strong position concerning the issue of making adequate preparation for large numbers of physically, mentally, and otherwise disabled individuals to be returned to competitive employment. A further complicating factor was the technological revolution and economic dislocation, which was changing the nature of the urban labor markets. This dictated a need for a more intensive type of job retraining than ever was needed before. These considerations led to the inclusion of the six- and eighteen-month evaluation periods in the administration bill submitted to the Congress.

The House committee was more deeply involved and gave greater consideration to vocational rehabilitation legislation than did the Senate at this time. First of all, most of the manpower development, economic opportunity, and educational grant programs were initiated in the House. Moreover, House committees had had a closer relationship with the National Rehabilitation Association over the years, so that their members could more readily understand the need for developing a new financial formula for vocational rehabilitation. In the past, legislation such as Public Law 565 favored the low-income states, and it was decided that the time had come to give the states with large urban populations the support that they would need to cope with their problems. As could be expected, the attempt to readjust the form of financial balance and create a new formula that would give greater sums to the high-income, high-population states led to conflict between the Senate and the House on this matter.

The House proposal was based on a simple consideration of people to be served, total state income, and total state population, which had the effect of giving the larger states a greater proportion of the money to be made available. However, the Senate under the leadership of Senator Hill would not accept this formula, and what eventually emerged represented a compromise between the two legislative bodies. Most important is that the principle of 75 per cent of federal support was maintained in Public Law 333, and since this is only for a three-year authorization, it will require substantial evidence of success for its continuation.

The amount of money made available to the states has increased spectacularly, rising from $300 million in 1966 to $315 million in 1967 and $400 million in 1968. In addition, the Extension and Improvement Program was raised to a maximum of 90 per cent federal support so as to encourage greater innovation and work with catastrophic illnesses.

Finally, an entirely new section—in many ways the most exciting of the act—was the workshop section. This permitted the establishment of many additional workshops to meet the needs of new populations. The workshop program consisted of several parts, dealing with the statewide planning for new facilities, assistance in construction of new facilities on a project basis, improvement of workshop functioning (both with respect to physical plant and staff), and the addition of specialists for professional medical and technical services heretofore unavailable to workshops. All of this was designed to establish national standards for workshops and enable them to qualify for training grants to be used in the rehabilitation of large numbers of disabled individuals. In spite of the fact that a great many workshops existed and a great many voluntary agencies were interested in sponsoring them, it was found that a surprisingly small number of vocational rehabilitation clients used the workshop as a way of entering the labor market in a given year. It was this fact, among others, that brought about the realization that an important rehabilitation resource was being neglected.

An interesting and important feature of Public Law 333 was a change in the requirement that all federal funds granted to states had to be used for statewide services. It always had been recognized that certain local communities and special interest groups might be willing to provide their own funds if these were matched by the federal government. This was now made possible in the new law with exciting possibilities of local participation in rehabilitation programs on a much larger scale than heretofore.

Other important features included the reenactment of the popular Expansion Grant Program with its use of specialists to speed up the rehabilitation process, the creation of cooperative programs with school systems, the creation of a commission to deal with the problem of architectural barriers that impede the rehabilitation of those who function in wheelchairs, and provision for a statewide planning organization that would determine rehabilitation needs up to 1975.

Several technical amendments also were adopted. These provided for four years of training support in the place of the former two years, establishment of interdepartmental research programs with data-processing and informational services, authorization of special services for the blind and the deaf, and, finally, federal participation in management services of the small business enterprises operating under the Randolph-Sheppard Act.

The Vocational Rehabilitation amendments of 1967 (Public Law 90–99) further improve the public vocational rehabilitation program. This new legislation: (1) authorizes project grants to states for rehabilitating disabled migrant workers; (2) authorizes the development and operation of a national center for deaf-blind youths and adults; (3) extends present authority for appropriating federal funds for the basic federal-state rehabilitation program for another two years, to include fiscal years 1969 and 1970; (4) authorizes one additional year (through June 30, 1968) of the present federally supported programs of statewide planning for rehabilitation services, facilities, and other resources; (5) eliminates residence as a requirement for receiving vocational rehabilitation services; and (6) specifies an allotment of 75 per cent for the District of Columbia to provide more equitable funding for this special jurisdiction.

The legislative story of vocational rehabilitation from 1920 to the present is but one link in the succession of dynamic events that have moved the American spirit in the past 50 years. It is a continuing response to a social consciousness, which seems to be growing generation by generation. As society learns more about disease and disability, the need for rehabilitating people formerly considered hopeless becomes ever greater. It is our hope and expectation that legislative advances will keep pace with the growing demands for vocational rehabilitation services.

DISCUSSION QUESTIONS

1. What will be the impact on rehabilitation of the growing numbers of disabled persons in the United States who could be, but are not, benefiting from rehabilitation services?

2. Of what significance is the emergence of nonvocational goals in rehabilitation, especially in relation to rehabilitation legislation and public support of rehabilitation enterprises?

3. Discuss the interrelationship between rehabilitation and broad American social movements, such as antipoverty programs, broadened social security provisions, changing attitudes toward the individual in American society, and the breathtaking pace of technological advance.

4. How relevant is present counselor function for modern rehabilitation practice? Is there a need for a redefinition of the counselor role?

5. As the rehabilitation movement serves increasing numbers of severely disabled individuals, will there be a shift from an immediate 30 days in suitable employment to more long-range rehabilitation criteria of success?

6. Should it be expected that all individuals who receive rehabilitation services will be able to occupy an autonomous

social and economic position in society? If not, what would be a reasonable goal?

7. As privately supported voluntary rehabilitation agencies come to rely ever more heavily on governmental financial support and program guidance, can they escape excessive bureaucratic influence and retain their unique and, at times, experimental functions?

8. Will it ever be possible for our society to value human dignity as much as financial independence as a rehabilitation goal for disabled individuals?

9. What is the relationship between autocratic types of social organization and the treatment of the disabled in such societies? Similarly, how does a democratic society influence attitudes toward limited persons?

10. What additional legislative enactments are needed to meet critical unmet rehabilitation needs?

PART TWO

PHILOSOPHICAL VIEWPOINTS

INTRODUCTION TO PART TWO

Rehabilitation can be viewed as a social intervention that seeks to promote human development. In view of the fact that disability tends to impede growth in many aspects of living, often leading to individual retardation or stagnation, social conscience and a utilitarian concern for human resources have stimulated both government and private groups to take measures to reverse this debilitation process. Moving empirically, the rehabilitation movement has inched its way forward toward a wider fulfillment of restorative goals without the benefit of a unifying theory that is consistent with, grows out of, and in turn shapes the philosophy of rehabilitation. In view of the momentous progress that has been made under these conditions, it seems gratuitous to suggest that a conceptual framework is needed to give greater direction to the future evolution of the field. Yet, the growing sophistication of rehabilitation and its prevailing interest in serving very severely disadvantaged groups whose problems defy simplistic solutions, suggest that the movement soon will need to relinquish its romantic and quixotic dependence upon pragmatic forces and turn increasingly for guidance to an overarching theory of rehabilitation.

The three theorists represented in this section constitute a specially select group. Each in his own way attempts to create a frame of reference that will help to explain the rehabilitation process more fully and give it surer direction. Despite the fact that each selects a different starting point for his penetration, they all arrive close to a common target at the locus of the rehabilitation circle. In effect, their formulations complement one another and, in so doing, provide hope that a unified rehabilitation theory may emerge at some future date.

Wright launches her exposition from studies of the attitudinal interaction between a disabled person and his social environment.

Unlike the nondisabled people who share this culture with him, the person with a disability is shaped in large part by the responses of others to him. These responses are almost always in the context of an individual-to-individual relationship, but these relationships are almost always conditioned by persistent culturally determined beliefs that more often than not constrict his development and necessitate early and intensive professional intervention. Although many disability attitude structures could be discussed, Wright zeroes in on four insidious myths: the myth that maladjustment and disability go hand-in-hand, the myth of tragedy, the myth of excessive frustration, and the myth of sin. While nondisabled "outsiders" perpetuate these myths more blindly than the rehabilitation in-group, a benign "fifth column" of rehabilitation workers maintains an emotional, albeit unconscious, alliance with the myth-holders and thus contributes almost unknowingly to the impoverishment and stagnation of the person with a disability. Wright's paper suggests that, unless the social-psychological situation of the rehabilitation client is understood, and unless rehabilitation can take positive steps to influence the social environment, treatment programs necessarily will be less effective than the situation demands.

Starting at another point on the circle, Roe launches her theoretical approach from an occupational sociology base. Perceiving employment as a continuing source of gratification and status for the "advantaged," she suggests that American society must offer the disadvantaged similarly gratifying rewards in connection with the work experience. Without receiving such rewards, a substantial segment of the population will fail to regard work positively and, to the extent that society remains work-oriented, they will continue to experience alienation and frustration in the work situation. In many respects the disabled can be viewed as a disadvantaged group. After suffering varying periods of vocational deprivation growing out of enforced idleness, limited opportunities, and lack of access to certain realistic but socially denied employment objectives, many disabled persons appear to be vocationally unmotivated.

Modern rehabilitation faces no greater problem than that of the emotional readiness to work. Without client motivation, the most enriched rehabilitation program tends to fail; with it, many of the most highly developed elements of rehabilitation service can be absent and progress will still take place. Consequently, remotivation has become a central concern for rehabilitation counselors. By applying Roe's formulations to this problem the rehabilitation worker may understand the motivational factor more completely. In her context, interest in work develops in large part from the individual's belief that status, education, and economic benefits can be achieved through this medium. Thus, it may be supposed that some of the failures in vocational rehabilitation derive from our inability to structure programs that reflect the convictions that ours is a relatively open society and that upward occupational mobility is not only possible for the disabled but is also the major fulcrum of the vocational rehabilitation service.

Super gets even closer to the vocational rehabilitation target by suggesting that vocational development is dependent upon how one uses his capacities in the life situation. As he sees it, disuse results in occupational stagnation and retardation. This concept has relevance for rehabilitation, because disability usually is accompanied by important vocational sequelae, not the least of which is prolonged vocational inactivity during both the acute and the recovery stages of illness and incapacity. Since disuse may be as crippling as the direct effects of the disability itself, the conservation of human resources requires us to concentrate more fully upon early case-finding and early client reentry into meaningful work, preferably that which is related to the individual's interrupted vocational development process.

Although some clients, especially those disabled early in life, are confronted by lifelong vocational development problems relating to their disabilities, a substantial proportion are handicapped by vocational development discontinuity. In this latter group the onset of the disability slows down development or brings it to a halt while the individual directs almost all of his energies to his illness. The longer the interruption, the more critical will be the long-range vocational problems that face the disabled person. Consequently, rehabilitation should be seen as a means through which vocational stimuli and interactions are introduced into a vocationally damaged life in an effort to shorten the period of discontinuity and preserve the individual's links with the world of work.

Taken as a unit, these three papers spell out three dimensions of the rehabilitation mission: (1) the social action dimension, which concerns itself with modifying attitudes toward the disabled; (2) the development dimension, which requires the construction of an environment building continuing links between the disabled person and the world of work; and (3) the resource dimension, which exposes the disabled individual to experiences that persuade him that major life satisfactions are possible for him through the medium of work. As a unit, these formulations suggest that rehabilitation cannot be unidimensional, but that it must strike out in at least three directions, affecting simultaneously, American society, the rehabilitation movement, and the disabled person himself.

IV

THE MEANING OF WORK IN A DEMOCRACY

Anne Roe

The title of this study assumes that work may mean something different in a democracy from what it may mean in some other political structure. Before examining this assumption, we had better be clear about what is meant by work.

The unabridged Webster fills almost two columns with meanings of the word "work." The one most relevant to the purpose at hand is the first, with its five subdivisions.

Work: 1. activity in which one exerts strength or faculties to do or perform

   (a) sustained physical or mental effort, valued as it overcomes obstacles and achieves an objective or result;

   (b) the labor, task, or duty that affords one his customary means of livelihood;

   (c) strenuous activity marked by the presence of difficulty or exertion and the absence of pleasure;

   (d) occasional or temporary activity toward a desired end;

   (e) a specific task, duty, function, or assignment, often being a part or phase of some larger activity.

These nicely cover most of the historical meanings assigned to work that have been reviewed by Tilgher, although perhaps not in the same mix; since only one of the subdivisions mentions any possibility of unpleasantness associated with work.

Tilgher, however, begins with the Greeks, which is rather late

63

in human history. It might be advisable to begin much earlier and examine the activities of *Homo sapiens,* his predecessors, and his living cousins. If we look at man's predecessors as well as at his modern relatives—the great apes—it is clear that by far the largest part of their daily round has been concerned with foodgetting. Since the apes are mostly herbivorous, this is very timeconsuming, but it requires neither tools nor particular skill. Man can no longer be distinguished as *the* toolmaker, however, for it is now known that some chimpanzees make and use tools, and that the australopithecines—creatures who were either man's ancestors or very like them—were also toolmakers.

Tool-using, however, makes possible additions to the diet. Chimpanzees shape pieces of wood or grass to an apparently set pattern, and then go off to a termites' nest where they use their tools to get at the termites. The chimpanzees have also learned that a particular plant has leaves with a spongy quality, and in the dry season they use these leaves to gather water from the boles of trees, where it would otherwise be unobtainable for them. That the australopithecines made tools is apparent from chips and other artifacts associated with their living sites. The tools were presumably originally used for defense, but were soon converted into instruments for hunting. It was doubtless the case with pre-man, as it is with modern chimpanzees, that each individual made his own tools. This seems to be the case with the most primitive societies living today. Certainly, then, both modern apes and pre-man did work in the sense of "engaging in occasional or temporary activity toward a desired end."

There is also a social aspect to work—a difference in the work roles of different individuals in the society. This social "division of labor" is probably even earlier than toolmaking. The basic division is an age-sex one, and the characteristic pattern appears not only in primates but also in many mammals that live in social groups: under threat, members of the group rapidly take up regular positions obviously developed for the protection of the young. Females and infants are centered, young adult males take up positions on the fringes of the group, and the older and dominant males interpose themselves between the group and the source of the threat. Many of these groups also have sentry animals, but, so far as is known, there is no understanding of how individuals are selected or tours of duty assigned.

Work—both in the sense of activity for personal ends and of regular individual variation in social responsibility—then, is older than man. It may also have been a factor in his becoming man. Vygotsky remarks that language arose because of the need for intercourse during work. Indeed, this could have been a factor, but if so, it can be conceived of only within the context of increasing the division of labor, which seems to be a rather general principle associated with developing man. We can readily see the immediate usefulness of language; for example, in conveying to stay-at-home members of a group the location of a particularly fine outcrop of rock usable for tools, or of a herd of edible animals some distance away. Since among chimpanzees and gorillas it is quite usual for young males to leave the troop for varying lengths of time, alone or with a few others, it is not hard to see that hunting parties could develop once food sharing became characteristic of the group. Some means for communicating their experiences would clearly have enormous survival value.

Not only has work been an essential part of man's life from his beginning, but as time went on, the increasing differentiation of the activities of different individuals within the group has been perhaps the most outstanding feature of cultural development. This is true of all cultures, whatever their political structure. Such specialization was early extended to differences in productive activities among cultures, also. The next question, then, concerns the effect the political structure may have upon the work structure of a society.

Clearly, in slave societies the hard work and the dirty work is relegated to the slaves, even though individual slaves have also been teachers and professionals of one sort or another. In caste societies, as is the case in India, occupations are strictly caste-related. However, in any aristocratic or oligarchic society, work, especially manual work, has been considered beneath the dignity of the wealthier levels.

In an agricultural society, in which most members of the group tilled their own land, other occupations were relatively few, and allocation to them was practically uncontrolled—it seems largely to have been a matter of chance and individual interest, although in either case family or place of birth may have played a role.

The degree of differentiation of labor is clearly related much more closely to the degree of industrialization of the society than to its political structure. However, the fact of industrialization it-self appears to cut across most other variables distinguishing societies. Inkeles (1960) has attempted to investigate the follow-ing proposition: "Men's environments, as expressed in the institu-tional patterns they adopt or have introduced to them, shape their experience, and through this their perceptions, attitudes and values, in standardized ways which are manifest from country to country, despite the countervailing randomizing influence of traditional cul-tural patterns." He was able to assemble reasonably comparable information for six countries; the USSR, the United States, Ger-many, Italy, Sweden, and Norway, for the realm of work. His find-ings are summed up as follows:

> We see striking confirmation of the differential effect of the job situation on the perception of one's experience in it. The evidence is powerful and unmistakable that satisfaction with one's job is differentially experienced by those in the several standard occupational positions. From country to country, we observe a clear positive correlation between the over-all status of occupations and the experience of satis-faction in them. This seems to hold, as well, for the relation between satisfaction and the components of the job, such as the pay, but the evidence is thinner here. We may expect that the relationship will hold for other components, such as the prestige of the job and the autonomy or independence it affords. Job situation appears also to pattern many values germane to the occupational realm, such as the qualities most desired in a job and the image of a good or bad boss.
>
> At the same time, we note that there are certain attitudes which position in the occupational hierarchy does not seem to influence. For example, all occupational groups agree on the relative ranking of the status or desirability of different jobs. And they seem to agree in favoring job security at less pay over a better-paying but less secure job. Yet in the latter realm we discover an interesting fact. When we add the special ingredient of a promise of success, promotion or advancement, we trigger a special propensity to risk-taking in those in more esteemed occupations, whereas those in the manual classes remain unmoved and stick to security. This alerts us to the importance of precision and refinement on seeking the exact nature of the values and beliefs which

differentiate the social groups on the basis of position in the occupational hierarchy, as against those which they share in common with all of their nationality or all who participate in modern society.

Inkeles also studied satisfaction with progress in life and concluded:

> We cannot entertain any other hypothesis but that the feeling of happiness or of psychic well-being is unevenly distributed in most, perhaps all, countries. Those who are economically well off, those with more education or whose jobs require more training and skill, more often report themselves happy, joyous, laughing, free of sorrow, satisfied with life's progress. Even though the pattern is weak or ambiguous in some cases, there has not been a single case of a *reversal* of the pattern, that is, a case where measures of happiness are inversely related to measures of status, in studies involving fifteen different countries—at least six of which were studied on two different occasions, through the use of somewhat different questions. There is, then, good reason to challenge the image of the "carefree and happy poor."

In equally industrialized societies, therefore, whatever the political structure, it would appear that many perceptions, values, and attitudes are similarly ordered to status ladders of occupation, income, and education. If there are major differences under different political regimes in the role of work in individual lives, then, perhaps they are related to the accessibility of work roles to all members of the society.

If the dictionary is resorted to again, this aspect of the meaning of "democracy" does not appear at all until Definition 5, which reads: "political, social, or economic equality: the absence or disavowal of hereditary or arbitrary class distinctions or privileges," and Definition 6 is: "A state of society characterized by tolerance toward minorities, freedom of expression and respect for the essential dignity and worth of the human individual with equal opportunity for each to develop freely to his fullest capacity in a cooperative community." Somehow this has an amazingly propagandistic ring to it. There is no such community on earth, including the United States. Perhaps one *can* say that although class differences have not been abolished, in America at least they are disavowed as an ideal.

How close does the United States, in fact, come to the democratic ideal of an occupationally open society? That an honest answer can only be "not very close" is not encouraging. We might attempt to see whether or not the United States is getting closer to or farther away from a completely open society. Inkeles (1953), in his discussion of social stratification and mobility in the USSR remarks that "the very fact of modern large-scale production—involving extreme division of labor, precise differentiation of function, emphasis on technical competence, and elaborate hierarchies of authority and responsibility—provides a natural basis for the development of distinct groups." Once developed, there is a strong tendency for social groups to perpetuate themselves, both as regards the individuals and their children. That the privileged do not want fewer privileges for their children than they have had for themselves, even though they had earned their own, is certainly a common human trait, whatever the political structure of the society. We need to consider both intergenerational mobility and intragenerational mobility, therefore, in studying the degree of openness of any society.

The degree of occupational mobility reported in any study is of course directly affected by the fineness of the occupational classification used. In most of the sociological literature on the subject, the rather crude classification of Professional, Business, White Collar, Skilled Manual, Semi-skilled, Unskilled, and Farmer is used, hence some comparisons are possible. Jackson and Crockett have reported an extensive recent study of data from a national sample survey collected in 1957, and compared these results with those of earlier studies. The analysis concerns 1,023 males for whom occupational data was available both for themselves and for their fathers. Some 30 per cent of the men were in the same occupational level as their fathers; when movement occurred it was usually to an adjacent or near-adjacent category; nearly a quarter of those in urban occupational categories had moved up, and about a sixth had moved down. The data was then compared with models for maximum stability and for equal opportunity. The full equality model assumes that the occupation of the father has no effect on that of the son.

The results show ". . . a tendency for sons disproportionately to enter their father's occupational category or one nearby. Inheritance beyond random expectation is especially marked for sons of professionals and farmers. Among sons of urban workers, deviations in the direction of upward mobility are larger and more common than those indicating disproportionate downward mobility. . . . About 85% of the sample would have moved under conditions of full equality; this compares to an observed movement of 70% of the men." This data was then compared with Center's 1945 national sample study, but the subjects unfortunately had to be restricted to white, nonfarm males who were employed full- or part-time. Although the differences were not large, it was clear that the latter sample had experienced somewhat more mobility than the earlier one. They both consider the possible influence of some age differences in the samples, the effect of the war, and, what they believe to be a more probable explanation, that ". . . the findings represent at least in part a long-term relaxation in the system of occupational transmission, due to such factors as increased educational opportunities and the decreasing importance of inherited financial capital in occupational success."

Increasing intergenerational mobility has been reported in other countries, for example, in Japan (Yasuda in *American Sociological Review;* including a discussion of methodological problems). In France there has also been some increase (Rogoff), but at present actual mobility there is not as high as it is in the United States. To some degree social mobility has decreased in the USSR in the last decade. (Inkeles, in Bendix and Lipset.)

Some groups have been shown to be more upwardly mobile than others, and there are individual differences in mobility within any given group. Bieri, Lobeck, and Plotnick studied these differences in 96 male adults in relation to religion (Catholic or Jewish), nationality of father, degree of dominance in the self concept, acceptance of authority, parental identification, family power relations, and intelligence. Their major findings were:

1. Jewish Ss are more mobile than Catholic Ss.
2. Those Ss with foreign born fathers are more mobile than those with U.S. born fathers.
3. Feelings of dominance are inversely related to mobility, especially for lower-class Jewish Ss.

4. In contrast to Catholic Ss, Jewish Ss are less accepting of authority, report less external forms of parental discipline, and perceive their parents as less controlling.
5. Parental identification appears to be more related to occupational choice than to mobility.
6. Education and intelligence are primary factors in these mobility differences. Jewish Ss tend to excel Catholic Ss both in amount of education and in intellectual attainment.

These differences seemed explicable ". . . in terms of cultural value differences between the two religious groups, and in terms of personality determinants of educational attainment and occupational choice."

If there has been a moderate degree of success in this country in developing intergenerational mobility, it has not applied equally to all racial groups. The nonopenness of society in this respect is now so much in the public mind that this will not be referred to here, except as a reminder.

How often, and why, people change jobs is not well studied. Longitudinal studies, such as would be required, are notoriously difficult and expensive. There are, however, some data, but mostly for special groups. It is reported, for example, that the average employee spends only 4.6 years with the same employer. Whether in changing employers he also changes type of work was not recorded.

Presently being studied are records of 804 men who had been at Stanford University between 1927 and 1933, whose occupational histories were reported in 1949. (A man was not recorded as changing jobs if he simply advanced within the same line in the same company.) The mean number of different jobs held by them during these years was 3.19. The distribution of numbers of jobs is shown in Table 1.

Table 1—Jobs Held

	0	1	2	3	4	5	6	7	8	9	10
N	14	136	188	172	136	79	37	13	21	7	1

Except that men who had been in graduate school recorded fewer job changes, it is not yet known what other factors may be related to the amount of change. The problem is complicated by the fact that the time interval includes the depression years and the war. (Military service was simply not counted.)

Obviously there are differences in the likelihood of change in different occupational activities. Becker and Strauss have discussed this in several papers, including the psychological stresses attendant upon mobility. They note that ". . . central to any account of adult identity is the relation of change in identity to change in social position; for it is characteristic of adult life to afford and force frequent and momentous passages from status to status."

Herman, after a study of vertical mobility, concludes that

> differences in class concepts and attitudes toward mobility need not be closely related to rates of mobility. American traditions may provide an incentive to strive for longer upward moves and lower resistance to the acceptance of a less prestigeful job, especially if it represents a rise in income; but, to a considerable extent, attitudes toward success and achievement seem to be too generalized to affect behavior. . . . The higher incomes of American production workers and greater standardization of consumers' goods, along with common democratic patterns of behavior in public situations, may provide as much support for the American belief in opportunity as the prevailing rate of vertical mobility.

Palmer has reported that both employers and workers value stability as much as variety in employment connections and that there has been a gradual decline in mobility rates in recent decades. While reluctance to sacrifice seniority may be the principal reason given by workers for not changing jobs, it is often accompanied by other attitudes that are not without significance. One such consideration is a general fear of the unknown. Established ties add an element of comfort to the feeling of economic security, since a worker knows what is expected of him where he is, and is familiar with the routine and with his supervisor and associates. Feelings of satisfaction in the particular job, expectations of better pay or advancement for the future, and, possibly, a sense of identification with a company, all reinforce his general reluctance to change. Identification with the nature of the work and other occupational attachments may create ambivalence in the attitudes of skilled workers to job changing, but they, too, are increasingly influenced by formal seniority patterns.

In a pilot study of changes in occupations after age 30, Baruch and this writer found that the subjects tended to explain occupational changes and the course of their careers in terms of contingencies and external influences rather than as a result of rational decision making on their parts.

In *The Psychology of Occupations*, the rewards of occupations in terms of satisfactions of different needs were discussed. There have been a number of recent studies that confirm that at different levels of occupations different kinds of satisfactions are available and expected. The pattern is a very clear one: for lower-level occupations, adequate income and security are major satisfiers. As the possibilities of intrinsic task interest become greater, so too do the expectations for satisfaction of desires for purposeful and challenging activity and for self-expression. In this book, and in other publications, the writer has taken the position that the occupational life has become so central for so many people just because it may, and frequently does, offer more levels of satisfaction than any other aspect of living. However, there are many in this society for whom the picture of satisfactions from work does not hold.

Davis, in a study of motivations of the underprivileged worker, writes that society must convince the underprivileged person that

> he can secure a better life by hard work, and he can be convinced only when he *sees* a fair number of under-privileged *people like himself* getting reasonably secure jobs, a place to live, and a chance for promotion. I am *not* saying that society has to provide every such worker with permanent tenure and homeownership, and likewise make him a foreman, in order to motivate him to work harder. But I am saying that the under-privileged worker will not improve unless he finds that there is a chance of his getting the basic social and economic rewards that I have mentioned. He must be given the realistic hope that the game is worth the candle. If he *does change* his work habits, if he does become ambitious, if he does begin to crave respectability, then industry and

society must have the homes and steady jobs and education to offer him in return for this greater effort.

We see that middle-class people work like beavers and have an insistent conscientiousness. They have the craving for respectability to drive them, and the hope of a better home, or better job, or higher status for their children to pull them. In order to make under-privileged people anxious to work harder and willing to bear more responsibility on the job, our industry, business, and government must convince them that they can get more out of life than they now get. This means that our system of production must expand so as to offer a larger proportion of the working class steadier jobs, good wages, and a decent place in which to live and to rear a family. Otherwise, a third or more of our white and Negro labor supply will become increasingly demoralized. In a society where even wars are won by the side with the largest skilled labor supply and the most efficient industrial structure, this is a vital consideration. In the future, our survival as a nation very likely will depend upon what happens to this one-third of our labor supply.

Before even beginning to solve the problems of the under-privileged worker, including the disabled, this society is in the midst of social changes that may alter completely its complexion and the role of work within it. For many of the disadvantaged, "work" has been a meaningless concept. The advent of the "Age of Cybernation" may well mean that work will lose its centrality for an even larger proportion of the population. What will there be to take its place? Something is known of the devastating psychological effects of joblessness in a society in which jobs are a major indicator of status, and not working is looked upon as a sign of personal incompetence of one sort or of another. Even apart from that, the possibilities for need satisfactions outside of some kind of institutionalized activity are limited. Unsatisfied needs for self-esteem and self-actualization are not only personally disruptive, but socially so as well.

American society also has unmet needs—needs for more educators, for cleaner cities, for more esthetic surroundings, and so on. As Berle points out, these are not wants that have commercial possibilities—no one is going to make money out of meeting them. To fulfill these wants, many more jobs are needed, and public funds will have to be supplied. In view of the astronomical sums being spent for the National Aeronautical and Space Administration (NASA), for example, it cannot be maintained that they could not be found. The problem is primarily one of facing up to the realities of the present and organizing effectively to respond to them.

It should be added, however, that no amount of clever organization can keep up with the situation if the population explosion continues at its present rate in this country, or in any other. We are faced with the absolute necessity of dealing positively with these problems, and the past does not offer any applicable guidelines for most of them. The affluent society is here to stay only if it recognizes itself for what it is and makes up its mind that continued affluence for the few at the expense of the many is a quick and simple road to the disappearance of a misnamed species.

V

THE DEVELOPMENT OF VOCATIONAL POTENTIAL

Donald E. Super

The wording of this topic is a welcome sign of the maturity of the vocational rehabilitation counseling profession, of the breadth of vision that now characterizes those who exercise leadership in this field. There was a time not long ago when vocational rehabilitation counseling tended to think in terms of talent. Now, many of those responsible for public policy are thinking in terms of disabilities and disadvantage. However, it should be noted that the focus of this discussion will be on potential.

In talking about potential, we are talking about everyone—the gifted and the retarded, the normal and the abormal, the advantaged and the disadvantaged, the functioning and the disabled. Everyone, no matter what his endowment, has some potential. Potential exists in possibility but not in actuality, it is becoming rather than being, it is in the making rather than in effect. No one—such is human imperfection—can be viewed as having become all that he is capable of becoming. A person may have a great deal of potential or only a little, but he is not likely to have realized all that he has. In thinking about the development of vocational potential, then, we think not just about the especially talented, nor just about the handicapped, but rather about everyone. Interest in the handicapped and in the disabled leads us to pay special attention to the development of vocational potential under adverse conditions, but we gain from recognizing that vocational rehabilitation is dealing with a special application of vocational development theory, not with a different theory.

WHAT IS POTENTIAL?

What is it that is potential, that may or may not be realized, that characterizes what the individual may or may not become? It is, of course, the aptitudes, the abilities, the interests, the personality traits, the motivations, and the concepts of self that have been isolated in clinical and psychometric studies and that have been observed to have direct or indirect bearing on vocational behavior. Sometimes the clinical assessments or psychometric measures leave a good deal to be desired in established reliability or validity. Sometimes their relevance to vocational behavior is more inferred than demonstrated. However, some of the measures are sound and some of the relationships are clear. In considering the development of vocational potential, it is these aptitudes and traits that are relevant to this discussion.

THE PROCESS OF DEVELOPMENT

The process of development has been shown, in many studies extending over more than a generation, to be one of interaction between an organism and its environment. The organism is born with certain capacities of development; development that is facilitated by some environmental conditions and inhibited by others. Thus, the common fruit fly has a solid gray belly under normal conditions but develops yellow stripes under other conditions, depending upon the absence or presence of X-rays, which are natural in certain parts of the country or artificially produced in a laboratory. Knowledge of such facts as these should have helped the psychologists of a generation ago to avoid the controversy over the relative importance of nature and nurture and to concentrate on more fruitful problems, such as that of the methods of maximizing the beneficial effects of the environment. It is obvious that whether or not the fruit fly develops his unique capacity to have yellow stripes depends upon the environment in which he is raised; it is also obvious that it is easier to control the environment of man than it is to control his heredity.

THE ASSESSMENT OF POTENTIAL

Recognition of the importance of the environmental control of development (or, rather, its "enhancement"—it *is* a more acceptable term) should not blind us to the importance of the assessment of potential. The environment offers so many possibilities, and the time available for their exploitation is so limited, that it is not possible to expose each person to all of the vocational development experience that might be opened up for him. Selection is necessary in adolescence and in adulthood, although in childhood the nature of the organism and of the experiences made available by society do fortunately permit a wide sampling.

The use of assessment methods provides grounds for selecting future experiences, for choosing from the environmental resources those that are most likely to contribute to optimal development. Sometimes the appraisal helps to identify potentials or assets that can be capitalized through training, and thus provide a basis for successful and satisfying experience. Sometimes the assessment points up deficiencies or limitations that can be remedied or for which some kind of compensatory development is possible. Although the psychometric selection model has tended to set the pattern in the use of test and other prediction data, it is not the only model. Rehabilitation counselors have been among the leaders in recognizing that the prediction of success or failure is not enough. They have, instead, stressed the identification of assets that can be utilized in mobilizing resources that may help to overcome the handicap and defeat a prediction of failure. Predictions need not be self-fulfilling—they may instead be self-defeating. It all depends on the elements in the prediction, and on how counselor and client seek to use them.

Guided by knowledge of the aptitudes, abilities, interests, needs, and self-concepts of the client as developed by his experience up to the time of appraisal, the counselor and client are in a position to make informed judgments about the appropriateness of educational, training, and employment experiences that might be open to, or opened for, the client. This process of assessment and planning is, of course, one that can and should take place, not just once in the life of the client at some one critical choice point but a number of times during the course of development, so that development may be guided rather than fortuitous, continuous rather than discontinuous.

THE STIMULI OF DEVELOPMENT

The main focus here, however, is not on assessment, but on the stimuli of development, on the resources that determine what happens to potential, and on the role of these resources in development.

WHAT THEY ARE

The stimuli of development may be classified, for present purposes, as human and cultural. Some of the determinants of whether or not potential develops are the people to whom the developing child, youth, and adult is exposed. Others are the social institutions and other cultural resources of the community in which he lives. The nature of the exposure to the environment is to a substantial degree a function of the people who mediate it.

HUMAN RESOURCES

The human resources that determine development have frequently been referred to as key figures, some of whom function as role models but many of whom are important influences without themselves serving as models. Parents, older brothers and sisters, relatives, neighbors, teachers, ministers or other representatives of organized religion, other adult and eventually peer-group friends, and characters encountered in books, movies, and television, are the key figures and sometimes the role models whose experiences, attitudes, values, and behavior affect those of the developing child and youth.

In childhood and early adolescence, role models tend to play a major part in the development of potential, for living or vividly portrayed exemplars of a capacity or a characteristic then have more meaning than do abstractions. The father's strength and power, the mother's kindness and understanding, the teacher's omniscience, the movie hero's omnipotence, the older friend's popularity, the physician's power to heal, the mechanic's ability to repair: these are the human embodiments of abilities and traits that appeal to the weakness and to the insecurity of the child; these are the role models that help him to see how he too may function "when he grows up." Thus, development along certain lines is stimulated and made easier by its manifestation in others.

Some of the people to whom the growing child or adolescent, and the adult too, is exposed influence him, even though not serving as models, because of the experiences to which they expose him. It may be a mechanical toy given to a child by a visiting uncle, a book lent to a youth by a neighbor, or a discussion with a friend that awakens the individual to a field of activity or a realm of ideas that he had not been aware of and by which he is challenged.

Role models appear, according to some studies (Henderson, 1958), to play a less important part in later adolescence and adulthood than in earlier stages of development. Factors contributing to this trend seem to be widening experience, an increasing number and variety of human and other sources of ideas, and greater ability to deal with abstractions. The more mature person is able to admire a trait without admiring the person in whom it is observed, to be interested in an activity without confusing it with the person engaged in it, and to aspire to produce something without considering it necessary to emulate its producer. He may even, as he gains skill and self-confidence enough to aspire to independence, seek to perform or to achieve in a way peculiarly his own, fully differentiating "self" from "other."

It is surprising, with all the shrewd observations that clinicians and sociologists have made about the importance of role models, with all the theorizing by psychoanalytically oriented writers, that there has been so little scientific study of the influence of role models in vocational development. Henderson's dissertation, at Columbia University, was unique in its attempt to measure father identification at the time at which it was planned, although by the time he had completed it several other attempts were made.

Subsequent studies, such as those by Ronald Schneider (1962) and Charlotte Breytspraak (1964), which deal objectively with parent identification and career orientation, have added to the knowledge of the contribution of this mechanism. However, parent identification is just one kind of modeling. A current study by

Alan Bell is the only attempt that is known to assess, in anything other than an impressionistic or direct self-report manner, the influence of key figures and role models, let alone to relate them to vocational development. Bell's task is a laborious one, for it involves a detailed content analysis of interview material. Once completed, however, it may both reveal more about role models in vocational development and point the way to improved methods of studying them.

There is a need to know what relationships exist between the characteristics of the individual, the type of role model he uses, and the use he makes of it; what kind of patterns, if any, exist in the sequence of role models used; and why role models are outgrown (if that is, indeed, an appropriate term to apply to the process). It is not even known whether role models help or hinder vocational development, or, to put it more scientifically, when and how they affect vocational development.

CULTURAL RESOURCES

The cultural resources that contribute to development have long been an important part of the armamentarium of the vocational and rehabilitation counselor. School curricula, extracurricular activities, clubs, libraries, museums, vacation and part-time jobs, volunteer work—these and other less formal social institutions and agencies have been sources of experience used by counselors. They have been used to assist students and clients to develop necessary skills, acquire needed knowledge, broaden their horizons, develop self-confidence, and acquire attitudes and values that would help them to orient themselves to, and adjust themselves in, the world of work. What they consist of and how they are used in education and in rehabilitation is the subject of regular courses taken by students of counseling.

It is helpful to view the use of resources as a kind of vocational behavior, and to classify such behaviors in very much the same way as life stages. Such a classification is only natural, as the names given to the various life stages by Buhler (1933) and used in this writer's text (Super, 1957) were derived from the types of behavior that were most characteristic of each age, although observed at most ages. Thus, vocational behavior can be viewed as exploratory, establishment, maintaining, and retiring.

In a volume published some years ago by the College Entrance Examination Board (Super *et al.,* 1963), these stages of development were related to the vocational development tasks encountered at each stage, and in a paper read at an American Personnel and Guidance Association (APGA) convention (Super, 1963), an attempt was made to separate the exploratory and establishment categories into more refined types of behavior. These were identified as floundering, trial, instrumental, stagnating, and establishment or stabilizations and advancement. The purpose then was to lay a conceptual foundation for the development of criterion measures suitable for use with young men in their early twenties, that is, in the late exploratory and early establishment stages. However, the same concepts are relevant to the present problem: that of understanding the vocational development process as it takes place in adolescence and early adulthood and again in rehabilitation after disablement.

In *trial,* the activity engaged in is viewed as one that may offer prospects of success and satisfaction; it is undertaken with the idea that it may prove to be a good choice, or that it may prove otherwise. If the former is the case, it is expected to provide satisfactory outlets or to lead the way to opportunities that will be satisfying. If the activity proves not to be appropriate, the expectation is that it will be dropped and that another trial choice will be made. The financial or emotional investment made in the trial is not so great but that it can be written off if necessary. Finally, the expectation is that a sequence of trials, if called for, will, through progressive elimination, lead to a sharper focusing of effort and to the finding of an activity that is truly appropriate to one's abilities and interests.

In *floundering,* on the other hand, the activity engaged in is chosen more or less at random, or, more accurately, is entered into simply because it is the convenient and obvious opportunity. The choice is made by default. When one activity is dropped, whether by the participant or by those responsible for it, the next move is made on similar chance grounds. What might have been learned about the self or the world in the position being vacated provides no basis for action. In floundering there is no sequential elimination of possibilities, no movement toward a more appropriate objective.

The behavior designated as *stagnating* is essentially floundering without movement from the position occupied. It is aimlessly staying in one place, and in a place that is, or will soon become, inappropriate. This happens easily in limited-choice situations, such as schools with few curricular alternatives, one-industry towns, families with rigid vocational traditions, and communities with limited perspectives on the employment of the handicapped.

In *instrumental* behavior, the activity engaged in is used as a means of preparing for another activity. There are thus two types of instrumentation: that which provides the resources with which to do something else and that which prepares one for an activity. Working as truck driver in order to earn enough money to start one's own earth-moving business is an example of the former; studying programming in order to get a job in data processing is an illustration of the second type. Instrumental behavior can be viewed as transitional from exploration to establishment, for when it involves preparation it provides opportunity for a late type of trial, a further testing of a choice already tentatively made.

In *stabilizing and advancement* behavior, the choice is more definite and the objective of making a place in the field is clear. In early establishment there is still a degree of trial, but with considerably more commitment than during the exploratory stage. The mechanical engineering graduate who decides, in his first regular job, that he is really more interested in management than in engineering can make such a change, but only at the price of giving up a substantial investment of time and money in order to shift to another field in which he has much to learn both on the job and in part- or full-time study. After this late trial behavior, we observe what is more truly and more clearly stabilizing and advancement behavior, as the individual consolidates his position and seeks to improve it.

Since we are most concerned here with the kinds of behavior that are frequently observed in vocational counseling, whether in education or in rehabilitation, it is appropriate to elaborate somewhat upon the various types of exploratory behavior. Trial and instrumental behavior are of particular significance, for in education and even in rehabilitation most emphasis is put on the latter, despite counselor recognition of the importance of trial, or what are often referred to in the literature as exploratory activities.

In his essay in the College Board monograph, Jordaan (in Super *et al.,* 1963) has surveyed the literature on exploratory behavior and examined its implications for vocational exploration. His concern is primarily with what is here referred to as trial behavior, but some of his points apply also to floundering, stagnating, and instrumentation.

Exploratory behavior, as Jordaan defines it, is undertaken with the avowed or unconscious purpose of finding out more about oneself or one's environment, of arriving at a basis for a decision, or of verifying a decision. It is vocational if it is viewed as having a bearing on choosing, preparing for, entering, adjusting to, or progressing in an occupation.

Exploratory behavior can be *intended* or *fortuitous.* As Jordaan points out, it may be engaged in with the express intention of learning more about one's abilities and interests or about the nature of some occupation. On the other hand, it may be the result of some other purpose or even of some accident. In the latter type of case, interest is aroused by the fortuitous experience, and purposeful trial results.

The trial may be *systematic* or *random,* depending upon the extent to which advance information is used in planning the exploration, the amount of planning that is done, and the evaluation of the experience that follows it. Ignorance leads to diffuse rather than focused action, but the kind of planfulness that is associated both with middle class values and with vocational maturity leads to using available information well in the planning of trial activities.

Another important dimension of exploration is that of *self* versus *environmental orientation.* The individual may engage in an activity primarily in order to learn more about himself, or primarily to learn more about educational or vocational demands and opportunities.

A final dimension that should be mentioned is the *motor* or *mental* quality of the trial, for not all behavior involves observable movement, "doing something," such as seeking a job or working as an orderly in a hospital. Essential to exploration or trial are the associated intellectual activities. It is possible to think about an activity before engaging in it, while doing it, and after having done it: the most important elements are having something to think about and doing the thinking. Although, unless there is at some point action such as reading, discussing, or working, there will be little or nothing to think about. Related to this dimension is that of *time,* for as has just been noted, the exploratory thinking can be based on memory of past experience, observation of current experience, or even fantasy concerning future experience.

It should be clear, after this discussion, that the use of cultural resources is as legitimate for exploratory or trial purposes as it is for instrumental or preparatory purposes. Vocational potential is developed not only through preparatory activity but also through the exploratory activities that first bring it to light and into contact with appropriate outlets. One of the major functions of the counselor is to see to it that the exploratory stage is well-utilized, that exploratory behavior is of the trial rather than the floundering or stagnating types, and that it leads in due course to instrumental behavior.

The effective use of exploratory experiences calls for some appraisal. As indicated earlier, the objective is to help in the planning of trial activities. Good appraisal calls for counselor-client collaboration in the selection and use of these activities, and it calls for similar collaboration in evaluating the experiences as they unfold and after they have been completed. Guidance is, at its best, the guidance of development rather than help in the making of a specific decision.

CONTINUITY AND DISCONTINUITY IN DEVELOPMENT

It was pointed out by Ralph LoCascio (1964), that vocational development theory has dealt largely with the continuities of careers rather than with their discontinuities. The very notion of a career pattern implies continuity, even though Miller and Form (1951) and others (Super, 1957; Mulvey, 1963) who have carried out research on, or constructed theories of, career patterns have taken due note of the unstable, multiple trial, and interrupted career patterns. Perhaps the reason for this has been that understanding the nature, extent, and dynamics of continuity has appeared to be the first step, after which the discontinuities become clearer and are more easily understood. They would then, to be sure, throw more light on continuity itself.

It has been shown in a variety of ways that the development of potential is in part a matter of use, and that continuity of use is essential to continuity of development. The classic studies of intellectual development conducted by members of the Iowa Institute of Child Welfare during the 1930's (Sheels, 1940) first clearly established the fact that intellectual development is stimulated by a culturally rich environment, such as that of a good foster home, and that it fails to develop as highly in an intellectually and emotionally impoverished environment, such as that of a typical orphanage. Studies of identical and fraternal twins, such as that by Newman, Freeman, and Holzinger (1937), have brought out the fact that personality development is even more affected by environmental differences. More recently, Owens (1953) showed that the longer the period of formal education, the longer the period during which mental ability continues to increase and the higher the eventual level of mental ability.

Benjamin Bloom (1964) has published a searching review and synthesis of research on stability and change in human characteristics, documenting the facts that change occurs more readily in early childhood than later, and that the longer the period of stimulation to growth, the longer the period and the greater the amount of growth.

One interesting conclusion to be drawn from these facts is that one of the best methods for insuring the feasibility of eventual rehabilitation (should it ever prove necessary) is to expose oneself to continuing stimuli to growth and change even after the normal period of exploration has been completed and after establishment has taken place. The retrainable person is the person who keeps on training. Failure to continue to develop potential—its disuse— can be the result of environmental deprivation, illness, or accident, or of some combination of these.

ENVIRONMENTAL DEPRIVATION

This phenomenon, with which psychologists have been familiar at least since the Iowa studies, suddenly became popular with the affluent society's rediscovery of the disadvantaged. The poor are indeed always with us: in the newspapers, on the radio and television, in the legislatures, and in the professional literature. The effects of socioeconomic deprivation are felt early and seen for a long time.

One other form of economic deprivation has been highlighted by the events of the past generation: namely, that of industrial or technological change. While socioeconomic disadvantage produces a low-grade continuity of many unrelated semiskilled and unskilled jobs, known as the multiple-trial career, technological and industrial change produce discontinuities that are sometimes more dramatic. Railroad workers, coal miners, and movie theater organists have suddenly found themselves jobless in an economy that offered no new opportunities for people with their skills and knowledge.

Despite the fact that the fear of technological unemployment dates at least from the seventeenth century, when sailors burned Papin's first steamboat on the River Rhine to keep steam from displacing men, shockingly little is really known about the effects of this type of environmental influence on the careers of individual men and women. Economists have tended to deal with technologically displaced workers as members of an amorphous and manipulable labor force, not as individuals whose careers are made up of a more or less meaningful and rational sequence of jobs. The few psychologists who have studied the displaced have viewed them as people with aptitudes and skills that might be used in other types of employment. They have matched men and jobs. However, no one has studied the careers of the displaced, no one has followed through to find out where they go next, how, and why.

It is recognized that deprivation is not just economic but also cultural, intellectual, and emotional. We are not as disturbed by the knowledge, but it is clear that, just as well-fed people have been found to suffer from dietary deficiencies, so well-to-do people may suffer from intellectual deprivation or emotional starvation. The effects are observable, not only early but also later in life. The high school student who has the ability to go to college but who enters semiskilled work and continues to work at that level will not, unless he develops unusual leisure-time interests, develop intellectually to the degree that would be true had he gone to college. The college graduate who takes a job that is devoid of intellectual challenge and conducive to a leisure of poker, bridge, golf, and fishing, will not grow as much intellectually during his post-college years as will the graduate whose work stimulates him to deal with complex issues and to study during some of his leisure time.

Environmental deprivation, however, has not come to be seen as one kind of handicap or disability, comparable to mental retardation, cerebral palsy, cardiac impairment, or paraplegia. Perhaps some day it will be classified with the other handicaps, but for the time being it benefits from standing on its own, spotlighted as one of the nation's most important problems, and defined primarily in socioeconomic terms.

DEPRIVATION THROUGH ILLNESS OR INJURY

This has been seen as the prime cause of discontinuity in vocational development, after or perhaps along with industrial or technological change. Studying the effects of discontinuity and finding ways of remedying it has of course been the major concern of rehabilitation counselors, although the problem has not usually been phrased in quite these terms.

Accident or illness sometimes destroys a skill and with it the potential for its development or redevelopment, as in the case of paraplegia and housepainting. Even in such cases, however, the potential is broader than the specific skill, and may be used to develop a kindred skill, such as painting toys. Sometimes the disability involves the skill but not the potential for redeveloping it, as in the case of aphasia and radio announcing. The extent of the discontinuity of vocational development therefore varies with the nature of the disability and with the availability of retraining programs.

When the development of potential has been interrupted, whether by environmental, health, or accidental deprivation, and the interruption has been of some duration, the resumption of development or redevelopment is made more difficult by atrophy and inertia. Although the physical analogy is probably too pat, unused muscles atrophy and unused aptitudes deteriorate with disuse. The ease with which young children acquire the accents of languages quite different from their own, and the difficulties encountered by their parents in learning to speak the same languages, well illustrate this fact. Inertia and other attitudes such as pride compound the problem, as ability to get along with sign language and unwillingness to make mistakes perpetuate inferior modes of adaptation and prevent the renewal and development of ability to make strange noises in strange sequences.

CONCLUSION

A case history may prove useful to illustrate what this paper has been saying in a rather abstract way. The case is of a young man whose vocational development was personally observed from the time he was 14 until he was 25 years old. These observations, it should be noted, were those of a disinterested behavioral scientist rather than those of a beneficently intervening counselor or friend.

Mike first came to attention when he entered high school, transferring from a K–8 school in a nearby rural district. His father was a laborer, an immigrant who had been in the United States since boyhood but had never attended school here. His mother came from the same background. The family lived in a shanty town on the outskirts of a small city, the father working wherever in the district he could find manual labor, the mother taking in laundry and doing domestic work as family responsibilities permitted and as the opportunity offered. When Mike was first seen he indicated his intention to leave school as soon as he reached the legal age of 16, certain that school had nothing to offer him that he could conceivably want. Mike was clearly a disadvantaged future dropout.

Two months later, in another interview, Mike volunteered: "You know, that school I was in last year was a lousy school!" When asked why, Mike embarked upon a detailed comparison of his elementary school and the school he now attended. He had, during the past month, discovered art and science, thanks to two creative and accepting teachers who had somehow stirred his hitherto well-hidden potential. Mike spoke also of the contrast between the facilities and curricula in the two schools. It was clearly the availability of both key figures and cultural resources that began, rather belatedly, to develop Mike's latent aptitudes and interests. He now announced that he would not drop out of school at 16, but would stay on to graduate. He wanted all of this kind of education he could get.

Mike was seen again, to talk to at some length, when he was in 12th grade. He was still interested in art and in science, but particularly in art. He wanted to continue an artistic education after high school, preferably in a school of design. His grades, test scores, and art work justified such plans. He was saving money from outside work for this purpose, and also found time to be active in school activities of types to which his family and neighborhood had never exposed him. Mike's potential was still developing, thanks to society's planned accident of schooling.

The next personal contact with Mike took place when he was 25 years old. He had not gone to design school after graduating from high school, for he had to work for a while to help out with home finances, and he had hoped to save some money for college. Actually, all he had earned had gone for family expenses. He was then drafted and served two years in the Army, saving enough money this time so that he returned to civilian life ready to go right to art school. However, circumstances intervened again, this time also to his detriment: his mother was seriously ill, and all his savings went for her medical expenses. Working in a routine clerical job at a salary that permitted no saving, Mike now had no plans for further study and foresaw no possibility of making any.

Mike's career from age 14 to 25 was discontinuous, with discontinuities resulting from socioeconomic deprivation and from social intervention. The deprivation was endemic in his home, his neighborhood, and his elementary school. Its first result was a lack of awareness of what education could offer him, and of the challenges of artistic and intellectual endeavor. Its later result was the repeated postponement of the higher education that he sought and that would have effectively opened up for him the better world he had glimpsed in high school. The social intervention first took place through the high school, with its stimulating curriculum and its effective teachers, and then through the Army, which offered him the occasion and the funds with which to start over again. Had these things transpired a generation later, Social Security might have intervened to provide for his mother's hospitalization, and thus have rendered the social intervention effective.

As it was, the socioeconomic deprivation was more powerful than the social interventions, and Mike's belatedly and partly developed potential was not strong enough to enable him to overcome his handicaps.

A counselor working with Mike at the right time, unlike the behavior scientist restricted to periodically studying his career development, might have brought to bear on Mike's case enough additional resources to have enabled him to surmount his difficulties. More knowledge of how higher education may be financed, more skill in managing family debts, and a better understanding of the worthwhileness of the higher-level objective for one with Mike's talents might have done the trick. This is the challenge to the counselor, to the skilled guide of vocational development.

VI   SOME PSYCHOSOCIAL ASPECTS OF DISABILITY

Beatrice A. Wright

Certain myths about illness and trauma have, over the years, become part of the American folklore that so strongly influences people in their attitudes toward the disabled. In discussing these myths, the convictions of large numbers of people are involved, not necessarily because they like them but because they seem so necessarily true. These myths are so compelling that both laymen and experts succumb to their power and either ignore facts that belie them or distort facts to fit them. What are some of these myths? From where do they get their blinding force? What mischief do they create?

THE MYTH OF GENERAL MALADJUSTMENT

The first of these is called "the myth of general maladjustment." In essence, it states that people with physical disabilities tend to be more maladjusted than the ordinary person. Aphoristically, this has been stated as "a twisted mind in a twisted body." What, however, are the facts?

There are literally hundreds of studies dealing with this question. Yet the results, no matter how they are ordered, cannot be made to favor the nondisabled group with even moderate consistency. To be sure, some studies show that the able-bodied have more mature and constructive personalities, but other studies show the reverse. It is true that a sheer frequency count would yield a large number of studies in the column favoring the able-bodied, but so often the results of such studies can be attributed to experimental artifact, if not artifice.

Too many studies, for example, use tests and measurements

91

that have been developed with normal populations and whose interpretation must be vastly different when applied to persons with particular disabilities. It can be seen that an affirmative answer to the question: "Do you hesitate to introduce people at a party," would have a different meaning when given by a person who is deaf than by a person with normal hearing. Yet, such differences in interpretative significance have too often been ignored. When a number of such invalid questions contaminate the experiment, the presumed result that the deaf are more maladjusted than the hearing may indeed be an experimental artifact.

Then there are studies comparing the adjustment of persons with disabilities and those without that ignore the possible influence of factors other than the disability that distinguish the two groups. For example, one study investigated the adjustment of college age, but noncollege attending, crippled girls in a charity camp by comparing their scores on a questionnaire with those of female college freshmen on whom the questionnaire was standardized. The former group was found to rate more emotionally maladjusted. In the wisdom of detached critical appraisal, it can immediately be pointed out that the difference in scores may plausibly be accountable in terms of differences between the two groups other than physical disability. It is important to note that girls attending a charity camp are quite differently selected, aside from their crippledness, from college freshmen. They may be expected to differ in socioeconomic status, intelligence, and personality on this basis alone.

One effective antidote to confusing the effects of other factors with disability is to entertain the "something-else-perhaps" query as a check on the "nothing-but" dogma. Instead of attributing the low adjustment scores of the girls in the aforementioned study to "nothing-but" the disability, this notion becomes as tenuous as quicksilver as soon as we introduce the possibility that perhaps something else may be held accountable. So it is that the insightful parent, teacher, and rehabilitation worker have learned to avoid the error of reducing all difficulties of the child to the fact of his disability by considering an array of possible contributing factors, not all of which are even connected with the disability.

There are other methodological pitfalls that have weakened the studies purporting to demonstrate the greater inferiority of persons with disabilities. At this time it can be said with considerable assurance that the great overlap in the level of adjustment of physically handicapped and nonhandicapped groups is at least as significant as the relatively small margin of difference found in some of the studies. Most persons with physical limitations make about as good (or as poor) a personality as do the nonhandicapped.

We can now inquire into the basis for the myth of heightened maladjustment and why the myth persists in the face of a lack of evidence to support it. One of the main factors has been called the "halo" or "spread" phenomenon. Briefly, this means that where a dominant characteristic of a person is negative, he will tend to be perceived negatively with respect to other characteristics as well; a parallel proposition holding for positive characteristics. Thus, a single fact of crippling tends to generate in the mind's eye the notion that the person is also less able mentally and less sound emotionally. To put it crassly, it is easier for man to think of another person as all good or all bad; all positive or all negative.

Since the spread phenomenon occurs unconsciously, it might be expected to have greater reign under conditions of heightened emotionality. That is why, aside from matters of disability, the positive halo so easily prevails when love is blind and negative distortion spreads with our enemies. That is also why the myth of heightened maladjustment thrives when there exists a deep fear, resentment, or guilt regarding disability.

Sometimes the spread phenomenon is even fed by personal advantage. It is not hard to see the role of personal motivation in underscoring the worst traits of one's enemies. In the case of disability, however, the motivation factor is often more covert, for to want to see a person with a disability in a bad light is morally indefensible. Yet, such a wish hides behind the demeanor and behavior of people more often than we like to think. It has been labeled "the requirement of mourning" when someone needs to reassure himself of his own status and well-being by insisting that the person with a disability is a suffering and unfortunate creature. The insistence is poured with an oozing pity that insidiously spreads the negative effects of disability. Persons with disabilities and those close to them, such as parents and spouses, have met this devaluating pity in the figurative pat on the head and crocodile tears that say, in effect: "Look how fortunate I am in comparison to you." Genuine sympathy is one thing; devaluating pity another.

The wish to emphasize the negative effects of disability and imagine them when they do not exist is also seen in some rehabilitation workers, who need to reassure themselves of the importance of their services and thereby of themselves. These workers tend to view their client as a child—helpless, defenseless, and vulnerable—and by their behavior will keep him in a subordinate position. Even parents and persons with disabilities themselves are not immune from the wish to make the worst case possible out of disability, for this wish can reflect the martyr complex, the need for self-pity, the need for self-punishment, and other needs in the search for secondary gains.

It is not meant to leave the impression that undue emphasis on the negative effects of disability always implies a wish to see the person with a disability in a bad light. Everyone knows that when there is a genuine interest for someone, there grows a concern about any matter that is troubling, such concern often tending to exaggerate the significance of the difficulty. Thus, parents and teachers sometimes see the child solely in terms of his shortcomings —the fact that he is poor in arithmetic, or lazy, or poorly coordinated—without permitting the child's strengths to help draw the proper perspective. The shortcomings are immediate and demand one's attention. As such, they loom large. The good points are not troubling. As such, they tend to recede into the background.

The question still remains, however, as to how people with a disability achieve more or less the same level of adjustment as their able-bodied counterparts. The explanation requires recognition of several factors. First of all, all human beings know rejection and frustration, disability being only one variant among many that contribute to social and personal difficulties. Second, negative psychological situations are not the only ones experienced by a person with a disability. Certainly respect, encouragement, and acceptance from family members and friends are not infrequent, and such interpersonal relations may well provide the main prophylaxis against the destructive personality effects of disability. Even the larger society looks up to a person who achieves in spite of his disability. Third, a society that gives weight to the dignity and value of each of its members facilitates adjustment by providing schools, work and recreation outlets, and other means that will meet the needs of persons with special problems. The fourth point is perhaps the most important of all: a human being is not an inanimate object becoming more and more scarred with each successive blow.

For clarification, consider the relationship between *degree* of disability and adjustment. One might assume that the more severe a person's disability, the more difficult it is for him to accept it or to achieve good adjustment. The facts, however, provoke serious question of this. Though some studies have shown a relationship between degree of disability and poor adjustment, other studies have shown no relationship, and still others have shown the reverse relationship.

To explain these inconsistencies, it may be postulated that a person with a mild disability may, because he is *almost* normal, have a greater need to hide and deny his disability, thereby thwarting his own adjustment. A person whose disability is so severe as to be undeniable has little recourse but to grapple with the problem of accepting himself as a person with a disability. On the other hand it may also be postulated that a mild disability, by imposing fewer frustrations owing to the barrier of physical limitations, should make adjustment easier. Doubtless there are still other factors associated with degree of disability, some favoring and some hindering good judgment, the resultant effect being quite removed from the objective fact of severity. Notice the shift from the physical fact of degree of disability to *psychological* concepts, such as the need to hide the disability, and the need for genuine self-acceptance, in order to account for the associated personality and psychological behavior.

In any case, the person actively works on his problems, reorganizing his own outlook and influencing environmental supports so that he can live a life in which to some extent he is master of his destiny. The success of this continuing process is simply unpredictable from the sheer fact of physical disability. Neither do such refinements as the duration, kind, or severity of disability help the prediction. We can only conclude that the common association between maladjustment and physical disability is a grossly oversimplified myth unwarranted by the facts. This is not to say, of course, that people with a disability are generally well-adjusted any more than we could say this about the population at large. All that can be said is that physical disability is an extraordinarily poor criterion for judging the mental health of an individual or group of persons.

THE MYTH OF TRAGEDY

The second myth is called "the myth of tragedy." It appears when the life of a person with a disability has been made equivalent with disaster, when there has been such a coalescence between tragedy and disability that nothing else is perceived but a life filled with suffering, frustration, and rejection.

The dictionary defines tragedy as involving "a fatal outcome of a hopeless struggle or at least subjection to extreme and protracted suffering, especially of a mental sort." If cerebral palsy, mental retardation, deafness, and blindness, for example, are tragedies, how can it be conveyed to people with these disabilities, or to their families, that their lives can be rewarding, "that they can partake of life's meaningful offerings," that not all of life is disability connected? These hopes are realities, and are not compatible with the perception of disability as involving a fatal outcome of a "hopeless struggle." The less-severe view of tragedy that defines the suffering as extreme and protracted might be applicable were it not for the fact that the modifiers "extreme and protracted" tend to be extended indefinitely in degree and time so that virtually all of life for all time is reduced to tragic aspects.

There are very few people who like to be looked upon as tragic, and those who do are accused of wallowing in self-pity or other uncomplimentary intentions. One might be willing to accept a particular *event* as being tragic, as when a loved one dies or when a crippling disease strikes, for this gives recognition to the great suffering and loss that is experienced. Even then, the person needs and wants help in realizing that the tragic impact will dissipate in time, that mourning is confined to a period of mourning and not to a whole lifetime. The tragic appellation *must be confined to be tolerated.*

The person with a disability, who has begun to accept the

fact of disability without the suffering of shame, sees life as encompassing far more than those experiences that are blocked by his disability. If, indeed, he felt that only through physical normalcy could worthwhile things of life be gained, then he would feel the tragedy of his fate and succumb either to abject resignation or active self-pity. Or, if he continued to contrast his existing state with an idealized and mythical "what might have been" or "what should have been," then the negative aspects of his situation would remain in focus.

However, the great majority of persons with a disability, even those with severe disabilities, have not allowed the disability to overshadow everything else. They have refocused their values so that the disabling effects of disability become more closely confined to objective limitations instead of engulfing all meaningful experience. In the process, physique becomes subordinate to other values, and the things the person can do become open to pleasure and satisfaction.

It is understandable, then, that the person with a disability resists, if not resents, being considered a tragic figure. He resists, if not resents, his life being dismissed as a tragedy, for the designation implies the futility of his efforts at reevaluation, efforts that have meaning to accessible life experiences. It undermines his struggle to emphasize the positive in his life, and threatens to make the negative supreme. To the person who has accepted his disability, the disability is not a tragedy entailing unabated mental suffering. Such acute suffering may be characteristic of a "period of mourning," but this is just one phase of the adjustment process known as "acceptance of loss."

So it is with the parent who has accepted and adjusted to his child's disability. He does not continue to suffer the mental torture of tragedy. He can and does find gratification in helping his child lead a purposeful life, and life begins to encompass not only suffering and despair but also accomplishment and satisfaction. The suffering and the satisfaction seem to oscillate, to come in waves, for acceptance of the child's disability is not an all-or-nothing process. The struggle to accept proceeds, even though at another layer of the personality the parent may still resent the disability and continue to experience distress over the loss of important values now denied the child and the parent. However, the distress does not remain as *the* characteristic of the parent's or child's life. It becomes tempered by adjustive forces; the heavy burden of nonacceptance becomes lightened; the depressed moods become less intense, less protracted, and less frequent.

In a certain sense, everyone might be ready to agree that cerebral palsy, mental retardation, blindness, and deafness are tragedies. That sense, however, must be carefully restricted to the time-bound deep experience of loss of important values when the person and his family are first faced with the impact of disability. Then it is that the loss aspects of the situation are necessarily in the forefront. In the case of loss of a loved one, all one can think of is the pleasure of sharing that will be denied forevermore. All one can think of in the case of disability, is the pleasure of those aspects of life that one assumes are denied for all time. Nothing else matters. However, this preoccupation with loss, with what "can't be had," "can't be done," "can't be enjoyed," and with what "might have been," dissipates with time. Gradually, the person discovers meaning in what he can have, can do, and can enjoy. Physical normality and its assumed benefits are no longer all-important.

A reevaluation of a basic and constructive nature is in process. The new perceptions, vying with the old, are threatened by the insidious equation between disability and tragedy. Yet, how unthinkingly the word "tragedy" is used as an epithet, even though its connotations run afoul of one's intentions!

THE MYTH OF EXCESSIVE FRUSTRATION

The discussion thus far should also cast suspicion on the common-sense notion that excessive frustration abounds in the lives of persons with disabilities. The little research there is, rejects this notion as a myth. When the lives of children with and without disabilities are systematically observed and evaluated according to the proportion of experiences that end in frustration and failure on the one hand, or satisfaction and goal attainment on the other, no difference is found in the two groups. The investigators conclude that the contention that motor disability necessarily implies more frequent occurrence of bad episode endings is simply not supported.

This does not mean that frustration is never tied to disability. Obviously, this is nonsense. All this says is that having a disability does not mean that the person is subject to *more* frustration. He may be subject to more of certain kinds of frustration, but evidently he becomes less exposed to other sources of frustration, the net effect being a frustration level that in general approximates the usual. Certainly, there are people with disabilities who are highly frustrated, but then there are people without disabilities who also are highly frustrated. A clinic or institution may tend to draw to its services the excessively frustrated and maladjusted, but such selection cannot provide the basis for generalization to the overall population of people with disabilities. Just as maladjustment does not show a progression with the fact or degree of disability, neither does the amount of frustration experienced depend on the fact or degree of disability.

It is well to examine the basis for the conviction that sees disability steeped in frustration. First of all, the nondisabled person, being uninitiated into the specific ways of circumventing limitations, tends to perceive the disability as an insurmountable barrier to the achievement of many goals. For example, many persons would be certain that the following activities are closed to those who are blind: playing ball, mowing the lawn, roller skating, and so on, until the list becomes frighteningly long. It is with surprise and admiration that many learn that none of these activities is denied, because the manner of carrying them out can be appropriately modified.

A second reason is that in empathy, we often react the way we think we would feel in the situation, without realizing that adjustive forces within our own psychic economy would so alter the meaning of the situation that the emotional reaction would correspondingly be different. The thought of taking so much extra time and energy to ascend stairs may be frustrating to the able-bodied, but to the person with an orthopedic handicap, climbing stairs may signal satisfaction at having gained in independence.

Still another reason is the tendency to reduce to the fact of disability whatever frustrations and failures a person with a disability may experience, even though they may be only indirectly related or not at all. Such reduction is a consequence of the power of physique to control judgments through the spread phenomenon.

Finally, the presumption that disability brings about frustration leads the observer to expect frustration: an expectation that conditions him to highlight evidence supporting it and to suppress or distort evidence conflicting with it.

Exploding the myth of excessive frustration does not mean minimizing the problems imposed by disability. On the contrary, it forces us to recognize the effectiveness of environmental accommodations and of adjustive changes within the person himself. Examples of environmental frustration-reducing accommodations are:

(1) considerations in the home that take into account the special needs of each person;
(2) school curricula geared to individual and group differences;
(3) architectural features that fit varying physical attributes of people;
(4) legislation on behalf of persons with disabilities;
(5) social attitudes of acceptance, and so on

Adjustive changes within the person that serve to reduce frustration center around accepting the disability as nondevaluating, thereby allowing the establishment of goals and patterns of behavior in accord with his abilities. Environmental accommodations and personal adjustive changes are the two foci that must be counted on in the rehabilitation effort, and exploding the myth of excessive frustration gives reassurance that this trust is well founded.

THE MYTH OF SIN

The last myth to be explored is "the myth of sin." This myth has to do with the perceived cause of disability and implicitly affirms that disability is a punishment for evil, usually on the part of the person himself or his family, but sometimes on the part of others, such as the doctor. Because this myth is so easily challenged by the rational scientific view that regards the cause of disability as an amoral fact, it is more often expressed covertly in the shame and guilt and need to blame that so commonly centers around disability.

An important basis for the myth has to do with the principle that a cause tends to be perceived as similar in kind to its effect, just as the imprint in the sand fits the shape of the foot that made it. Positive effects must have positive causes; negative effects must have negative causes. In the case of disability, amoral casualty, being neutral, does not fit the perceptual requirements. To make the cause sufficiently negative to match the negative state of disability, it must be blameworthy.

Another aspect of the matching between cause and effect has to do with man's need to bring harmony into his world by aligning existing reality with what ought to be. In short, it is wrong for the good to be hurt and the bad to be blessed. Such injustice is rectified either by changing the lot of the person as a reality, or by alerting the judgment of good and bad. So it is that the myth of sin finds fertile soil in the event of disability. The disability is a reality, and, especially where it is an unchangeable one, harmony is restored when, seen as a punishment for sin, it is felt to be deserved.

No one is completely immune from these forces, and the silent, often unconscious, accusation of the general public is one of the important barriers to understanding.

The person with a disability himself may feel pervasive, and sometimes overpowering guilt, although its content may be vague. In less anguished form, self-accusation is seen when a person, beset with a series of misfortunes or continuing disablement, feels that "it is someone else's turn," as if he had suffered enough and paid his debt for any sin. In asking the seemingly naïve question, "Why did this have to happen *to me?*", is not the person in some obscure way searching for a personal offense that might justify his hurt? A slight change in the question to "Why did this happen?" represents a major change in the meaning of the disability, a change in which objective, impersonal attribution is uppermost and guilt less potent.

In some instances, the source of the disability may be attributed to the negligence of a second person, in which case it is often felt as willful negligence, even though objective consideration may deny premeditation. Imputing an intention augments the sin to a level appropriate to the disastrous consequence.

Thus, hardly any parent of a child who has a disability can escape being bothered by the thought that in some way avoidable mismanagement was a contributing cause, if not the cause, of *the* disability. The mother may blame herself or her doctor for the sedation that might have caused the birth injury of her child. The father may blame himself for the accident that occurred, or he may blame others. Someone has to be blamed, for disability is perceived as having its source in wrongdoing.

It is important for the person, his family, and the wider public to become aware of the need to blame—why it is psychologically so pressing—for the insight will help in viewing disability as an amoral fact, capable not culpable, whose problems must be met, worked through, and lived with so that life can continue to unfold worthwhile experience.

There are many other myths that should be challenged. The four that have been selected: namely, the myth of general maladjustment, the myth of tragedy, the myth of excessive frustration, and the myth of sin, are among the most disabling, not only to the person with a disability himself and those who are closer to him but also to the ordinary person who, by them, becomes ill-prepared to meet the challenge of disability.

It may be noticed that in this discussion the phrase, "the person with a disability" has been employed rather than "the disabled person," in the belief that the former, though more cumbersome, far more adequately expresses the enormously important fact that a physical disability does not necessarily or even typically disable the *whole person,* myths notwithstanding.

DISCUSSION QUESTIONS

1. How does the occupational mobility of the disabled compare with that of the able-bodied? If there are differences, what are the implications of these differences for rehabilitation practice?

2. How far should a democratic society go in providing special occupational opportunities for the disabled that are not available to others in that society?

3. Some countries, for example, Britain and Denmark, mandate the employment of disabled persons in industry. This is in contrast to the voluntary hiring practices found in the United

States. Which of these approaches is philosophically more sound and which is the more practical in maximizing job opportunities?

4. Since work satisfies some fundamental human needs, and since social and technological change in the future may reduce the number of workers needed to perform society's tasks, should attempts be made to satisfy these needs for the disabled primarily through avocational means?

5. If work continues to be a major satisfier of fundamental human needs, should employment opportunities be made available only to those disabled persons who can meet the acceptable minimum production requirements of competitive industry and sheltered workshops?

6. To what extent does vocational rehabilitation make conscious use of vocational development theories? In what ways could greater use be made of these theories in everyday rehabilitation practice?

7. The concepts of aptitude and potential are practical realities for rehabilitation counselors and their clients. How do these concepts relate to the central rehabilitation problem of converting potential into tangible achievement among disabled persons?

8. Vocational behavior may be viewed as occurring in four stages: exploratory, establishment, maintaining, and retiring. How do these stages differ from the norm among disabled persons, if at all?

9. "Acceptance of disability" may be viewed both from the context of a society and an individual. What do we expect from an individual who "accepts his disability"? What do we expect from society in "accepting the disabled"?

10. Usually, forces external to the disabled individual are identified as causing negative societal attitudes toward exceptional individuals. What part does the disabled individual's own behavior play in the formation and reinforcement of such negative attitudes?

PART THREE

THE VOCATIONAL
REHABILITATION PROCESS

INTRODUCTION TO PART THREE

A popular conception of the rehabilitation counselor is that of an officebound worker who, in a face-to-face confrontation with another individual, engages in both verbal and nonverbal behavior that he expects will produce desired changes in that individual. In many respects, this is a glamor model of the counselor role, since it embodies a special mystique that is dimly understood by the lay person and, in many instances, by the professional as well. The interactive view of the rehabilitation counseling job is attractive to most counselor trainees, since it bears a close relationship to high-prestige psychotherapeutic processes, it allies the counselor with psychiatrists and other mental health practitioners, and it provides entree into an area in which "mysteries" and "magic" abound. To a certain degree, almost all rehabilitation counseling jobs offer opportunities for face-to-face counseling of this type, but, as McGowan reports, other types of rehabilitation counselor activities predominate, especially in state rehabilitation agencies.

If anything distinguishes rehabilitation counseling from other types it is action coupled with interaction. Primarily, this action appears to be in the form of diagnosis, analysis and planning with particular reference to environmental change. From the outset it should be recognized that counselor action would have limited effect but for the face-to-face interactive counseling that accompanies, supports, and clarifies it. However, the rehabilitation counselor is essentially a doer, who functions within a well-structured activity framework that channels his energy and provides sequence to the rehabilitation process. In fact, this doing aspect of rehabilitation counseling may be the most powerful dynamic in the rehabilitation experience. Thus, while interaction occurs in rehabilitation counseling, it leads to, and acquires significance from, the activities undertaken both by the client and the counselor outside the counseling room.

The three papers in this section describe the scope of counselor activities and suggest the skills that are required to make them productive. In some quarters there is a tendency to demean the evaluative, training, placement, and follow-up concerns of the rehabilitation counselor. Those who hold this view perceive the counseling relationship and its consequent interpersonal transactions as the key to rehabilitation. Although this may be so, the evidence that is now at hand questions the attributing of special contributions exclusively to counseling. On the contrary, much of the benefit of a vocational rehabilitation service seems to derive from the action that clients and their counselors undertake, singly and together. Consequently, both environmental and personal interactions are critical ingredients in rehabilitation. At the very least, the action functions of the rehabilitation counselor are an integral part of the counseling functions and, in many cases, are instrumental in shaping the direction and effectiveness of the rehabilitation process.

This being the case, referral, evaluation, training, placement, and follow-up cannot be separated from counseling, per se. In his paper, McGowan suggests the range and variety of competencies required to admit and assess a client and to prepare him for subsequent vocational rehabilitation experiences. Sinick notes similarly in his paper the complex skills required in offering training, placement, and follow-up services. In both instances, high-level counselor judgments are essential, as is the capacity to take reasoned decisive action in cooperation with clients, their families, and their communities. These judgments and decisions are no less vital in determining the course of rehabilitation than the judgments and decisions made in the counseling room.

A comparable but somewhat different situation prevails in relation to research. In this area, in which action is also central, the counselor should engage in diagnostic activities to ascertain the relevance of studies for his own practice. Since counselor growth rests heavily upon awareness of the effectiveness of various interventions, Rusalem makes a case for each counselor's having research functions, whether or not he perceives himself primarily as a researcher. Unless counselors maintain favorable attitudes toward research and take appropriate consequent action, a gulf develops between innovative practice and the everyday clinical service—a gulf that increases the probability of counselor obsolescence. Thus, to be good practitioners, counselors must be imbued with research values.

As the reader considers the papers in this section, he may wonder about the almost unreasonable richness, diversity, and complexity of the rehabilitation counseling job. This feeling is well founded. The field is still grappling with such professional problems as the establishment of a role model for the rehabilitation counselor, the reality limits of the rehabilitation counseling job, the disparate roles, and the values and limitations of developing professional and subprofessional specialties within the field. The three papers in this section may play a part in fashioning the reader's viewpoint.

VII

REFERRAL, EVALUATION, AND TREATMENT

John F. McGowan

Rehabilitation is a process that is applied to disabled persons in an effort to help them achieve fuller development. This process usually is a complex interaction of professional interventions and client responses. At no point can one identify clearcut demarcations among the steps in the process, since all are interwoven in a single fabric. However, so that we can examine referral, evaluation, and treatment in depth, they will be discussed as discrete units. The reader should remember that this is a matter of convenience and rarely, if ever, appears in this fashion in real life.

Before discussing referral, evaluation, and treatment in turn, it is advisable to present some operational definitions of terms that will be used in this chapter.

(1) *Vocational Rehabilitation*—The process of restoring the handicapped individual to the fullest physical, mental, social, vocational, and economic usefulness of which he is capable. (Key word is "fullest.")

(2) *Disability*—A condition of impairment—physical or mental—having an objective aspect that can be described by a physician. (Medical disability.)

(3) *Handicapped*—Accumulative effect of the obstacles that disability interposes between the individual and his maximum functional level. The handicap is the measure of the loss of the individual's capacity, however evident. It is an individual thing, composed of the barriers that the handicapped person must surmount in order to obtain the fullest physical, mental, social, vocational, and economic usefulness of which he is capable.

(4) *Vocational Rehabilitation Counseling*—(This definition was

prepared at a previous guidance training and placement workshop of Vocational Rehabilitation Administration supervisors.)—A process in which the counselor thinks and works
in a face-to-face relationship with a disabled person in order
to help him to understand both his problems and potentialities
and to carry through a program of adjustment and self-
improvement to the end that he will make the best obtainable
vocational, personal, and social adjustment.
(5) *Vocational Rehabilitation Counseling* (McGowan's definition)
—For me, the vocational rehabilitation counselor's unique
contribution to handicapped clients consists of intrinsic interest
in their problems: special training and supervised experience
that have prepared him to combine medical data from the
physician, psychological data from the psychologist, psycho-
social-vocational data based on his own special training in
testing and counseling, and information about the world of
work obtained from the employment services and other sources
—all utilized in the counseling process with a client in such
a way that a vocational plan, acceptable to both the client
and the counselor, is arrived at that promises the client the
best possible chance of achieving job satisfaction and vocational success.

The Vocational Act (Public Law 565, 1964) makes the
following statement: The purpose . . . "to render the disabled
individual fit to engage in a remunerative occupation . . . and
to provide the disabled individual with the rehabilitation services
needed to achieve the best possible vocational adjustment."
It should be emphasized that vocational rehabilitation, as
perceived by Congress, is concerned with the individual's vocational
adjustment. However, this emphasis on vocational adjustment does
not eliminate the rehabilitation counselor's interest in the personal
and social aspect of his client's adjustment. Again quoting from
Public Law 565: The counselor is responsible for ". . . all of the
health, personal, and social problems related to the disabled
individual's best possible vocational adjustment."
Thus, the vocational rehabilitation counselor is concerned
with his client's personal and social problems, but only insofar as

they affect his vocational adjustment. This appears to be one of the main differences between the work of the clinical psychologist and the rehabilitation or counseling psychologist. Traditionally, the clinical psychologist is more concerned with the "process" of adjustment, while the rehabilitation counselor is concerned primarily with the final outcomes, or "product," of the services offered.

To me, the program seems to be founded on two assumptions: First, that every member of a democratic society has an inherent right to the opportunity to earn a living and to make his contribution to society; second, that society has the corresponding obligation to equalize, as best it can by special services, the disabled person's opportunity to earn a living equivalent to the opportunity possessed by nondisabled members of society.

As we are all aware, this concept has resulted in Congress' passing a fantastic amount of social welfare and/or rehabilitation legislation within the past several years. This was best exemplified when President John F. Kennedy remarked in his 1962 State of the Union address: "To help those least fortunate of all, I am recommending a new program of social welfare (and rehabilitation), stressing services instead of support, rehabilitation instead of relief, and training for useful work instead of prolonged dependency."

Starting with the Smith-Fess Act of 1920 through the Vocational Rehabilitation amendments of 1968, the legislation related to vocational rehabilitation has resulted in the establishment of a state-federal service that provides what is commonly known as the vocational rehabilitation process. The process begins with the initial case finding and referral and ends with the successful placement of the handicapped individual on a job. The unique characteristic that distinguishes and differentiates the vocational rehabilitation process from all other forms of counseling is its primary objective, which is a realistic and permanent vocational adjustment of the handicapped individual.

The rehabilitation process is a planned, orderly sequence of services related to the total needs of the handicapped individual. It is a process built around both the problems of a handicapped individual and the attempts of the vocational rehabilitation counselor to help solve these problems and thus bring about the vocational adjustment of the handicapped person.

There are several basic principles underlying the process. These are:

(1) Action must be based upon adequate diagnostic information and accurate and realistic interpretation of the information that is secured.
(2) Each rehabilitation client must be served on the basis of a sound plan.
(3) Guidance and counseling of clients and close supervision of all services are essential at each step of the process.
(4) Each service must be thoroughly rendered and followed up.
(5) The cooperation and involvement of the client and all others concerned with his rehabilitation is necessary and must be secured before adequate rehabilitation can be accomplished.
(6) Adequate records must be kept.

There are several basic steps in the vocational rehabilitation process. These are:

(1) Selection and preliminary investigation;
(2) Accumulation of client study data:
    a. medical evaluation,
    b. social evaluation,
    c. psychological evaluation,
    d. vocational evaluation;
(3) Formulation of a vocational rehabilitation diagnosis:
    a. identification of problems,
    b. determination of eligibility,
    c. vocational appraisal for the purpose of selecting a job objective,
    d. identification of rehabilitation services needed;
(4) Planning and arranging rehabilitation services;
(5) Selective placement and case closure;
(6) Evaluation of placement and case closure.

This chapter will now treat in greater depth three major components of the vocational rehabilitation process: referral, evaluation, and treatment.

REFERRAL

The two basic questions to be answered when considering the matter of referral are: first, where do the people come from?; second, what do they want from rehabilitation?

Data on referral sources from 1957–1963 indicate that about 12 percent of the people who are declared rehabilitated in any given year came to the agency as self-referrals. The other 88 per cent are referred from a wide variety of sources: Approximately 30 percent are referred by physicians or hospitals; 12 to 15 percent by welfare agencies; 10 to 12 percent by educational institutions; with the remainder being referred from many different sources. These sources would include such agencies as labor unions, crippled children's service, Old Age Security Insurance, and the employment service.

These data clearly indicate that year after year, when national figures are considered, from 80 to 90 per cent of the clients who receive rehabilitation services are referred. Nevertheless, it should be pointed out that the actual source from which any given counselor will receive a majority of referrals will vary greatly from region to region, from state to state, and from counselor to counselor. In the Midwest, if a counselor is assigned to a county or a town where a state hospital is located, he may carry a large number of referrals from such a hospital on his caseload. Another counselor will receive a substantial number of referrals from local welfare offices, from a school for the mentally retarded, from a prison, or from any number of such agencies or facilities that may be located in his specific territory. In New York City or Chicago a counselor's entire caseload may consist of referrals from one facility or agency.

Data on the type of disabling condition served by vocational rehabilitation indicate that approximately 40 per cent of the people served have some type of orthopedic disability. From there, the figure drops to 10 per cent with some form of visual difficulty or blindness, 5 per cent mentally ill, 5 per cent mentally retarded. The remaining percentage is distributed among all different types of disabilities.

As is true in so many other areas, a disabling condition seems related to social class, with chronic limitations of activity most prevalent among low income families. Approximately 21 percent of persons in families with incomes under $2,000 per year had some degree of chronic limitation of activity. This proportion decreased steadily to only 7 percent with activity limitations in families with incomes of $7,000 or more.

In rehabilitation, as in medicine and related fields, one of the problems involved in planning facilities and services has been the lack of up-to-date information on the number and characteristics of persons with chronic diseases and impairments. However, under legislation enacted by Congress in the summer of 1956, a continual national health survey has been inaugurated, which is providing current data, on a regular basis, on the health status of the general population.

There are great differences in the way referrals are made to rehabilitation agencies as well as great differences in the quality of the referrals. The personnel of one referring agency may have accurate knowledge about the type of services that rehabilitation is in the position to provide, may understand eligibility requirements, may refer clients as early as possible, and may refer only people for whom there is a reasonable expectation that vocational rehabilitation services will be helpful. The personnel of another agency may have either little or inaccurate knowledge of vocational rehabilitation, may refer people who are ineligible or not feasible, or may refer clients only when their own agency has exhausted all of its resources and given up.

It should be pointed out that there is a great influx of technical, subprofessional personnel into all of the helping relationship areas. This has been caused by the great demand for personnel created by current legislation in the fields of vocational rehabilitation, welfare, and, more specifically, provisions of the Economic Opportunity Act. Because there is simply not enough trained personnel available to staff existing positions, one by one the disciplines involved are assigning certain duties to personnel with minimal training. As long as these people are adequately supervised and provided with in-service training, the system may work. However, more and more rehabilitation agencies are receiving referrals from people who have little actual knowledge of the services rehabilitation is in a position to provide. There is also the possibility that many cases will be referred by untrained personnel who are neither sure of themselves nor of the services that they are supposed to provide, and who may unfortunately project many of their own feelings of inadequacy and uncertainty onto the personnel of the agency to whom the client is referred. It may be that the use of technical subprofessional personnel will require a restructuring of existing and established interagency policies and relationships, especially in large metropolitan areas such as New York City.

By way of summary on the topic of referral—a counselor would want the agencies who are in a position to refer clients to know the community resources, to understand the eligibility requirements of various agencies, to have a realistic picture of the services provided, and, finally, to appreciate the importance of referring clients as soon as possible. Although research data on the relationship between the time of disability, referral, and initiation of treatment services are fragmentary, it has been found that the sooner a rehabilitation counselor can establish contact and initiate services the better the chances will be for a successful outcome.

EVALUATION

Vocational evaluation is defined as the process of gathering, interpreting, analyzing, and synthesizing all vocationally significant data, that is, medical, social, psychological, that have been collected regarding an individual and relating them to occupational requirements and opportunities. Before discussing the three areas of medical, social, and psychological evaluation, consideration should be given to the determination of eligibility.

The physician who serves as medical consultant has the obligation to evaluate the medical information that has been secured and to determine if a physical disability exists. However, the vocational rehabilitation counselor must gather additional data, which will be used to determine if the client is eligible for rehabilitation and if there is a reasonable expectation that the provision of services will result in a successful closure. The 1954 amendments state that eligibility shall be based upon:

(1) the presence of a physical or mental disability and resulting functional limitations or limitations in activities;

(2) the existence of a substantial handicap to employment, caused by the limitations resulting from such disability; and

(3) a reasonable expectation that vocational rehabilitation services may render the individual fit to engage in a remunerative occupation.

The newest legislation (PL 333) recognizes that the counselor cannot readily obtain enough data to determine the eligibility of certain applicants who have complicated problems or severe disabilities. It authorizes that full vocational goods and services be provided to these severely handicapped people for up to six months as the usual maximum. For the mentally retarded, and applicants with catastrophic disabilities as designated by the Secretary of Health, Education, and Welfare, vocational goods and services can be rendered up to a maximum of eighteen months before evaluating the eligibility of the applicant. Within this six- or eighteen-month period, the state agency can observe the applicant's response to services and thereby be better able to predict whether further services would make him employable.

The term eligibility is not to be confused with factors that may cause an otherwise eligible case to be rejected or not accepted for services. The Regulations Governing the Vocational Rehabilitation Program (1954, Sec. 401.18) state: "If a State is unable to serve all eligible persons who apply for service, the State agency establishes a system of priorities for determining the order in which individuals are accepted for service." As an example, while a person requiring extensive medical restoration may meet the eligibility requirements on the basis of his disability, because of a state's priority system he may legally be refused vocational rehabilitation services, or the services may be delayed.

Prior to PL 333, economic need was another factor that was considered in relation to eligibility for some services. As far as the federal government is concerned, the new law removes any previous requirement that the handicapped individual must prove his economic need before certain services (for example, physical restoration) could be provided. State agencies no longer have to use an economic needs test to distinguish an applicant's entitlement for certain services from his basic eligibility. However, the new legislation gives each state the freedom to retain (or introduce) a needs test as it deems necessary. The intent of the new law is to encourage states to eliminate tests of economic need in an effort to see whether this will result in larger numbers of people rehabilitated yearly.

In practice, the rehabilitation counselor usually has little difficulty in determining eligibility. He utilizes the client-study material that he has gathered about the applicant and relates it to three areas that must be considered for every individual who is given further services: medical, psychological, and social.

The major purposes of the medical diagnostic study and evaluation in vocational rehabilitation are:

(1) to establish, through competent medical judgment, that a physical or mental impairment is present that materially limits the activities that the individual can perform (as one aspect of determining the individual's eligibility for services as a "disabled" person);

(2) to appraise the current general health status of the individual, including the discovery of impairments not previously recognized, with a view to determining his limitations and capacities;

(3) to determine to what extent and by what means the disabling condition can be removed, corrected, or minimized by physical restoration services; and

(4) to provide a realistic basis for selection of an employment objective that is commensurate with the disabled individual's capacities and limitations.

This is an area of the rehabilitation counselor's work that presents some rather unique ethical problems. Through the authority of the physician who serves as medical consultant for his agency, the counselor is provided with extensive medical data about his clients. This raises the immediate question of how much training the counselor needs in order to be able to use medical information adequately as a part of the counseling process. It seems obvious that serious and permanent harm can result if inaccurate medical interpretations are made to clients. Most authorities appear to agree that before a counselor can effectively utilize medical information and the services of his medical consultant, he needs training in the following areas: medical terminology, basic information about types of disability, limiting effects, residuals, and the probable effects of physical restoration.

The general procedures that a rehabilitation counselor goes through in obtaining medical information are relatively standard. A general medical examination is usually obtained. This examination can be given by the family doctor, by the referring agency, or by local physicians who are known to the agency and who are willing to give the exam for the fee allowed under the state fee system. The general medical is usually reviewed with the medical consultant, and in many cases the client is then referred to medical specialists for more complete medical information.

Once the medical reports are in, the counselor has an opportunity to again discuss with the medical consultant what medical services are needed and what permanent limitations are involved. The physician or physicians involved retains primary responsibility for interpreting medical data to the client. However, this is often not done in actual practice, and the counselor ends up with the job of interpreting medical limitations to the client when occupational choices are being discussed. Everyone entering the field of vocational rehabilitation counseling needs to be aware of the responsibility he incurs when working with medical information, and to realize that each counselor must accept personal responsibility to become as well prepared as he can in this area.

By way of a brief summary: the counselor is the principal recipient of medical consultation services. All medical consultation services, whether administrative, educational, or local, have the effect of refining the counselor's role in relationships with his clients. He can clarify, expedite, interpret, and make decisions with greater effectiveness through the use of medical consultation.

The counselor cannot expect to develop all the skills necessary to solve the complex problems presented by disabled persons. Regular medical consultation can be of assistance to the clients and to the counselor in overcoming some of the barriers to successful rehabilitation. It should cover the variety of disabling conditions brought to the attention of the counselor and be available to him as needed.

The counselor can expect to utilize medical consultation services more effectively by better understanding the following:

(1) The medical terminology, physical findings, diagnoses, and recommendations contained in medical reports.

(2) How disabling the client interprets his condition to be, and how he relates it to employability.

(3) How physical restoration may improve the client's employability.

(4) The skills of specialists in the diagnostic study and treatment programs.

(5) The residuals of a disabling condition: the limiting effects, the physical stability of the client, and the progress of a client under treatment.

(6) How the regulations regarding eligibility, services, training, and employment are both related to, and affected by, medical evaluation and interpretation.

In preparing cases for the services of a medical consultant, the counselor should:

(1) Review all cases to determine the need for medical consultation and select those cases presenting problems for presentation to the consultant.

(2) Select cases recommended for treatment, surgery, and prosthesis and cases presenting multiple disabilities.

(3) Present cases where a conflict of information has occurred. This could be between physician and patient, counselor and client, physician and physician, or physician and consultant.

(4) Prepare his material so he can be brief and to the point in presenting cases to the consultant.

The psychological evaluation of a client obviously forms an integral part of the client-study process. Evaluation involves more than mere psychological testing. It includes the study of the client's past behavior as well as conclusions drawn from observations of his current behavior during the initial interview and outside contacts. The evaluation of the client's behavior is in no way limited to the preliminary phase of the study, but continues during the entire rehabilitation process. The professionally trained rehabilitation counselor is continually checking his observations and predictions against the client's overt behavior and modifying counseling techniques and possibly even tentative job objectives on the basis of these observations.

The rehabilitation counselor bears the responsibility for determining both the need and extent of psychological evaluation. It is his job to provide either directly for the evaluation, if trained to do so, or to secure the information from other sources. In most rehabilitation agencies, psychological evaluation may be provided by the counselor himself, by psychologists on the state staff, by consulting psychologists on the state staff, or by outside psychologists, if they have special training in the area of diagnostic work with the handicapped. Nevertheless, the ultimate responsibility for the application of the information obtained lies with the counselor. He is professionally obligated to make use of the information gained during the psychological evaluation to help the client know and understand himself and to help him in arriving at a reasonable vocational objective. During the initial phase of the case study, the psychological evaluation provides valuable information in the determination of eligibility and feasibility.

Counselors obviously want and need as much information as can be secured about a client's ability, interest, achievement, and personality. Unfortunately, norms based on disabled or handicapped persons are not readily available, and in many cases such data as are available are based on very small samples. In using personality scales the evaluator has to be aware that many personality factors may be directly related to the disability and resulting environmental stress. Who wouldn't show depression and hysteria spikes on the Minnesota Multi-Phasic Personality Inventory (MMPI) if confined to a chronic neurological or orthopedic surgery ward?

The psychological effects of physical disability can be roughly classified as falling under three headings:

(1) Psychological effects arising directly from the disability—as in the case with cerebral palsied, brain damaged, and so on;
(2) psychological effects arising from the client's attitude towards his disability. We can never be sure of his reaction, since we do not have data about his predisposition. His reaction will depend in large part on
   (a) his adjustment prior to his disability,

(b) the amount of fear or tension involved,

(c) information he has received,

(d) reaction of family and friends, and

(e) hope for regaining independence and security; and

(3) psychological effects arising from the attitudes and behavior of others toward him.

All three of these areas are extremely difficult to evaluate for a number of reasons: the individual's own awareness of needs and fears; pain thresholds and frustration tolerance (differences); reaction of others we cannot control; and previous adjustment levels.

Finally, a brief word on social evaluation. Working on the assumption that "past performance is the best prediction of future performance," a study of the client's social history and present environmental stimuli must be viewed as an integral part of the rehabilitation process. A complete social history is necessary for an evaluation of the client's total problem and is the background against which a probable solution to the client's difficulties is formulated.

The full understanding of a client's disability requires complete and carefully selected information concerning the extent of his disability and the nature of his response to this and other life experiences. A social history is necessary for a diagnosis of the total problem and is the background against which a probable solution to the disabled person's problem is formulated. The social evaluation should be as thorough as possible. It reflects the life style and the individual characteristics of the client.

Pertinent information is secured in relation to what appears to be the client's problem(s). Some of the content included in the history may be contained in the routine "survey." However, this may be supplemented in narrative recording as additional problems are identified or further information is obtained. The history should not be cluttered with irrelevant information. The client is encouraged to tell his own story in his own way, but the counselor guides the interview, keeping in mind the information that is desired. Notetaking or recording should be kept to a minimum if an easy, relaxed atmosphere is to be maintained. If the client gets the impression that the counselor is asking questions and then recording the answer, he will soon learn to wait for the next question.

In the recording of the history, the primary source of information is the client. If the agency is a member of a local social service exchange, then the counselor can obtain a record of the social agencies that know the client. Reports from these agencies should be obtained and significant material incorporated under the appropriate headings in the psychosocial history. Information other than that obtained from the client may be incorporated in appropriate sections of the history, with the particular source identified.

The techniques of history taking and writing are developed through practice. It is necessary for the counselor to hear as well as listen. He must bear in mind the importance of the sequence of events, associating the appearance of certain reactions with particular experiences. For example, was there any change in the health picture following divorce or trouble on the job? The counselor should explain that, in order to plan for successful rehabilitation, he must know the client as a person, which means he should know about his health history; how and where he has lived; his education; his interests; and so on. There is no set form or procedure for the taking of a history, but usually the major disability is a logical beginning point. If the counselor simply asks the client to tell about the trouble he is having, he will generally have little difficulty in getting a detailed description of the current disability.

TREATMENT

Throughout this chapter the premise that each client's needs must be considered individually has been emphasized; that is, the rehabilitation process is an individual process. This is especially true in the provision of rehabilitation services. The rehabilitation counselor has a great amount of freedom and flexibility in formulating a plan of services for each client; however, this freedom should be exercised with discretion and foresight. The services provided a client should not only meet his present needs but, insofar as possible, encompass future needs. A capacity to develop adequate plans of service for disabled individuals is one of the necessary and unique qualifications for rehabilitation counseling.

Generally, the rehabilitation counselor can provide whatever services are reasonable and necessary to insure the best obtainable vocational adjustment for his clientele. Vocational rehabilitation legislation has authorized a wide range of services that can be utilized in the rehabilitation process. There is also a great deal of latitude within each service, that is, the counselor and the client may select a training facility from several possible colleges or vocational schools.

Peterson, in a study done at the University of Missouri (completed in 1963), analyzed the various services provided in a random sample of 213 Missouri vocational rehabilitation clients who had been closed as rehabilitated. He listed eighteen possible services, that is, intake evaluation, medical evaluation, counseling, prosthetic appliance, referral to another agency, vocational evaluation, vocational training, medical treatment, trial placement, mobility training, and so on. The results of his investigation indicated that over 98 percent of the clients received intake and medical evaluation. All subjects in the study were provided at least two different services. The largest number of services provided to a single client was thirteen, the least number was two, and the average number of services provided to clients was five. He also reported a wide variation in the types of services provided.

In most states a planned program of services is generally approved prior to the actual authorization for any vendor to begin providing services. A written authorization is sent to the vendor with a description of the type of service, proposed expenditures, and method of reporting and billing. If the cost of a portion of the service is to be paid by the client or other resource, the vendor is informed.

The client is informed of the services, starting date, conditions of contract, and regulations of the agency pertaining to the services. If release forms, receipts, or other signed statements are required prior to initiation of services, they are secured by the counselor. A written statement is sent to the client confirming the plan of service prior to the starting date. Sufficient time is allowed between approval and starting date so that the client can reasonably be expected to meet the schedule.

The counseling relationship continues during the entire period of service. In cases where the client is from out of the district or state, and is under the supervision of another person during the period of services, complete information needs to be sent to the supervising office. The client is then informed of the availability of counseling services in the district or state where he is presently residing, and the supervising office arranges for continual counseling.

SUMMARY AND CONCLUSION

The main issues that are involved as the counselor attempts to implement the rehabilitation process have to do with his role as either a "coordinator" of services or as a "counselor." Both of these models are very much in existence in both our training programs and in field practice today. The counselor model sees the counselor working primarily as a professional counselor, whose main contribution to the rehabilitation process is the counseling services that he provides. The coordinator model sees him working primarily as an interdisciplinary-oriented coordinator of services, who provides or arranges for many client services, one of which is counseling.

This does raise the very interesting question of how much counseling is actually being provided and how clients react to these services. A brief review of three doctoral dissertations that have been completed at the University of Missouri, and that deal with this topic, may shed some light.

Doctor Carroll Smith completed a study on the opinions of various counselor roles. He compared the attitudes of state directors, VRA counselors, and counselor trainees. He studied their opinion of the counselor's role in the following areas: counseling, testing, office routine, placement, incidental services, occupational information, public information, and self-improvement. These three groups agreed on the need for self-improvement but disagreed on nearly all of the other factors. They disagreed most on their perception of the counselor's role in the area of testing and placement.

Doctor Ron Peterson, who is now at Flagstaff, Arizona, did a study on the amount of counseling being provided in a typical state agency. He concluded that counseling is "provided to less than one-half of the clients served—and of this group another half received less than 50 minutes of counseling."

Doctor Tom Porter, who is now at the University of Georgia, tried to determine if counseling made a substantial contribution to the outcomes of the counseling process. He was basically interested in seeing if the client who received counseling was more adequately placed and more satisfied with his job. His study failed to indicate any significant difference. Actually, in some ways both Porter and Peterson found some negative results. Their studies suggested that counseling in a typical rehabilitation agency was provided primarily on a "demand" basis to those clients who needed it the most and who, as a result, were often most severely handicapped and had the most severe social-psychological problems. As a result, the incidence of failure among this group was actually higher than among the group that did not need, and hence did not receive, counseling services.

In closing, let us consider the rehabilitation counselor at his worst and at his best. At worst he represents a person who is hired through direct entry into a field with little training or without any interest in his clients. He often rejects clients and looks upon them as people that he would not hire himself. He provides a mechanical type of coordinated services, often resents his agency and his supervisor, and ends by disliking himself. Since he has a good deal of authority to either control or extend services to clientele, they sometimes end up worse than they were when they started. At best, a rehabilitation counselor represents a person professionally trained in the field, who is interested in his clients, who respects them as human beings, and who provides a form of sound professional service that makes a real difference in the life of the handicapped individual.

VIII

TRAINING, JOB PLACEMENT,
AND FOLLOW-UP

Daniel Sinick

In considering various principles and practices that pertain to training, job placement, and follow-up as important aspects of the vocational rehabilitation process, we must also examine and discover disparities that impede proper training, job placement, and follow-up. Disparities between principles and practices are frequently encountered in prospective employers of the clients of rehabilitation agencies. Awareness of such disparities can enhance the effectiveness of job placement activities. Heightened awareness is also needed of the numerous disparities between principles and practices that exist in rehabilitation agencies themselves and among rehabilitation counselors. Increased perceptiveness in this regard might bring about increased effectiveness in all agency and counselor activities pertinent to training, job placement, and follow-up.

Lack of effectiveness in these three areas sometimes results from ineffective activities and sometimes from lack of activities. Not at all uncommon are errors of omission as well as errors of commission. Failure to do things that need doing is probably more common in these three areas, indeed, than in other areas of the vocational rehabilitation process. For the sake of comparison, though perhaps somewhat invidious, consider the following three areas of the vocational rehabilitation process—evaluation, treatment, and referral. Each of these areas is a source, of course, of both types of error. In each area, things that need to be done are left undone, and the things that are done could stand improvement. There seems less likelihood, however, that evaluation, treatment, or referral is neglected than that training, job placement, or follow-up receives insufficient attention.

This is a very general statement with, admittedly, many exceptions. Job placement is not infrequently done, for example, on the basis of inadequate evaluation. A familiar phenomenon, on the other hand, is excessive evaluation, as is overextended treatment, both frequently representing avoidance behavior rather than professional behavior that approaches client problems. Referral, too, is often used to avoid dealing with client problems, although it can constitute a valuable service in itself. Surveys of agency services have consistently found the one service most commonly offered to be referral.

While training is sometimes based upon avoidance motivation, as will be discussed later, it tends to share the relative neglect accorded job placement, if not the gross neglect given follow-up. The topic to be dealt with then is how training, job placement, and follow-up are neglected through inadequate action, how they are impeded by inappropriate action, and how they suffer from disparities that exist between principles and practices. Out of the discussion of such negative considerations—many stated and others implied—there will emerge, it is hoped, positive guidelines for effective practices based upon sound principles.

TRAINING

As a phase of the vocational rehabilitation process, training basically means preparation for employment in a suitable occupation. The broader term, preparation, reflects the principle that training in job skills alone frequently does not suffice. Such training may be insufficient for either getting a job or holding a job, if a client requires preparation in the area of personality. He may need assistance in the development of what has come to be called a "work personality."

The quotation marks around that term indicate that it has not been fully accepted. Some object to "work personality" for the same reason they object to the term "vocational rehabilitation." The qualifying words, "work" and "vocational," are regarded as limiting too much the possibilities that exist for both personality development and social rehabilitation of wider scope. The unqualified terms are seen as keeping pace with the rapidly moving trends that, in parallel fashion, have properly subordinated the concept of "the economy" to the larger concept of "the society."

"Work personality" is objectionable to others on other grounds. Work may be accepted as of such central significance in this culture as to warrant a heavy vocational emphasis in the fields of rehabilitation and guidance. Within a vocational emphasis, client personality characteristics of possible vocational significance are, in turn, properly emphasized. What these objectors dislike is the pragmatic interpretation of "work personality" as a personality that works. Molding a personality to meet the needs of business and industry may develop conformity instead of individuality. Is the "organization man," ask these objectors, the desired product of rehabilitative efforts?

Be that issue as it may, the principle still holds that both skills and personality need attention in the preparation of clients for employment. Skills of some sort are needed for the performance of job duties. It is common knowledge that personality traits outweigh job skills as a source of difficulty in obtaining and retaining employment. How may clients be assisted in acquiring relevant skills and traits, within the framework of training rather than psychotherapy?

INSTITUTIONAL TRAINING

Schools at various levels have been used to impart to clients basic educational skills as well as specific job skills. There is ample evidence in the experience of most counselors, however, that schools have not proved maximally effective in achieving these goals of training.

The imparting of basic educational skills is sometimes impeded by previous educational impoverishment suffered by many severely disabled clients. The previous education of these clients, both in and out of school, has frequently been delayed, interrupted, or disrupted as a consequence of the disabling condition. Whether because of limited physical mobility, limited mental ability, or limited emotional stability, or because of severe sensory impairment, these clients have had reduced exposure to the world. The enriched and individualized educational experience they need is not readily provided in the usual school situation.

Tutorial training can be provided within an educational institution as well as through private tutors. Such individualized instruction can start with the student where he is and proceed at a pace appropriate to his capabilities. His particular gaps in knowledge can be filled and future gaps prevented.

A relevant principle here has broad implications for the training, placement, and follow-up of severely disabled persons. The severity of their disability, and the obstacle it may become to their employment and adjustment on jobs, suggests that their training ought not to be ordinary training. Whenever possible, their basic educational skills and their specific job skills should be brought up to a level about that of prospective competitors for employment. Overcompensation, or at least compensation, for a severe disability can be one of the aims of training.

For consideration with disabled clients, as with the nondisabled, is the possibility of two years of education beyond high school, if not more. For some clients, a two-year technical institute will furnish the highly specialized knowledge and skills they need for competitive employment in an increasingly technological economy. The same goal frequently can be achieved through two terminal years at a junior college or a community college.

There are many additional reasons for exploring the possibility of a two-year college. A major reason is the opportunity thus afforded for a client to explore himself and to become better oriented to the world around him. As a consequence, the two years may lead to still higher education and even better preparation. "Late bloomers" sometimes blossom in junior colleges, and clients previously lacking in educational motivation find themselves and, in turn, find themselves desirous of additional education.

Additional education in itself must be pointed out as a possible path of error, for client and counselor alike. For a client, further schooling may simply prolong the sheltered atmosphere he has comfortably experienced. Staying in school is fine for some, but for others it merely postpones the inevitable confrontation with the real world, which is, after the hothouse the school often represents, a cold world.

For a counselor, additional client education may constitute a way of getting a client "off his back." Some counselors are adept in postponing the inevitable by finding some sort of "dumping ground" for the client. The process of evaluation, whether through tests or in a workshop, is not infrequently used as an avoidance technique. Training is similarly used as a dumping ground. Many severely disabled clients have spent years in college, which yielded no economic return. The cultural gain from a college education is important, but it is too often offered as a facile rationalization for a counseling failure.

The reverse of this technique of employing training to avoid client problems is to avoid training even when it is highly relevant to what the client needs. Why would a counselor minimize the use of training with his caseload? He may regard training as a postponement of closure. If he is oriented toward fast and frequent closures as a prerequisite to fast and frequent promotions, he may aim at "counseling and placement only" closures. Such counselor conduct is, of course, political instead of professional.

In the use of institutional training, a counselor should be aware of various traps and pitfalls. One of the most common is to base choice of training on local availability of training. This practice often combines two separate errors. When availability of institutional training is the basis for choice of training, it may also be the basis for choice of occupation. Occupational choice must be broadly enough based so that a single factor does not carry excessive weight.

The other error is basing training, or occupational choice, on purely local possibilities. This sometimes happens because of a counselor's geographically limited knowledge of training facilities. He has failed to become informed about training opportunities outside his local area. The error is at times, however, of a more general nature. The counselor may assume erroneously that the client must be confined to the area in which he is being counseled. The assumption may stem from presumptions of limited physical mobility or of strong family ties. Or it may be a function of the counselor's own limited perspective. Certainly a principle pertinent to training, as to every phase of the counselor's work, has to do with his use of imagination and ingenuity.

A related "training trap" involves unimaginative stereotyping of training, at the expense of individual differences. Straight stereotyping on the basis of disability causes some counselors to put all paraplegics, for example, into watch repair training. Traditional practice is replete with such examples as all deaf persons being trained in printing and all blind persons being trained for darkroom work. The counselor is himself working in darkness who fails to flash light on the client's individuality.

Light must also be cast on the dark dealings of some schools.

Since many schools are private, profit-making institutions, they may be tempted toward questionable practices. They may try to recruit for training in their institutions clients lacking in the potentials the schools assert to be present. They may try to lure clients with false promises of job placement. Regarding clients in training, they may provide progress reports of a highly exaggerated nature. The training traps, and others, must be familiar to the rehabilitation counselor.

Two additional traps with regard to skills training through institutions involve specificity of training versus breadth of training. While both are important, an overemphasis on either may constitute a trap. Training that is too broad and general is frequently sparse in spots. It may fail to provide the high degree of specialization commonly called for by our economy.

Since the economy is constantly changing, however, training that is too narrow and specific may inadequately prepare the client for occupational mobility, whether horizontal or vertical. Technological developments often necessitate changes of jobs, within plants or offices or from firm to firm. Overspecialization sometimes reduces the needed adaptability. It may also reduce the possibilities for advancement to higher level jobs, for these jobs often are at a lower level of specialization. If this paradox regarding promotion is perplexing to the reader, be assured that it is perplexing to management, too.

Technological developments create or aggravate a general shortcoming of institutional training in skills. Most job skills involve the use of equipment or machinery or apparatus of some sort. Schools find it financially difficult to furnish their classrooms, shops, and laboratories with the most modern equipment, especially with the tremendous changes constantly occurring in the design of such equipment. Clients trained on outdated office or shop machines may not be regarded by employers as the best prospects for employment.

NONINSTITUTIONAL TRAINING

The shortcoming just mentioned, and other limitations of institutional training of many clients, may be overcome through training in work settings. In actual offices and shops, employers are compelled to meet competition by maintaining up-to-date equipment. In other respects, too, training may be more realistic and advantageous in settings where actual work is being done.

Arrangements for such training are possible through apprenticeship training programs, less formal programs for training on the job, and rehabilitation workshops. These three approaches differ in their availability in particular localities and in their desirability for particular clients.

Long recognized as highly desirable in equipping workers with the skills needed in craft occupations, apprenticeship training is for consideration wherever it may be accomplished. Combining concurrent classroom instruction with practical experience on the job, apprenticeship training has turned out large numbers of butchers and bakers and cabinetmakers.

The formality of apprenticeship agreements and the number of parties involved, however, reduce the availability of such programs. Those who must agree to the arrangement usually include the state apprenticeship agency, an employer, a union, the client, and the sponsoring agency. Difficulties can arise from any of these sources, but a prime difficulty in the past has been the operation of restrictive practices on the part of many unions. Despite the invaluable role of trade unions in the socioeconomic advances made by labor, unions unfortunately exemplify, perhaps as much as employers, one of the numerous disparities between principles and practices.

"On-the-job training" is used here not in the general sense of "in-service training," often provided regular employees to enhance their effectiveness, but in the special sense of an arrangement whereby a client is employed on more or less a trial basis with the opportunity, through training on the job and consequent performance, to achieve regular employment. The term "on-the-job training," therefore, is broader than the term "apprenticeship training."

While somewhat less formal than arrangements for apprenticeship training, which ordinarily is of greater duration, an on-the-job training arrangement is best drawn up as a document signed by the three interested parties: the client, the employer, and the sponsoring agency. The union business agent may be a fourth signatory.

Each has important responsibilities, which can be specified in the written agreement. The client's basic responsibilities are to perform his duties as a conscientious trainee, to profit from his supervision on the job, and to improve his performance until he approximates the productive quality and quantity of a regular employee doing the same work. The employer's basic responsibilities include the provision of qualified supervision with regard to increasingly varied and complex tasks. The responsibilities of employer and agency and union vary in some respects in accordance with the type of training plan spelled out in the agreement.

There are four general types of on-the-job training plans:

(1) Trial job placement.
    If the client's preparation for employment in a particular job is adequate, the plan may call for only the same employer supervision provided other new employees, with the agency counselor collaborating in fairly close consultation with the employer. The client is paid by the employer and receives no pay from the agency.

(2) Sliding wage scale.
    With clients less well-qualified for a particular job, added supervision by the employer may be required, accompanied perhaps by closer counselor consultation. A wage scale is set whereby, at specified intervals, payments by the employer increase and payments by the agency correspondingly decrease.

(3) Fixed wage scale.
    When clients require even more supervision by the employer, the plan may call for no payments by the employer at all, the agency providing payments to both the client and the employer. The agency counselor also provides as close consultation as is needed.

(4) Training placement.
    With clients requiring still more employer supervision, as well as continuing close counselor consultation, the plan may again call for no payments by the employer, the agency paying the employer only and furnishing the client not pay but the usual subsistence provided trainees, whether in school or on the job.

Although not strictly on-the-job training, volunteer work, without pay, may offer similar opportunities for acquisition of work experience and job skills. Some communities have a volunteer bureau to facilitate the employment of volunteers in numerous settings. In this arrangement, the client would be expected to receive

The

Individuals With

N

→ <u>Directional Hypothesis</u>

There will be a

Based upon previous

The will be a positive
relationship of between ind w/
cancer and ind. degree w/d. med

The relationship b
The rpo of in w/c & w/d
will be

The career patterns of ind with
cancer will be similar to the
career patterns of indw. with
a history of diabetes nell.

the normal supervision on the job provided other volunteers; his agency would again provide subsistence and counselor consultation.

Rehabilitation workshops and rehabilitation centers, although less traditionally utilized for training purposes, loom large as additional sources of noninstitutional training. They can be regarded as noninstitutional to the extent that they differ from schools. They have tended to develop in ways that distinguish them from schools. Even the so-called "shelter" of such shops is more closely geared to the real world outside of schools. For convenience, the term "rehabilitation workshops" is used to replace sheltered workshops and to represent the workshop aspect of the services offered by rehabilitation centers and related agencies.

The role of rehabilitation workshops with regard to skills training has been enhanced, together with on-the-job training, in other settings, as a consequence of the Manpower Development and Training Act. Through subcontracts with the Association of Rehabilitation Centers, which has a prime contract with the U.S. Department of Labor, workshops are enabled to establish on-the-job training programs. An interesting feature of these programs is that they are to train the disabled for jobs in which they can serve the disabled. This parallels the plan described by Pearl and Riessman * for training the poor to serve the poor.

Rehabilitation workshops share the general superiority of noninstitutional training over institutional training with respect to development of "work personality." The frequently inadequate translation of school skills into job skills is more than matched by inadequate translation of school personality into work personality. The skills, traits, and attitudes that are effective in school are not necessarily effective at work. Rehabilitation workshops and on-the-job training programs provide a more realistic setting and a firmer focus for work-personality development.

Where work is going on, clients are more readily motivated, if only on the basis of face validity. They are more likely to develop such desirable worker traits as dependability, accuracy, attentiveness to work, and persistence. They grow in frustration tolerance, acceptance of supervision, and interpersonal effectiveness.

---

* Pearl, A., and Riessman, F., *New Careers for the Poor* (New York: The Free Press, 1965).

They may learn the meaning of responsibility, so that they do not find themselves in the position of the job applicant who was told, "For this job, we need someone who is responsible," and who replied, "That's me. On my last job, whenever anything went wrong they said I was responsible."

In workshops, care must be exercised to distinguish training from evaluation and employment. These are overlapping functions, but each is more effective if kept relatively distinctive. The same work task would be differently administered, for example, depending upon whether the client is being trained or evaluated. If a transitional client in training becomes so competent as to be made a terminal employee, a gross disparity is evident between principles and practices.

Since on-the-job training has not been sufficiently capitalized upon by rehabilitation agencies, it merits more attention. It is applicable to almost all occupational fields and occupational levels. It develops both skills and personality. To suggest the promise of this underused approach, other advantages to clients and employers are specified here, together with certain cautions to be observed.

On-the-job training advantages for clients (and rehabilitation agencies):

> More suitable than institutional training for particular clients; better preparation for particular occupations; often the sole preparation for self-employment; relevant institutional training may not be available locally; equipment on the job generally more up to date; often of shorter duration than institutional programs; frequently less costly to rehabilitation agency; usually provides income (earning while learning); facilitates self-evaluation in a realistic setting; facilitates occupational exploration; serves to broaden or narrow occupational choice; facilitates acquisition of proper work attitudes, habits, and skills; enhances readiness for placement on regular jobs; provides employment for trainees who might not be hired as employees; sometimes serves as a step toward regular employment with the same firm; and demonstrates to employers the employability of disabled persons.

On-the-job training advantages for employers:

Preselected trainees instead of "walk-in" applicants; extended tryout period for further selection; trainees generally well-motivated, conscientious, dependable; trainees amenable to employers' procedural preferences; pay geared to successive levels of trainees' performance; may constitute low-cost training program for new employees; may contribute to reduced turnover of new employees; provides "ready reserve" of replacements for employees who leave; may fill demand for specialized workers in short supply; and may constitute an employee recruitment program.

Cautions regarding on-the-job training:

Use for its appropriateness, not as a last resort; should meet client needs, aptitudes, personality; should realistically implement a vocational plan; content, length, and progression of training should be appropriate; possible exploitation of client is to be anticipated and avoided; explicit program should be spelled out and agreed on; counselor consultation should make sure program is carried out; frequency of counselor contacts should be adapted to specific situation; and evaluation of program's progress a continuing counselor responsibility.

JOB PLACEMENT

Since the discussion of training embraced work personality and job skills within the broader framework of preparation, the term "readying" is used in this section with regard to the counselor's role in preparing both clients and employers for job placement. "Role" is used to refer to either the counselor's responsibility for job placement or his function in job placement, or both. There will be more discussion of these terms later.

Two other terms that cause considerable confusion in the field of rehabilitation counseling are employment and placement, or employability and placeability. These terms need to be clarified and, if possible, distinguished, so as to clarify in turn the counselor's role with respect to job placement.

"Employment," to start with, has two different uses: one pertaining to a state or condition, the other to an act. A person who is now employed (a state) at some point became employed (an act). At the risk of further confusion, there is a parallel with disability (a condition) and disablement (an act), two other terms worth distinguishing.

Employability is most appropriately related to employment as a condition. It seems best interpreted as including both work personality and job skills as prerequisites to suitable employment. A client possessing both sets of needed characteristics would then be employable; he is ready for the state of employment. In state employment service terms, he is "ready, willing, and able" to work.

He may not be ready, however, for the act of employment. Although employable, he may not be able to get someone to employ him. The act of employment, of course, involves the applicant for employment and the employer. To the employer, the act is generally known as hiring. From the rehabilitation counselor's point of view, the same act is one of placement. An employable client's placeability, therefore, may be in question.

The major basis for the question regarding a client's place-ability may be a lack in the client with regard to getting a job or it may be the fault of employers. Both these areas of possible inadequacies are ordinarily attacked in effective job placement. The present discussion similarly adopts a doublebarreled attack, largely withholding its fire from a third target: availability of jobs for which the client may be ready.

READYING CLIENTS

Clients who may need readying for placement are presumably already "ready for employment," a DVR term in accord with the terminology employed in this discussion. Regarded as employable, they are designated as Status 6 by DVR (Division of Vocational Rehabilitation). Studies of clients in Status 6 have frequently revealed, however, that some clients so designated are not really ready for employment or do not remain ready.

An important principle in job placement is to recognize the need for continuing evaluation of clients. Evaluation, indeed, is far more than a phase of the vocational rehabilitation process; it pertains to all the phases from case finding through follow-up. Follow-up, incidentally, is another term that could be interpreted as applying to every step of the entire process.

Evaluation at this point sometimes finds that the vocational plan is not suitable. Various pressures may have caused the counselor to settle for a plan not worth implementing. The client may not be aware of this, but "ready for employment" is an unsuitable objective. Or he may be aware of this and displaying apparently poor motivation. Motivation toward improper goals is not one of the aims of counseling.

The *Placement Training Handbook,* issued by the U.S. Vocational Rehabilitation Administration, presents a whole unit (Unit Two) on evaluation of both readiness for employment and readiness for placement. Numerous questions are raised to serve as criteria for ascertaining these types of readiness on the part of a client. Some space is devoted to the kinds of occupational information that are relevant to the client's physical readiness, psychological readiness, occupational readiness, and placement readiness.

Several emphases are not specifically made, in that in-service training aid might be made at this time. One is that evaluation of client readiness must be accompanied by evaluation of factors outside the client. While this is perhaps an obvious point, it is another example of the many disparities between principles and practices.

The professional or personal orientation of some counselors causes them to deal with clients more or less in a vacuum. Sealed off from the outside world, these clients are examined like microbes under a microscope. The counselor's office and the testing room are no microcosm, however, of the world outside. Readiness for employment and readiness for placement depend upon the interaction of internal and external variables.

With regard to readiness for employment, for example, a client's low tolerance for frustration or slow but accurate test performance has to be weighed against the realities of occupational requirements. There may be occupations that don't tax his tolerance or exceed his speed. A client's readiness for placement cannot be judged by his level of job-seeking sophistication, similarly, without regard to relevant labor market information.

Occupational information and labor market information are two more terms that cause confusion. Occupational information is the broader term, including information bearing on occupational choice and information bearing on job placement. For the latter, there is the more specific term, labor market information or job market information. Unit Three of the *Placement Training Handbook* uses the intermediate term "placement information."

What is lacking is a parallel specific term like occupational choice information. That term is inadequate on two counts, for occupational choice involves information about clients as well as about occupations and is itself inadequate as a term descriptive of a developmental process. "Vocational planning information" would share the first of these drawbacks.

While appropriate and distinctive terms would be useful, it is the conceptual distinction that is necessary to improve both vocational planning and job placement. Without such conceptual clarity, a counselor might routinely apply to long-range vocational planning current information about job openings. Some job placement specialists even believe they should be present during the initial counseling interview.

The shoe should probably be on the other foot. To guard against the short-circuiting of long-range plans, it would be useful for the counselor to be in close touch with a job placement specialist, who may be serving the counselor's client. Such a specialist, and the counselor himself, may sometimes overemphasize variables outside the client; in this instance, to the detriment of a client's inner needs. An overemphasis in either direction would tend to violate the interactive principle regarding internal and external variables.

Evaluation of client readiness for placement may reveal areas where further readying is needed. In the physical area, for example, the client may be able to perform the duties of a job and get around within a plant, but travel to and from the plant may be beyond him. He may need readying with regard to the psychological climate of a particular plant or to differing work shifts. He may need readying, above all, for the job-finding process.

There is a wealth of material on job-seeking and job-finding, issued by public agencies and private companies and frequently free of charge. Unit Five of the *Placement Training Handbook* delineates some of the specifics involved in helping a client to find a job. Certain emphases, however, seem deserving of mention here.

"Helping a client to find a job," the expression just used, reflects one important emphasis. Whenever possible, the client is readied to the point where he can find a job himself, instead of having it found for him. Aside from the well-known fact that most job placements are self-placements, why are self-placements to be sought?

For one thing, a client who finds his own job may experience enhanced satisfaction and self-esteem. He has demonstrated treasured independence and responsibility for his own future—enough to make both the existentialist and the pragmatist happy. However, independence and responsibility must be more than one-shot affairs, for the client may be called upon more than once to find his own job. The problem-solving learned in effective counseling needs to be paralleled in effective placement.

A cautionary note is in order. Just as independence can be overdone in adjusting to disability, or to adolescence, it can be overemphasized in regard to job placement. "Never accompany a client to a job interview" is an overgeneralization that overlooks the special needs of particular clients. Some mentally retarded clients and some blind clients, for example, require this added service.

Recognition of individual differences is the basis for another important emphasis. Stereotyping of placements is to be avoided. Lists of jobs for particular disabilities are less than ideal in meeting individual needs. More insidious, perhaps, are such lists that accumulate in a counselor's mind out of his placement experience. This disparity between principles and practices frequently results from routine application of facile formulas.

Related to such stereotyping is the role of diagnostic labels. These are to be avoided, of course, in the counselor's presentation to a prospective employer of a client's assets and liabilities. Functional terms familiar to a layman are far more effective than categorizations like "mentally retarded" or "epileptic."

In readying the client for job-seeking, diagnostic labels present additional problems. Job application forms generally request information regarding disabilities. The question a client often has to answer is, "To tell or not to tell?" Should he enter on the form a former disability from which he has recovered, such as so-called mental illness? Should he enter arrested tuberculosis or controlled epilepsy or other "invisible" disabilities?

The client's dilemma involves the present and the future. He may get the job now with the disability concealed, but he may lose it later if the disability is revealed. The client's dilemma becomes the counselor's dilemma, moreover, if the former asks the latter what to do.

There is no easy answer to this question. Examination of the APGA and American Psychological Association (APA) ethical codes discloses no specific principle to serve as a firm guideline to practice. The implementation of any principle would have to vary, anyway, with the individual features of the particular situation. Client qualifications and job opportunities might be relevant variables. It might be best for one client to tell and another client not to tell.

A counseling principle could be invoked here as a placement principle: that is, the principle of freedom of choice on the part of the client. Unimpaired freedom of choice is as basic, valid, and applicable in regard to job placement as it is to other phases of the vocational rehabilitation process. In his readying of the client for placement, the counselor ought not to hinder but to heighten the client's ultimate freedom.

READYING EMPLOYERS

The readying of employers has two major aspects. One has to do with long-range educational efforts to create a more favorable or receptive atmosphere for the employment of disabled persons. The other aspect involves the more immediate aim of helping to find a job for a specific client. These two aspects are, of course, interactive: an improved employer atmosphere will increase the number of specific placements, and effective placements serving employers as well as clients will improve the atmosphere.

The presentation here will focus on the counselor's more immediate responsibility for job placement of a particular client. Much material on long-range education of employers has become available through the President's Committee on Employment of the Handicapped and similar committees at the state and local levels. The *Placement Training Handbook* deals with the general approach in Unit Four and with the specific approach in both Unit Four and Unit Five.

A principle applicable to contacts with employers parallels a principle in counseling with clients. It is a phenomenological principle, which suggests perceiving the world from another person's frame of reference. Understanding the employer's viewpoint is often a start toward his understanding the viewpoint of the counselor and of the client. A counselor who gets under an employer's skin in a Rogerian sense is far less likely to get into the employer's hair.

Once in the employer's shoes (Rogers and his metaphors are highly mobile), the counselor realizes that the employer is there to be served. Favors are not to be sought from him or poorly-qualified clients foisted upon him. If he is concerned with profits and productivity, the counselor must share his concern.

Constantly alert to specific needs of the employer, the counselor makes every effort to fill these needs. He tries to provide qualified clients for current and anticipated job openings. By being of consistent assistance to the employer, the counselor may come to be looked upon as a consultant.

The counselor can be of added assistance to the employer by continually adding to his knowledge of the physical and other features of the plant. Through repeated visits to the employer, tours of the plant, and informal job analyses, the counselor can better serve both employer and client. A counselor skilled in job analysis can create job opportunities by suggesting adaptations of work methods, equipment, or physical facilities. Further preparation of the client might also be indicated by the findings of the plant survey.

An effective working relationship with an employer might even get him to do some visiting in return. Employers who have visited rehabilitation workshops have invariably been impressed by the work performance and personality qualities of severely disabled persons. Such visits sometimes open the door to the plant for demonstrations by disabled clients of proficient job performance.

While demonstrations are a highly desirable way for employers to become acquainted with client capabilities, counselor dialog with employers is the usual way. The counselor must develop expertise in presenting the positive possibilities of employment of qualified clients. Negative possibilities are so commonly emphasized by the employer that the counselor must know how to counter them. This countering of employer objections is covered in Unit Four of the *Placement Training Handbook,* but this responsibility is of such central importance in job placement that it cannot be omitted from the present discussion. Here the *Handbook* material is somewhat expanded, although the same format is followed by presenting a series of employer objections and counselor counter-actions.

In attempting to overcome many of the objections, the counselor might have with him a supply of supportive publications put out by government agencies, insurance companies, labor unions, and employer organizations. A counselor's seemingly un-founded faith in his clients will be given greater credence if accompanied, for example, by reports of studies conducted by the National Industrial Conference Board.

Here, then, are objections employers raise and possible counteractions by counselors:

(1) Productivity is lower.

Productivity of impaired workers has consistently been shown to be equal to or higher than that of unimpaired workers.

(2) Turnover rate is higher.

Lower turnover rate is shown by studies, together with greater loyalty. Difficulty in obtaining employment causes disabled workers to stick to their jobs.

(3) Absenteeism is greater.

Less absenteeism is shown, plus greater punctuality and dependability.

(4) Accidents increase.

Reduced accident rate is found, and usually reduced severity of injuries.

(5) Workmen's compensation rates rise.

As rates are based on accident experience of the company or industry, reduction in accidents would reduce these rates.

(6) Liability for total disability results from injury on job.

Second injury funds maintained by many states reduce this liability by distributing it equitably among covered employers.

(7) Costs of health and insurance plans rise.

Rates of such plans are based on sex and age, and utilization of these services by disabled workers is lower.

(8) Higher costs will somehow result.

Broken down into specific objections, this general expectation is dissipated. Employer costs are reduced, indeed, through reduced taxes resulting from the conversion of disabled tax-recipients to productive taxpayers.

(9) Physical plant cannot accommodate disabled employees.

Where this is a factor, it can usually be overcome through appropriate adjustments, with little or no cost to employer.

(10) Preemployment medical examination rules out disabled applicants.

Medical examinations are often unnecessarily restrictive, setting up arbitrary hurdles comparable to excessive educational requirements.

(11) The union won't approve the hiring of disabled persons.

Printed statements issued by unions favor such hiring.

(12) Supervisors or coworkers won't approve.

Supervisors and coworkers in studies approve of disabled persons they have worked with. Disabled workers are found, in fact, to improve the group morale.

(13) Customers won't approve.

Numerous disabled workers are in successful contact with customers. Improved public relations may result from loyalty displayed by these workers and humanitarianism ascribed to the employer.

(14) The disabled have emotional problems or disagreeable personalities.

Stable and attractive personalities are common among disabled persons.

(15) Special consideration is required.

Disabled employees generally avoid requests for special treatment.

(16) The disabled can work at only low-level jobs.

All occupational levels are represented by disabled employees.

(17) Adaptability to different jobs is lower.

Individualized training and selective placement are

geared toward versatility and flexibility, for increased horizontal and vertical mobility.

(18) Firing or layoff is more difficult.

Regular personnel policies are applicable to disabled employees, who seek neither unearned seniority nor undue sympathy.

(19) We have enough disabled employees of our own.

Are they less productive or effective employees?

(20) We have other sources of job applicants.

This added source offers qualified applicants, pre-selected to save employer time and money.

(21) We prefer people who find their own jobs.

Other applicants use help in coping with the complex labor market. Are those who use help less effective employees?

(22) We don't like to deal with government agencies.

Not to be confused with regulatory agencies, this agency offers service, without any fee, to meet your needs.

(23) You people aren't familiar with our operations.

Indicate familiarity or request plant tour.

(24) Why experiment on us? Vague expectation of unknown risk.

Effectiveness of disabled employees has been nationally demonstrated and previous successful placements have been made in this community. What specific concern have you?

COUNSELOR'S ROLE IN PLACEMENT

The counselor's role in placement was previously indicated as including his responsibility, his function, or both. The distinction between responsibility and function is essential to a consideration of this vital professional matter. Everyone might agree that the counselor is responsible for the ultimate job placement of his client, without agreeing that it is the counselor's function to ready the client, ready the employer, and engage in other aspects of actual job placement. The distinction involves the difference between seeing that something is done and doing it oneself.

There are points to be mentioned on either side. The trend appears to be toward separating the placement function from the counselor's responsibility. Although retaining the responsibility, the counselor is, to an increasing extent, relinquishing the function. The function has tended to be taken over by a placement specialist within the agency or by specialists in placement agencies; for example, the employment service offices.

Nor has this been a reluctant relinquishment for many counselors. They may fall into either or both of two categories: those who dislike doing job placement and those who feel they cannot do it effectively. Other reasons offered are generally rationalizations supporting one of these two positions. Rationalizations tend to make either position appear weaker than it is, for there is a rationale for the separation of function from responsibility.

Such a division of labor into areas of specialization frequently makes for increased efficiency. Each professional can attend more intensively to a more limited area of functioning. Mastery over labor market information, whose specialized nature has been discussed, is thus left to a specialist. He can also concentrate on areas of specialization not previously mentioned: placement involving employment in rehabilitation workshops, in homebound employment, and in self-employment. Specialists in small business enterprises have been traditional in some vocational rehabilitation agencies.

In addition to differences in competencies required for counseling and placement, moreover, there is the matter of differences in personalities required. The kind of person who is effective in counseling might not be effective in placement, and vice versa. Frequently emphasized in institutes on placement is the notion of "selling," a concept alien to most schools of counseling.

Counselors ought not to look down their noses at placement, however, for it offers far more professional challenge than the "pavement pounding" it is often regarded as being. Psychological knowledge and skill are needed in the effective countering, for example, of employer objections. Manifest and latent content are to be distinguished with employers as with clients. Establishing and maintaining meaningful rapport in the face of manifold resistances constitute a challenge in placement as in counseling.

Continuity of professional contacts with a client can be more readily maintained, furthermore, when one person has both the responsibility and the function. Forwarding and feedback of information regarding the client may be less subject to distortion; when two persons are involved in this process, something is sometimes lost in the transition.

Robert Hoppock makes a strong plea for continuity and unity of placement responsibility and function in his book on occupational information. Under the heading, "Counselors Should See Their Clients Through Placement," he says: "We could make tremendous improvements in the quality of vocational guidance if we could require all counselors to do what good rehabilitation counselors do—follow the client through the process of placement and stay with him until his record indicates that the placement and the counseling have been successful."

This quotation leads very aptly into the last portion of the tripartite topic, "Training, Job Placement, and Follow-Up." It should be noted at this point, however, that such topics are relevant to the work of a counselor whether or not he himself does placement and follow-up.

This principle applies to all the phases and aspects of the vocational rehabilitation process, starting from case finding and including all treatment procedures. Counselors are more effective when they understand intake, whether or not they do it themselves. Counselors are more effective who understand prosthetic procedures and occupational therapy and—perhaps closer to home—psychological testing and psychotherapy, even though they may not do these things themselves. Certainly this principle applies to placement and follow-up.

FOLLOW-UP

Many of the same principles, practices, and disparities evident with regard to job placement are relevant to follow-up. Counselors who are not interested in placement are likely to be even less interested in follow-up. Agencies concerned with closures may regard follow-up as a postponement of "successful placements."

The quotation marks around "successful placements" indicate the need for follow-up. Hoppock has suggested the need to continue services with the client until successful placement is assured. The recent report of the House of Representatives' Committee on

Education and Labor stressed follow-up as one of the vocational rehabilitation services requiring early improvement.

Follow-up must be recognized as an essential part of the services provided the client. Terminology regarding this topic again creates difficulties. Follow-up has long been recognized as a procedure employed in studies of the effectiveness of services. Such evaluative studies are vital in bringing about improvements in services to make them more effective. Follow-up in research is geared to groups, however, and not to individuals. Follow-up as a service to individuals is the matter presently under discussion.

Despite the utility of clarity regarding the dual use of this term, it is important to realize that follow-up as a service can also serve a research function. The counselor who is ever searching for ways of improving his own practices will gain many clues to improvement from a follow-up of his clients. Increased counselor concern over improved professional practices can eventually reduce the disparities between principles and practices.

The terminological trap might be avoided through the use of separate terms: "follow-up studies" or "follow-up research" as against "follow-up service" or "follow-up services." The term "post-placement services" has been used. To be borne in mind in this connection is that "placement" itself has several uses. The two most pertinent to the present topic involve placement in training and job placement.

While both types of placement require follow-up, the discussion here focuses on follow-up after job placement. This is closer to the ultimate criteria of effective vocational rehabilitation services. Much of what is said about follow-up after job placement, however, can readily be translated into terms of follow-up after placement in training. In either situation, similar questions are to be asked of the client and his employer or trainer.

Many such questions have been enumerated in Unit Six of the *Placement Training Handbook,* which also spells out the purposes of follow-up with respect to the client, the employer, the counselor, and the agency. Included as well are procedures employed in follow-up after job placement. Just a few emphases, therefore, will be made in the remaining discussion on follow-up.

One emphasis is related to a general principle applicable to all phases of the vocational rehabilitation process. Though the phases of the process usually occur in a particular sequence, they are not entirely separate and discrete. Intake and field counseling overlap and, as has been discussed, counseling and placement overlap.

A corollary to that principle concerns the need for articulation of the phases of the vocational rehabilitation process. A familiar concept in education, articulation has many applications to rehabilitation. Special education and vocational rehabilitation, for example, are both less effective, if not articulated to create transition for disabled youngsters from one to the other. Transition from one vocational rehabilitation phase to another similarly increases the effectiveness of the whole process.

The emphasis with regard to follow-up, then, is for this service to be anticipated during earlier phases and articulated with placement. This articulation may be represented by the assistance a counselor can provide in the induction of a client into a job. Having found the job and having been hired may not necessarily be the end of the placement phase.

Although holding the job is usually associated with follow-up service, job retention is often related to initial orientation and, perhaps, to adaptation of the client to the job. The counselor can be of help regarding the physical layout of the plant, company rules and regulations, personnel policies and procedures, and other matters. Many employers welcome such assistance on the part of the counselor, and clients requiring it generally appreciate it.

Another emphasis has to do with the three general categories of criteria of vocational adjustment. These are suitability, satisfactoriness, and satisfaction. Satisfaction is based upon the client's perceptions and feelings with respect to the other two sets of perceptions and feelings, and more, for satisfaction and satisfactoriness do not always add up to a successful placement. Suitability involves such dynamic dimensions of the client as his potentials and his aspirations. The counselor's best professional judgment must be called upon before a case can properly be called closed.

Effective professional follow-up obviously requires time not often allowed the counselor. Lack of time, together with lack of emphasis on this service, generally results in lack of follow-up, at least any functional follow-up. Instead of a meaningful follow-up, there is a nominal follow-up. After a period of one month or three months, if lack of satisfaction or lack of satisfactoriness has not been reported, the case is closed.

A reason sometimes suggested for not following up a client is that dependency is thus fostered. While weaning a client away from dependency is a common counselor responsibility, the client's ultimate adjustment is a greater responsibility. If follow-up would serve this end, it should be conducted with weaning occurring concurrently. Follow-up activities could be planned so as to taper off appropriately.

Before this discussion tapers off appropriately, it should point out that a further function of follow-up is to help create a balance in the client between dependence and independence. Too much of either frequently hampers adjustment. A fetish is sometimes made of independence in a world in which everyone is interdependent.

Professional interdependence is, indeed, a theme pervading this entire discussion, if more often implied than made explicit. Interdependence in operation can enhance the effectiveness of training, of job placement, and of follow-up. Each of these phases of the vocational rehabilitation process can profit from the counselor's interactions with others.

A final principle is that counselors with sufficient courage and insight to recognize their need for assistance from others are the most likely to be effective in assisting their clients. To call upon supervisors, colleagues, or community resources for added perspective in the service of one's client requires professional humility. It requires less ego and more ego strength. Counselors with the inner security to listen to other voices in other rooms can add a touch of poetry to the prosaic vocational rehabilitation process.

IX   THE RESEARCH ROLE

Herbert Rusalem

More than a decade ago, a project was launched under a Social and Rehabilitation Services (SRS) grant to establish a systematic method of processing vocational rehabilitation cases. The goal of this investigation was to develop a more efficient manner for state rehabilitation agencies to deliver services. The customary procedure in this area had been for an itinerant counselor to provide the gamut of rehabilitation services, acting in turn as a counselor, buyer, arranger, and coordinator. The experimental condition introduced in this research was that of having the counselor assume a more delimited role: providing counseling while other team members offered related services.

Among the results of this project were the following:

(1) The experimental procedure did not result in an increased number of rehabilitation case closures.

(2) The experimental condition proved superior in total service to severely disabled persons with mental problems, clients receiving on-the-job training and subsequent client wages, advancement, and job retention.

Despite the apparent significance of these findings, few instances have been reported in which other vocational rehabilitation agencies based current practices upon the data derived from this experience. Although large sums of money and many hours of manpower were invested in this project, much of the rehabilitation structure in the United States functions as though this study had never been made. If nothing else, replications of the experiment would seem to be in order.

Writing in the *Rehabilitation Record* of July–August 1965, Usdane indicated that ". . . it takes from five to ten years to propel and generalize into application projects which have as their source

155

basic research in human interaction. . . ." There is obviously a gap between the accumulation of knowledge and the application of such knowledge to practical rehabilitation problems.

The purpose of this paper is to examine some of the facets of this gap and to suggest means of narrowing it. The basic matter that will be discussed is: How significant research findings can be implemented at the earliest possible moment so as to assure disabled persons the maximum degree of rehabilitation. Other writers have dealt with the anthropological and sociological implications of this problem. For example, Rogers and Schumacher in *Diffusion of Innovation: A Cross-Cultural and Communication Approach* (New York: Free Press, 1967) have drawn parallels between the acceptance of innovation in other societies and the implementation of planned change in our own. In drawing their parallels, they placed stress upon the role of opinion leaders and change agents. On the other hand, Glaser and Marks, reporting on a three-year project supported by the Social and Rehabilitation Services, placed their emphasis upon organizational aspects of the problem and experimented with different types of communication and consultation. They concluded that innovations do not spread automatically and that face-to-face communication is the most effective way of sharing the results of research and demonstration projects. They believe that psychological consultation to agency management facilities change and encourage innovation.

In contrast to other writings, this chapter will focus upon the more immediate situation that confronts rehabilitation workers and will apply selected generalizations to the research utilization conditions prevailing at the practitioner level today. Applying research to service is a common concern in all the behavioral sciences. Perhaps, without being aware of it, most clinicians engage in a day-to-day service process that resembles research. Using diagnostic procedures, the clinician gathers information and formulates hypotheses about the client. These hypotheses are tested both in interview and activity situations. Analyzing the feedback from team members, the practitioner constantly reexamines his hypotheses and from time to time restructures the client's rehabilitation program.

In many ways this process is comparable to a research intervention in which an N of one comprises the sample, and treatment is the independent variable. As the rehabilitation program proceeds, the counselor accumulates data concerning the impact of the intervention upon the individual and, in time, formulates generalizations that may have relevance not only for this client but for other clients as well. To some extent the rehabilitation worker's case records are research reports. Although the clinical procedure lacks the controls and precision that usually characterize formalized research, it contains many of the elements of such research and, in some instances, yields equally useful results. Consequently, good rehabilitation counseling often embodies an implicit research orientation unbeknown to the counselor who, on a conscious level, may deplore the "excesses" of the research method.

This concept of the practitioner as researcher is particularly relevant to an examination of the issues concerning the use of research findings by clinicians. All too often the researcher and the clinician view each other as antagonists pursuing individualized goals on divergent avenues, while, to some extent, all of us are practitioners and researchers simultaneously. In rehabilitation, both are searching for improved techniques of serving the disabled, using methods and concepts that differ more in emphasis than content. Yet, divisions frequently separate the two groups, and rivalry prevails in their ranks for funds, clients, and publicity. Where such rivalry exists, it is an unproductive exercise in futility, since it drains the resources of both participants needlessly and consumes energy that might better be devoted to enhancing the chances for rehabilitation of the severely disabled.

"Hard-headed" practitioners often question the essential values of research in the behavioral sciences. Alfred D. Lasker, the founder of modern advertising, is reputed to have stated publicly that research is something that tells you that a jackass has two ears, implying that much research is preoccupied with minutiae far removed from the concerns of the practitioner. An executive of a well-known rehabilitation agency took a comparable position at a national meeting, stating that the only value that research has for the practitioner is that of confirming what is already known to be a fact. When this executive was asked what his position was when research findings contradict what he already believes, he responded that he felt no conflict about the matter. "Obviously," he said, "the research is wrong." Yet, for the open-minded practitioner, research can be a highly functional form of problem solving and can generate practical and desirable alternatives to existing practices.

Research differs from everyday experience in that it is conducted under certain accepted rules. Although these rules alone do not guarantee excellence nor usefulness, they do assure the research consumer that certain minimum standards have been observed in structuring and conducting the research, thus ruling out, to some degree, the influence of irrelevant and contaminating factors. The research process usually includes an examination of the current status of a problem through observing and reviewing the literature, people, events, and settings in which the problem is imbedded. Through this means, the problem itself is identified and examined in detail and, in many instances, clarified, as well. Hypotheses are formulated suggesting possible solutions to the problem, and a method for testing these hypotheses is developed. Data then are gathered under the conditions stipulated by the method and are analyzed in accordance with accepted statistical procedures, leading to an acceptance or a rejection of the hypotheses. Finally, the data are related to the original problem and practical implications for service or further research may be drawn from the experience.

Rehabilitation research is at least 150 years old. In the eighteenth century, John Howard in England studied the problem of rehabilitating individuals who had been imprisoned while awaiting trial. Although many of these subjects were innocent, they were subjected to long periods of pretrial incarceration. Howard found that the delay in trial almost invariably forced the imprisoned to accumulate substantial debts. Consequently, upon acquittal they were almost immediately imprisoned again because of their unpaid obligations, and while being held for trial a second time accumulated further debts. This early researcher was able to describe a trial and imprisonment cycle that previously had not been documented. Subsequently, Howard's work led to judicial reform and to the provision of rehabilitation services to many of the victims of this system. Even then, the lag was deplorable.

Many generations later, in some American states, divorced men who had failed to keep up with their alimony payments were detained in jail and prevented from working until they raised funds to pay their debts, paralleling the situation described by Howard. Deprived of their earning capacity, they too fell further behind in their alimony payments. In this way their infractions were compounded and their jeopardy was increased. Thus, even today we can learn something from Howard's research. For example, the

"resistive" rehabilitation client who rejects some agency requirements or fails to follow a counselor-approved plan is generally excluded from service. Labeled as an uncooperative individual, his
unsatisfactory experiences may handicap him even more thoroughly
in the future when he once again seeks service. Indeed, the more
times he is excluded from rehabilitation, the more "unreachable"
he may become.

Are Howard's findings concerning a cyclical debilitating social
process with recurring crime-and-punishment sequences being re-
enacted today? In accordance with his findings, might not research
reveal that humane objectives would be better achieved by some
approach other than rejection of a client as "nonfeasible" or "non-
susceptible"? This question is particularly relevant today when the
rehabilitation of the socially disadvantaged is becoming a major
focus of state rehabilitation agency programs.

The rich and varied texture of rehabilitation research history
cannot be fully covered at this time. However, one other instance
of the lag between research and application may serve to highlight
the problem.

In 1848, Dorothea Lynde Dix appealed to the American people to consider the deplorable status of inmates of public mental
hospitals. When emotional appeals failed to stir the conscience of
the people, she turned to "hard" data gathered in "eight years of
sad, patient, deliberate investigation," marked by more than 60,000
miles of travel. Her efforts to "assure accuracy, establish facts beyond controversy, and procure, so far as possible, temporary or
permanent relief" produced an invaluable body of information already partially familiar to the mental health practitioner of her day.
The day-to-day experiences of these "professionals" had led them
to similar conclusions, but Dix's more systematic research, effective
only after long and arduous educational campaigns, proved to be
one of the critical elements in the launching of social action on behalf of the emotionally ill. There was a special cogency to her remarks when she said:

> I have myself seen more than nine thousand idiots, epileptics,
> and insane in these United States, destitute of proper care
> and protection . . . in jails, poorhouses, and private dwell-
> ings . . . , thousands bound with galling chains, bowed be-
> neath fetters and heavy iron balls, attached to drag-chains,

lacerated with ropes, scourged with rods, and terrified beneath storms of profane execrations and cruel blows.

From a modern research point of view, Dorothea Dix's methodology leaves much to be desired, as does the emotionality of her prose. Yet, the incontestable facts that she gathered were the "clincher" that convinced Congress of the need for immediate remedial action. It is ironical that after both houses of Congress passed legislation favorable to the emotionally ill, President Franklin Pierce vetoed it, turning back the clock on the fledgling mental health movement. However, this research was not in vain since, even today, it is widely used as a justification for more humane treatment of the emotionally disturbed.

The dimensions of the cultural lag in research are so great that in 1937, almost a century after Dix's work, Albert Deutsch described similar and no less shocking conditions in American state mental hospitals. His exposé, also based upon a personal research project, temporarily aroused the American conscience. Today, more than thirty years later, some of the institutional conditions described by Dix and Deutsch are still present, hopefully in less acute form. If the passage of recent legislation establishing community mental health centers is an indicator of changing attitudes, the gap between research and practice finally may be closing, and we can look forward to the application of other related findings of thousands of researchers, whose work confirms the fact that mental illness, in most cases, is a treatable disease and those who have it benefit most from community- rather than institution-based therapies.

The barriers that separate research from practice have many roots, but this discussion will focus upon those that evolve from the practitioner-researcher relationship. Four of these will be explored in some detail: (1) the "style" of the rehabilitation researcher, (2) the controls imposed by the researcher, (3) the researcher's affinity for records, and (4) the tools of research.

THE "STYLE" OF THE REHABILITATION RESEARCHER

By nature, the rehabilitation researcher is an inquiring, searching, doubting individual, whose activities can be an irritant to the practitioner. The latter functions on the basis of certain cherished assumptions painstakingly built up in the course of training and experience. Among these may be a belief in the sanctity of the legislation that shapes his practice, firmly established agency policy that determines some of his professional behavior, and personal beliefs about a variety of rehabilitation issues that suggest the most efficacious means of working with people.

Although he may question these basics from time to time, the practitioner engages in a selective perception process, which not only protects these ideas from the threats of dissonance but may actually enshrine them on an unassailable altar. In time, even though he may have had original reservations about them, he may become less doubting and, in doing so, less open to reassessment and possible restructuring of such notions. Entering this more or less stable system of belief, the researcher questioning almost everything, including some of the clinician's most sacrosanct ideas, is not likely to win any popularity contests. For example, the clinician may happily close as "rehabilitated" the case of a very severely disabled individual, feeling that suitable employment has been achieved at a level of functioning that is congruent with the client's capacities. Subsequently, the very source of the counselor's job satisfaction may be threatened when the research worker casts doubt on this achievement by questioning the success criterion used by the clinician as a parameter of his accomplishment.

It is evident that the probing, questioning, and doubting aspects of the researcher's style can be troublesome to the practitioner, heightening the possibilities of tension developing between them. Yet, such tensions can be prevented by a few simple devices to be suggested later in this paper.

THE "CONTROLS" IMPOSED BY THE RESEARCHER

Another aspect of the researcher's behavior that weakens his relationship with clinicians is his advocacy of data-gathering controls. This problem is one that arises in action research projects. Such an instance occurred in a demonstration project in which two different placement approaches were used experimentally with randomly-selected samples of physically and emotionally disabled

clients. Throughout the demonstration strained relationships prevailed between the practitioners and the researchers on this project,
centering around the researchers' demands for rigid adherence to a
design in which the practitioners had no choice in determining which
clients were to receive a vigorous field placement service and which
an employment counselor service. In instance after instance the
practitioners' judgment suggested that one or another of these approaches would be more favorable for certain clients, but this
judgment was not permitted to influence the experimental service.

Time and again, the practitioners sought to free themselves
from the design restrictions to practice in the manner that was
most consistent with their diagnostic skills—a course of action that
was not permissible within the research. As a consequence, the
practitioners, frustrated by these limitations, sometimes used subtle
means of circumventing the design and aggravating their research
colleagues. Although various means of accommodation were sought,
the problem never was fully resolved. At the conclusion of the
project, the counselors still resented the researchers' rigidity, and
the researchers complained about the covert resistance of the counselors. Both were delighted to see the project end.

In this project, no less than in other research situations, the
practitioner was committed to the principle of giving the client
every advantage that was owed him, ethically and legally. His over-
riding value was the client, first and foremost. On the other hand,
the researcher was committed above all else to the research design.
He felt no hesitation in denying clients in a control group certain
presumably effective services in order to preserve the integrity of
his study. The inevitable clash of these value systems played an important role in weakening this important investigation. Yet, practitioner involvement in the design and implementation of this study,
and more thorough indoctrination of the researcher in the service
process, might have ameliorated and perhaps eliminated the problem.

THE RESEARCHER'S AFFINITY FOR RECORDS

Researchers use words and symbols as freely as counselors use
interpersonal interactions. Dates, numbers, ratings, scores, and
other quantitative representations are the research worker's stock

in trade. He consumes recorded data at a fearful rate and takes as much pride in well-punched arrays of IBM cards as a practitioner does in the positive modification of client attitudes and behavior. To the researcher, abstract and case data are the essence of the human experience. Therefore he builds a professional way of life that is consonant with symbols, categories, designs, orders, ranks, tables, and graphic representations—all reflecting a mystique that has limited meaning for the clinician.

On the other hand, the practitioner often prefers the practitioner role because he is a fugitive from paperwork and abstract symbols. Negatively conditioned to quantitative data, his tolerance for records, reports, and other symbolic representations is fragile, indeed. Ordinarily, he rankles just at the thought of keeping ordinary day-to-day client records. Consequently, when required to do the additional paperwork demanded in a demonstration or research project, his flow of adrenalin quickens. Confronted by additional record keeping responsibilities, he may generalize his hostility to all research, whether performed by his agency or not. This experience may reinforce skeptical elements in his belief system about research, converting him into an adversary of the investigative process.

In operant conditioning terms, live clients increasingly become positive reinforcers, and written words, reports, and numbers become negative ones. In time the entry of a real client into the office suffuses the practitioner with warm feelings of comfort and security. Conversely, encounters with research materials and products generate negative responses. A form to be filled in, a record to be written, a rating to be prepared, or a research paper to be read, stirs up aversive reactions. Such aversive reactions are intensified by the turgid style of research reports, and the burdensome detail demanded in research and demonstration projects. Having experienced each other in unfavorable contexts, the practitioner and the researcher are reaction sensitive to each other's attitudes in their professional encounters and tuned into possible conflict.

THE TOOLS OF RESEARCH

Like any craftsman, the researcher takes pride in his tools and their effective use. Yet, accustomed to his own organismic and less-structured techniques, the clinician has little understanding of and patience with tools that stress precision, sequence, detail, and quantification. While the researcher feels comfortable with organized data, defined samples, and statistical treatments, the counselor is trained to respond to people on a one-to-one basis and to avoid generalizations about the human organism, which he regards as a unique configuration. Thus, practitioners tend to function well when confronted by the single case and to draw back from any tools that classify people into groups. While the researcher struggles to develop a representative sample of subjects, the practitioner delimits his sample to an N of one.

Since the inferences of the researchers flow out of multiple subjects, while those of the practitioners are applicable to a single case, the two groups place little stock in each other's findings. Researchers scoff at the apparent intuitiveness of the clinician's findings, and the clinician has little confidence in quantitative methods that seem to obscure human individuality. For the clinician, the truth lies in the judgments of a sensitive practitioner and not in the manipulation of allegedly objective measurement tools. Consequently, differing not only in the nature of truth but also in the routes used to arrive at it, researchers and clinicians go their separate ways, eschewing reasonable attempts to reconcile their respective positions.

Differing as they do in style, controls, records, and tools, the two professional groups reject each other's data and, in some instances, each other as well. Some counselors, however knowledgeable, practical, and sophisticated they may be, attempt to exclude researchers and their products from service agencies, especially if their acceptance would modify "normal" service procedures or established counselor-client relationships. The strain becomes intensified when administrative mandates compel the counselor to record research-relevant ideas, facts, and thoughts that ordinarily have little direct application to the immediate treatment process or to introduce research-derived approaches to the treatment situation that he "knows" from long experience will not contribute to client growth. Indeed, all too often, the recommendations of the rehabilitation researcher seem naïve and impractical to the experienced counselor. As a result of this attitude, barriers are established to the free development of research and demonstration projects in many service settings and the free use of new research data in the ongoing rehabilitation process.

Remedies for this schism are difficult to devise, because the gulf between practitioners and researchers is usually too broad and encompassing to be bridged by such usual means as the distribution of research reports, publication of research articles, and attendance at professional meetings. Consequently, innovative and imaginative approaches to the problem are needed. Sensitive to the need for a rapprochement between researchers and practitioners and improved channels of communication between the two, Social and Rehabilitation Services engages in varied activities designed to facilitate the flow of research-generated ideas toward clinical personnel. Some of these efforts follow well-established patterns, such as the publication of annotated listings of SRS projects; dissemination of project reports to clinicians and their agencies; sponsorship of research-oriented papers at meetings; publication of selected research "briefs"; publication in *Rehabilitation Record* of summaries of various projects; conduct of regional, state, and local conferences; and direct action of influential SRS personnel in cultivating more favorable attitudes toward rehabilitation research, in general.

In addition to these procedures, SRS has established university research institutes that plug into both research activities, generating publications and conferences that give rehabilitation research a broader exposure. Furthermore, SRS calls the practitioner's attention to the problems of using research findings through research-oriented meetings and a task force concerned with the current problems of research utilization. In all, SRS has taken creative and functional steps toward reducing the gap between practitioners and researchers and, through these efforts, has brought the problem to the attention of many rehabilitation workers.

Administrators also are not immune to misconceptions about rehabilitation research. Confronted with compelling rehabilitation management problems that demand early solution, they sometimes perceive rehabilitation researchers as a group that will provide them with guidelines for prompt and decisive action or justification for action already taken. The environmental stresses under which administrators operate grow out of immediate situations that call for expediency and will not wait for carefully planned research pro-

cedures. Consequently, the caution, detachment, and controls that
trouble practitioners are similarly irksome to action-oriented administrators. In some agencies, research function has become the
handmaiden of administration. Under such conditions, the value of
research is diluted by the administrator's manipulation of the quest
for truth. Here the search is for verification, and the chips may not
fall where they may.

Even when a rehabilitation agency administration encourages
the pursuit of truth, the researcher needs time, reflection, and resources that cannot be mobilized on short notice. While the administrator grapples with the immediacy of his problems, the researcher cautiously explores every aspect of the problem, struggles
with the development of designs, procedures, and methodology, and
slowly gathers his data. Not infrequently, the time required to organize a research effort may be so lengthy that in the interim the
administrator's perception of the problem undergoes substantial
change or more compelling new problems arise. For example, behavioral science researchers were deeply concerned with the developmental problems associated with retrolental fibroplasia during
the early 1950's. This disease, a major cause of blindness, brought
with it numerous psychosocial sequelae. Sampling problems retarded the organization of behavioral science projects related to
this disease, despite an immediate administrative need for data in
this area. By the time the researchers had found the means of
coping with the research challenges of the behavioral aspects of
retrolental fibroplasia, medical interventions had been introduced
that virtually eliminated this condition as a major cause of blindness. Consequently, large-scale investigations concerned with infant
development in cases of retrolental fibroplasia were no longer
needed, since the wave of young children with the condition had
passed.

Similarly, the problem of voluntary versus compulsory entry
into treatment of narcotic addicts was an attractive research area
for both administrators and researchers during the early 1960's.
Once again, sample and design problems delayed the implementation of actual study procedures. During the interim, new legislation
in New York State added a compulsory component to the addict
rehabilitation scene. Now that the original problem was no longer

important, the administrator's interest turned elsewhere and the initial research efforts lapsed.

Along with pacing, the administrator finds much rehabilitation research to be irrelevant. Even the most carefully contrived research solutions have little value for him if they require funds, personnel, and time that are unavailable to him. Although the final product of the researcher may be superior, the administrator views it with a pragmatic eye and often finds it wanting. As a result, he may grow increasingly impatient with research in general and commit agency resources to other enterprises. In the extreme, he may consider all research as a time-consuming adventure in futility and reject the widespread use of research results in his agency.

Since administrators make many key research decisions, the researcher's responsibility is a compelling one as well in this area. He must find ways of communicating to the administrator a realistic picture of the possible outcomes of research and the fact that, despite its limited value in parochial and pragmatic situations, it has a critical long-range role to play in rehabilitation. Once this is understood, good working relationships between researchers and administrators become possible. As an example, the Federation of the Handicapped in New York City, a service-oriented organization, is deeply concerned about the need for immediate upgrading in services available to homebound persons. Despite the intensive pressures of the immediate service situation, the administrator of the Federation of the Handicapped, having an understanding of the research process, was able to deviate from long-standing evaluation policies to sponsor, in cooperation with SRS, a programmatic research project that will generate few immediate solutions, but that, in the long run, will produce data and recommendations that will reshape services to homebound persons throughout the United States. An informed leadership was prepared to deal with the consequences of diverting agency resources from currently compelling service issues. Not all administrators would make the same decision.

Yet, administrators should know that the long-range service implications of research have important administrative implications. For example, SRS-sponsored research on deaf-blindness conducted at the Industrial Home for the Blind (IHB) eventually led to the enactment of a bill creating a national center for the rehabilitation of deaf-blind youth and adults. Although administrative pressures could have funneled this research into relatively narrow and short-term considerations, the administrative choice at the IHB was made by a well-informed executive with a longitudinal perception of the research function at his agency. In the long run, the benefits derived from this research far exceeded anything that might have resulted from a preoccupation with a search for solutions to immediate service problems with this client group or an evaluation of the existing program.

Research can be a powerful tool for both the practitioner and the administrator if perceptual congruence of its uses can be established and if unreal administrative expectations can be eliminated. Under such favorable circumstances, research procedures will not be muddied by administrative demands and conditions, and administrators (and practitioners, too) will not be led to expect rapid, definitive, and "practical" answers to narrowly pragmatic questions. If productivity is to be a criterion of rehabilitation research, it is probable that such research flourishes best and is most productive of useful information when it follows its own bent toward the truth, unfettered by the demands of other rehabilitation workers and left free to evolve its own structure. This is less true, of course, in reference to the rehabilitation demonstration project: a more immediate, pragmatic, compelling, and practical assault upon rehabilitation problems through evaluation. Unlike more basic research, the demonstration is evaluative in nature and imbedded in a service setting where the structure is determined in large part by practitioners.

Improved communication of research results lies at the heart of many rehabilitation research problems, since it could establish a common meeting ground for both researchers and practitioners. Currently, much valuable research material is unread and unnoticed, owing to the form in which it appears. Furthermore, much too often the researcher is a captive of his own language. Writing in the rarified atmosphere of theoretical and scientific pursuits, he tends to obfuscate rather than clarify his findings insofar as the practitioner is concerned. This dependence upon obscure language, trade talk, and technical jargon widens the gulf between the rehabilitation research producer and the rehabilitation research consumer. Even a cursory examination of the rehabilitation research literature reveals that important findings are concealed in technical publications that are not only physically forbidding but are difficult to read by any criterion.

In view of the mounting volume of significant rehabilitation findings, it is mandatory for researchers to find means of disseminating data in terms that are meaningful to a "hard-headed" practitioner. Efforts are moving forward to educate some researchers about improved means of presenting their findings to non-researchers. Hopefully, these measures will bear fruit. At the same time, however, there appears to be a concurrent need for a middleman—perhaps a research disseminator—who can serve as a bridge between researchers and practitioners. Such an individual would have sufficient technical background to understand research reports and adequate communication skills to distil their essence and present them in brief, attractive, and readable form. Although communication theory eventually will suggest long-term theoretical frameworks to guide this process, the current schism will be eased even if we do nothing else but employ audiovisual aids, "discovery" methods, and multisensory inputs of present findings to clinicians.

At present, relatively few research results seep through to the practitioner in a reasonable period of time. Under more favorable communication conditions the time lag could be reduced materially. One way of doing this would be to insist that all grant applications include provisions for disseminating the findings of the project through means that are best calculated to stimulate interest and involvement. Perhaps then, the vast body of rehabilitation research data could be made available to all clients wherever they may be. Additional suggestions include: (1) make research training a required area in all counselor education programs, (2) insist that all service programs have an evaluative component, (3) involve practitioners in research activities of their own choice, and (4) disseminate results on a person-to-person basis through the medium of a change agent.

SUMMARY AND CONCLUSIONS

It has been suggested that rehabilitation progress depends in part upon the speed with which new rehabilitation research findings make their way into everyday rehabilitation practice. The present lag is due in part to the contrasting styles, techniques, and interests of rehabilitation researchers, administrators, and practitioners, and the relative physical and linguistic inaccessibility of many research reports. The gap between research and practice may be closed by more thorough training of practitioners in the research philosophy, improved preparation of research workers in dissemination practices, dialogues between the groups stressing mutual understanding of each other's needs and response styles, improved procedures for disseminating research information so that it becomes physically accessible to research workers, and the preparation of readable research publications that briefly and interestingly reach the practitioner in his frame of reference. Movement in this direction would enrich rehabilitation enormously, for if we can reduce the lag between the publication of research results and their subsequent implementation in research programs, we will have accomplished a substantial victory over the communication barriers that now serve only to deprive disabled people of the best available professional knowledge.

DISCUSSION QUESTIONS

1. Researchers and practitioners tend to blame each other for the slowness with which research data finds its way into everyday rehabilitation practice. Which of the two groups—the creators or the consumers of research—has the major responsibility for this state of affairs? Why?

2. Some clients who complete their rehabilitation programs still are not ready for placement. Should such clients be considered rehabilitation failures? Why? What are some of the factors that, despite extensive rehabilitation service, contribute to a client's lack of placeability?

3. It is widely believed that adequate levels of personal adjustment are necessary for the placeability of disabled persons. Is it possible for an individual to be inadequate in personal adjustment and yet be considered vocationally adjusted? Explain.

4. What is the relationship between vocational and other social roles in the vocational rehabilitation process?

5. In many discussions of vocational rehabilitation, the evaluation process and the counseling process are treated as separate entities. Is this realistic? Most effective? Why?

6. Some rehabilitation specialists have noted that the evaluation, training, and placement phases of the rehabilitation process are an analog to the steps in a research project. Is the drawing of such a parallel justified? In what way?

7. Select a research that deals with some aspect of vocational rehabilitation and suggest how it might be applied in the rehabilitation process.

8. Counselors differ in their feelings about the placement function. Do you believe that every counselor should be the placement worker for his own clients or should he depend primarily upon specialized placement counselors for this service? Why?

9. The term personal adjustment training seems to encompass a wide range of activities. What is your concept of this type of training and what components do you believe should be included in it? What are its goals?

10. Vocational training occurs in various settings, sheltered shops, schools, industry, and so on. What are some of the things counselors have to consider before referring a disabled client for a training experience? Does the training setting make any difference?

PART FOUR

COUNSELING

INTRODUCTION TO PART FOUR

Counseling is the synthesizing function in rehabilitation. Confronted by a conflicting welter of information, experiences, and perceptions, the rehabilitation client and his counselor struggle to elicit meaning and direction from the multiple inner and environmental factors that impinge on the client's problem. Through means that are not yet entirely clear, they sort out disparate and, at times, contradictory elements and gradually unite them into a conceptual structure that has order, consistency, and unity. Integration emerges out of confusion, and both the counselor and the client, now supported by increasingly congruent and consistent perceptions of the client's incredibly complex life situation, move forward together toward implementing their common and, now better organized, understanding of the problem. Through counseling, they work together to create a rehabilitation plan that puts the client on target, eliminating, insofar as possible, his aimless wandering through the underbrush of his own inchoate yearnings and undirected efforts.

Although they generally agree on the synthesizing nature of counseling, rehabilitation counselors have persistent difficulties in harmonizing their concepts of the counseling process. In the face of contending counseling orientations, approaches, and techniques, counselors are more conscious of a seeming "chaos" than of real "wholeness" in their own field. Thus, while assisting clients to attain perceptions that have organic unity, rehabilitation counselors themselves need assistance in developing unified perceptions of their own field. All too often counseling theorists have contributed to the confusion by functioning as "hard-core" advocates of extreme positions in counseling, holding that the keys to the kingdom are theirs exclusively and that only by zealous adherence to the unique attitudes and behaviors that differentiate their approach from all others can the counselor truly achieve his counseling goals, if indeed agreement could be reached on these goals. Out of this situation have come sacred rites practiced by the inner circle of each counseling orientation designed to produce guilt and doubt in the heart and mind of the disbeliever.

In this section, Schwebel, Patterson, and Lofquist turn toward a more fruitful view of the counseling function, substituting reasonableness and reconciliation for the divisive extremes of earlier counseling theorists. Each of the three writers is conscious of the brotherhood of counseling and finds commonalities in the ranks that bind rehabilitation counselors in a unity of purpose, content, and technique that previously had been considered nonexistent. Each in his own way synthesizes the current counseling experience into a *Gestalt* that should reduce confusion and frustration among practitioners. Each communicates the message that apparent differences in "schools" or "theories" are differences in emphasis rather than in essential content, that, reassured by a common base of concepts and understandings, rehabilitation counselors no longer need to feel that they are combatants on a battlefield of ideas in which their energies are to be directed to thrust and counterthrust in support of theoretical positions.

The hope offered by these three authors is a real one for clients. Acceptance of their ideas will not only improve the level of rehabilitation counselor performance, but it will also free counselors from an internecine war of ideas. This will enable them to share in a peaceful coexistence based upon a respect for difference among counselors, knowing that such difference exists in a framework of mutuality.

The three authors achieve their synthesis through different avenues. Schwebel establishes a common ground among rehabilitation counselors through providing them with roots in personality theory and then by organizing apparently divergent personality theories into a family of ideas that has system and order. For his part, Patterson moves one step closer to the specific problems of the rehabilitation counselor by indicating the relationships between counseling theories, and by his observation that all seem to be talking about the same aspects of man in about the same ways. Through this means, counseling theory becomes systematized, and differences become less consequential than similarities. In turn, Lofquist finds a common base for rehabilitation counselors in sophisticated, modern technology, and suggests that the need to learn about the client and his environment cuts across all types of vocational counseling and that solutions to the problem lie in the use of simplified and mechanized information systems.

In most areas of cognition, the perception of difference is often easier than the perception of similarity. Indeed, the espousal of difference often brings benefits to an individual in reinforcing his individuality and insuring him a recognizable place among his colleagues. History rewards the idiosyncratic individual who casts off the mediation of the consensus and strikes out on his own innovative path. In the future, as in the past, such individuals will be needed to cross the new frontiers of knowledge, but the organizers and synthesizers of knowledge will be needed just as well. To bring order out of chaos, to make rehabilitation counseling a process that can be communicated to students, is a notable objective. This is what Schwebel, Patterson, and Lofquist have attempted to do.

X   IMPLICATIONS OF PERSONALITY
THEORY FOR COUNSELING

Milton Schwebel

All professionals use theory. Every counselor uses theory every single day of his work, often doing so unknowingly. In that circumstance there is a severe limitation in the use that he can make of the theory, and of the value the theory has in his work; for then he cannot evaluate whether the theory has been tested and found purposeful and valid. Furthermore, the possibility exists that he is unknowingly engaging in "theory-jumping": shifting from theory to theory without rational basis for such action. Let us consider, for example, a man who has been dropped into a thick wood and is lost. How does he find his way out? He may apply some kind of theory consistently, long enough at least to establish its validity for his purposes; or, in contrast, he may shift his theories erratically, running frantically in one direction as he is guided momentarily by one theory and then in another and again in still another direction. In the former situation (working with a consistent theory) he may be relying upon the sun or the stars to guide his steps and to find a way out of the forest, or he may even have something of greater all-round dependability, such as a compass, so that even if he cannot see the sky or find the sun, he may still solve his problem.

This comparison gives a reason for the conscious use of theory. Actually, theories are nothing more than the summations or crystallizations of past experience, which have been tested and found to be helpful in predicting behavior and in problem solving. Their value is well characterized by Kurt Lewin's oftquoted statement that even a poor theory is better than no theory at all. At least the man lost in the forest who employs a poor theory will end up at some point other than his destination and recognize the need to try another approach. This is better than aimless wandering.

A formal definition of theory is that it consists of principles supported by considerable data and is proposed as an explanation of a group of phenomena. It is interesting to see how a theory is tested. For example, we note that people tend to be influenced by words, especially if suggestions are made in a particular kind of way. So a hypothesis is set up: that a word presented in a particular fashion, repeated in a particular way, and at a certain time, will influence people in a specific manner. This hypothesis, in fact, is intended to explain the phenomena of human reactions to suggestion in the form of words.

As a test, let the reader concentrate on the big toe of his left foot—nothing else but the big toe of his left foot. If he dwells on his big toe, he will shortly feel a sensation. Repeated often enough, quite a few would experience this sensation, with the conclusion that the words (that is, the suggestion) are capable of influencing the body. Now, if this were an experiment, and after repetition it was consistently found to operate the same way, then it would be concluded that, yes, under certain conditions, human beings are subject to suggestions of a certain kind.

A distribution of suggestibility would surely be found with some at one extreme tending to fight and resist the suggestion, some at the other giving in quickly, and others in the middle range. To the extent that these hypotheses turn out to be valid, we have principles that explain groups of phenomena about human behavior; and personality theory really is—at least is presumed to be—a body of organized data that explain phenomena about the behavior of people.

Before turning to the practical aspects of theory (that is, their applications and implications), it might be wise to discuss briefly certain features that should characterize personality theory. First, a theory must not be regarded as the last word, because personality theory, like any other, is dynamic and everchanging. The Freudian system today is very different from that of 1890. In fact, we have merely to read what Freud wrote at the middle or near the end of his life, and contrast it with his earlier work, to see how much his thinking changed—so much so that he insisted he was not a Freudian!

A second essential feature of theory is that personality must be recognized as an attribute of a biosocial organism whose biological states (for example, fatigue and tension or the effects of food and drink) and organic defects (for example, motor or neurological) have their psychological counterparts and/or consequences. It is obvious that the behavior of the organism is modified by alcoholic beverages, which affect the personality of the individual. Alcohol acts upon the biochemistry, the brain, and the "psyche," usually relaxing inhibitions, although the degree and form of relaxation vary among individuals in any given population. Similarly it can be seen that the food diet (stimulating or tranquilizing) and the activity outlets of a person's occupation all have an effect on the expression of the personality.

Some of the conditions once considered to be personality disorders and now recognized as minor disorders of the central nervous system have an impact on the personality of the individual. Premature birth is a case in point. Although the extent to which premature babies are afflicted with minor central nervous system disorders is not yet known, such children rather consistently have a higher degree of emotional, behavioral, and learning problems than do fullterm children. The evidence is indisputable that personality is part of, and inseparable from, the physical organism and is influenced by physical states.

A third necessary feature of a viable personality theory is that learning is a key to human behavior, and that much of the human being, the very personality itself, is, to a large extent, the result of learning. The learning process involves a social being in a social condition. Every word we use has been learned from someone else; every thought comes from a relationship with other social beings. This is why the intrapsychic interpretation of behavior is questionable; that is, the kind of interpretation that speaks of a superego, id, and ego and of a development of personality emerging from instinct in the individual, without recognition of the crucial influence of the society in character development.

This is not to suggest that physiological impulses are unimportant, or that there are not biochemical differences among people that are related to behavioral and personality differences. The interesting study of children by psychiatrist Alexander Thomas and his colleagues reported in their *Behavioral Individuality in Early Childhood* (New York University Press, 1963) shows that children have consistent modes of response within days or weeks after birth that persist at least during the early years of life. This suggests that constitutional factors are operative in personality development, and it implies that a learning or environmentalist theory is just as incomplete as an instinctual or constitutional theory of personality development. The only defensible alternative is an interactionist approach that says, in effect, that our personalities develop as we, a biosocial organism, interact with our social and natural environments.

Let us examine the implications of personality theory for counseling practice. By providing an explanation of behavior, personality theory determines both the mode in which problems are conceptualized and the kinds of diagnoses made by counselors. The Freudian therapist or counselor diagnoses in terms of the psychosexual development of the individual, the balance among superego, id, and ego, and the mechanisms used to defend against anxiety. The learning theory therapist diagnoses conflict in terms of stimulus-response patterns and the reinforcement agents. The behavioral therapist establishes a hierarchy of causes of anxiety in the client, ordering them by their potency in immobilizing him. The nondirective counselor makes no diagnosis at all. So, personality theories are so different they lead some to say: "I don't want to hear anything about the individual's past because this will influence me," and others to regard such a stance as downright irresponsible if not unethical.

When we examine the relationship between personality theory and the treatment aspect of counseling, we find the former tends to determine or at least to explain or rationalize the latter. For example, consider this case situation. It is the third interview and the counselor feels he is reacting to the client with great understanding and empathy. Suddenly, following one of his statements, the counselor is surprised by the client's angry response. What are his alternatives in handling the client's outburst? For the naïve counselor, whose interpersonal response patterns are still not much different from those of the layman, the tendency would be to react intensively, either by being apologetic—saying, "What did I do to you?" —or by reacting in anger—"Where the devil do you get the nerve to speak to me this way?" Being in a position of authority, the counselor can crush the client, or, if nothing else, can so anger him as to discourage continuation in counseling. This is one way of dealing with the case and surely not a desirable one, yet it occurs more frequently than one would like to admit.

Consider another approach—a counselor who is not naïve, someone who is knowledgeable about counseling theory but not about personality theory. This counselor would respond to the client's outburst in accord with the kind of counseling technique he had learned. He might say, "Uh huh," or, "You feel very angry with me," or remain silent—a response that, in terms of counseling theory, is considered perfectly acceptable and may be found in the standard textbooks. Lacking knowledge of personality theory, he is engaging in an exercise of technique without an understanding of the dynamics of the interpersonal relationship and the conflicts of the client that elicited the outburst.

Now consider the sophisticated counselor who is knowledgeable about general principles that explain behavioral phenomena. He knows that one of several things is operating in this situation. For one thing, he may be encountering resistance, which all counselors experience at one time or another for it is one universal reaction of an individual to sources of intense anxiety. Faced with real danger some people run from it, some surrender and become immobilized, and some strike back with anger. The same is true in our response to anything that threatens us, no matter how imaginary it may be. One method of fleeing from anxiety is by using our energy to resist being conscious of the source of it. This we frequently do at a cost, as for example, avoiding sexual anxiety by resisting thoughts about it. Another possible explanation (in the mind of the sophisticated counselor) is that the client is exhibiting one of his defense mechanisms. All individuals have such mechanisms and use them quite unconsciously when faced with threat.

The question in diagnosis is what kinds of mechanisms are being used and how often are they employed. In this particular case, the mechanism displayed might be projection. Whatever was being discussed with the client might have threatened him and aroused feelings of hostility, which were then ascribed to the counselor. Therefore, his outburst against the counselor might simply have been a projection of this hostility, having nothing to do directly with the counselor himself. Saying it another way, this is what might have occurred: the counselor had developed a warm, reassuring relationship with the client, but now, suddenly, some feelings are aroused that frighten the client; in fact, he might be frightened by the closeness developed with the counselor, so that the expression of hostility is quite inappropriate to the situation and yet clearly understandable if one comprehends how the client has experienced the relationship.

Consider now the transference aspect in the relationship just described. It is still the same client and counselor in their third session, and they have just experienced this outburst of anger by the client. The possibility is that if the counselor is a male, the client has come to perceive him as a father figure, so that the perception and the consequent emotion exhibited were inappropriate in this situation. However, perhaps they would not have been irrational if the counselor really had been his father and had interacted with him as his father had. Similarly, if the counselor were a woman, the transference reaction might have involved a perception of her as a mother. Actually, much irrational behavior in life, in classrooms, and in jobs, as well as in counseling or therapy, is a result of the transference phenomenon; that is, counselors are seen as authority figures from the past, whose motives are ascribed to the counselors regardless of their actual behavior. Furthermore, the client acts and reacts in the ways that he reacted to these figures in the past.

There is still another explanation for the client's outburst: perhaps it is the result of certain culturally conditioned responses. In the client's family group the expression of anger or of angry-sounding words may be a fairly common response even to the mildest of annoyances; maybe even a necessary mechanism to get attention in a large and vocal family even in the absence of provocation of any kind.

Another explanation of the client's outburst may be found in the phenomenon of countertransference. Being human, counselors also have their problems, and sometimes these creep into the counseling situation. Counselors, too, use the relationship as a means of expressing hostility, serving power motives, manipulating people, and controlling their own anxiety-provoking impulses, including the sexual. Unbeknown to ourselves, the involvement with another person calls forth emotions so fearful to us that we must squelch them, and to do so we squelch the other person. Thus, it may well be that in our fictional situation, what the counselor thought was a warm, reassuring statement in a good relationship, actually was something else. It may have been a reaction to some threat posed by the client in a countertransference context, as in the case of the counselor misperceiving the client as a sibling rival.

Rehabilitation counseling is especially subject to the trap of countertransference. Instead of a relationship of respect and acceptance between counselor and client, it evokes pity or sympathy for the physically-afflicted client. These emotions do not form a sound basis for a rational approach to overcoming the disequilibrium that impels people to seek professional help. Emotions like that sometimes motivate the counselor in his work with members of minority groups, who react negatively to such expressions of pity or sympathy.

We could go on to indicate how the implications of personality theory for counseling relationships lead some counselors to be more passive, others more active; some more personal, and still others impersonal. The existentialist counselor does not hesitate to talk about his own problems in the belief that this serves as a bridge to the client. The traditional Freudian shudders at the thought of that behavior, because it is so alien to his way of viewing people and the therapeutic relationship.

Specific personality theories have important and sometimes very different implications for counseling. The neo-Freudians have given Freudian thinking an interpretation more consistent with twentieth-century developments in the behavioral and social sciences. They agree that instinctual impulses are important in motivating behavior, but other things besides sex and aggression are important, perhaps of even greater importance, in determining behavior. They make the point that precisely because of the overemphasis of sex and aggression as determining factors in the development of personality, the basic premise of Freudian theory is false. This they say without denying, nor would any of the other theoretical groups deny, the importance of sex in human life. Aggression is another matter, for, notwithstanding the work of Konrad Lorenz and the other ethologists on aggression in animals, there is no convincing evidence that man has to gratify an aggression instinct.

In the work of socially-oriented neo-Freudians like Erich Fromm and Karen Horney, behavior is viewed as a biosocial phenomenon arising from the interrelationships between people. An individual is a product of his biology and of a kind of social history that reflects the many other people and situations in his life in the present as well as the past. As a dynamic being, he can be aware of himself and of his ability to make decisions and to take responsibility for himself. There are important principles with which the counselor has to struggle if he is to firmly believe the client has the capacity to make the best choice for himself and to be willing to accept the client's right to choose his own directions in life. Do counselors really believe this or do they merely have a kind of half-hearted conviction about it? This question arises very often when dealing with the problems of adolescents. Do counselors really believe that the adolescent has the ability and the right to make his own decisions?

If a study were made to see what brought about the greatest changes in people in the last ten years, perhaps it would be found that these did not take place in schools or universities, in counseling or therapy offices. They may have taken place instead on the streets of Birmingham or Little Rock or Montgomery. Why? Because individuals were motivated in an existential way to take their destiny in their own hands and were responsible for their own experiences. Isn't this what humble counselors and therapists attempt to get their clients to do? ("Humble" because counselors work and plod along in circumstances that are very different from those that guide great events.) These events were great, not because someone pushed people to participate but because people were motivated to do it on their own. Are clients given this right to say "No, I don't want your help. No, I don't accept your values. No, I don't want to do what you say the tests say I ought to do. This is what I want to do"?

In applying learning theory to psychotherapy, Dollard and Miller point out that a person must want help if he is to receive any benefit from the therapeutic situation. He must want a change from his present state, which is more painful than the pain of change and the pain of exposing himself to a counselor and the pain of paying for his counseling or therapy. In other words, one's present status must be more painful than any status that might be created by change before people can make effective use of counseling. This, of course, is often a problem in working with children, because it is not only the children who are in pain but also their parents, and sometimes the children have averted much of the pain through some compensatory or protective device. This is sometimes the case in rehabilitation counseling, when clients do not come because they want counseling but are seeking some other kind of service.

The behavioral therapists (like J. Wolpe) would say that anxiety is a product of learning, but that no matter when it was learned and what was learned, it can be changed. They disagree with the Freudian concept, supported by others as well, that since most significant learning takes place prior to the age of five, change is difficult, and requires long treatment and a recreation of the past. The behavior therapists say it does not matter when learning occurred; if it has been learned, one does not have to engage in archeological forays nor delve into the psychodynamics emerging from a lengthy history. All one need do is find the present causes of anxiety and devise methods to reduce the anxiety. They say, in effect, that it does not matter what will help change behavior so long as change occurs.

Having learned personality theories, the counselor is still faced with the important task of selecting one, or a synthesis of several, that is compatible with his value orientation and personality style. Regrettably, he cannot base his choice on evidence from empirical studies, nor can he find even indirect evidence that any one of them has yielded great results in psychotherapy, as Hans Eysenck has reported even if too stridently and not without bias against all the therapies except the behavioral type. So it is left to each counselor to make a choice, to find a compass that is most meaningful, that helps him understand and interpret, and that becomes part of himself. I shall briefly describe my orientation.

What makes our species human and different from animals is our kind of consciousness, which enables us, so to speak, to step back and view ourselves and our behavior. As counselors, our sphere of activity is consciousness: we attempt to expand and develop it no matter whether we are general counselors or specialists in vocational, educational, or personal adjustment. We have a client who is anxious about a new experience—let us say one involving a heterosexual social situation, because he automatically experiences himself as an unwelcome member of a group. We help him reduce his anxiety by modifying his perception of himself as an inadequate and uncommunicative person, by which action we help change his behavior and his consciousness.

Another example is the reaction of the person applying for a job, who is immediately questioned by the boss. He begins to think and feel the way he did when he was in school and the teacher called on him, and the way he felt at home when one or both parents questioned him. Let us say this is a case of transference and we talk about this with the client. Now, what is happening? We are helping the client realize that he is neither in school nor at home and that this is a different situation. We help him realize that his anxiety develops from a deep sense of inadequacy and a feeling that he has been applying for this job as if he were a child imploring for attention and acceptance.

Take still another case, that of a client who just cannot make up his mind. He has choice anxiety, for he cannot decide about a job or about a mate or about anything, for that matter. This is a problem that plagues many people. Perhaps he becomes very anxious the moment he becomes self-assertive, with the result that he cannot allow himself to start going in any direction. Indecision is his defense. We try to help him change his consciousness through information, interpretation, and suggestions, and by confronting him with the actual reasons for his indecision, which usually have little or nothing to do with the relative merits of the alternatives. It is through new knowledge and awareness of oneself that behavioral change occurs.

My effectiveness is greatest when I am not the prisoner of a theory that makes me passive; a theory that tells me that I must say this or that, or that does not permit me, in a sense, to be assertive in the counseling relationship. I reject any theory that discourages my active and spontaneous intervention, even in the form of suggestion or advice.

My professional work is always in the context of the history of man's developing consciousness, which has permitted him to achieve ever greater control over his physical and social environment. Greater intellectual freedom from superstition and faith, and greater reliance on observation, objective evidence, and his own powers of reason have given him greater power. This is no less true for individuals, and through my interpretations and my behavior, I want to convey this point of view to my clients.

Theory and practice are inseparable: the theory determines my interpretations about what prevents us from using the great potential strength of the human mind; my behavior conveys a sense of openness, understanding, and courage. Realism and optimism are combined, so that realities are not denied but seen in the light of human potentialities, especially when people work collectively to achieve change. Life is there to be used, to be lived, and to be changed, and my job as counselor is to help people gain enough strength for them to take greater initiative in shaping their own destiny.

For example, realistically there are not enough jobs to go around for all the people who want them, and there are not enough decent houses for people who need them. We live in a society where the value of a person is measured to a large extent by the profit he can produce for someone else, and the fact is that many handicapped people are not valued because they cannot contribute to the profits of some firm in private industry. These are realities that unfortunately sometimes permeate the counselor-client relationship, and I want to be able to convey to a handicapped client that some of society's values are antihuman. Granting that this may be very little to offer to a client and that it has little practical value, yet it is important to convey to the client that even if circumstances are "stinking," there is at least one thing he can do. He has the power to join with others in our society to help make things better. This happens to be an exceedingly therapeutic measure for all of us: to be part of a group that brings about change and improvement. Handicapped people, like any other group, can also band together to make things better for themselves.

This is the essence of what a useful, personality-adapted, synthetic personality theory means to me: one that has been filtered through other theories, and enables me to use my strength as a human being, in particular my cerebral cortex, and my feelings, to help other people acquire strength. This is what counseling is really all about: a process of helping people become stronger so that they can cope with life more effectively and with a greater sense of fulfillment.

XI   THEORIES OF COUNSELING

C. H. Patterson

A survey of the major theories or approaches to counseling or psychotherapy (Patterson, in press) reveals considerable diversity. Various points of view appear to differ widely in philosophy and concepts, in goals or objectives, and in methods or techniques. Not only do the points of view differ as presented by their principal proponents, but there are often schools within schools. In addition, there are differences among individual practitioners. Every counselor or psychotherapist considers himself different or unique in some respect.

This diversity, and even disagreement, has led some observers to despair about the state of counseling or psychotherapy. Ungersma (1961, p. 55) writes as follows:

> The present situation in psychotherapy is not unlike that of a man who mounted his horse and rode off in all directions. The theoretical orientation of therapists is based upon widely divergent hypotheses, theories and ideologies. . . . Individual practitioners of any art are expected to vary, but some well-organized schools of therapy also seem to be working at cross-purposes with other equally well-organized schools. Nevertheless, all schools, given favorable conditions, achieve favorable results: the patient or client gets relief and is often enough cured of his difficulties.

This equal success of apparently widely different approaches constitutes a problem requiring some explanation.

Rogers (1963), who admits to having had hopes that therapists would be able to come to agreement on what constitutes psychotherapy, has recently expressed his disillusionment. Whereas he had felt that "we were all talking about the same experiences," he now feels that "we differ at the most basic levels of our personal

191

experience." He concludes that "the field of psychotherapy is in a mess," although he also feels that the present confusion is a healthy climate for new ideas, theories, methods, and concepts.

There is an old adage that "where there are many medicines the illness is incurable." Does this apply to the field of counseling or psychotherapy? Is there no agreement, no commonality, among the diverse approaches, no way of integrating them into a unified approach? The following pages review the basic divergences in various points of view, and attempt to sift out convergences to arrive at an integrated approach to counseling or psychotherapy.

DIVERGENCES

PHILOSOPHY AND CONCEPTS

While there are numerous specific differences among theories of counseling or psychotherapy relating to the nature of man and the nature of emotional disturbance, these may be reduced to a single basic difference in what Allport (1962) refers to as the image of the nature of man. Allport describes three models. The first is that of man as a reactive being. Here man is viewed as a biological organism reacting to stimuli from his environment. He is determined by his experiences, by his past learning or conditioning, and by potential reconditioning. The concepts representing this point of view include the following: reaction, reinforcement, reflex, respondent, reintegration, and reconditioning. This is the image of man assumed by the behavior theorist and by counselors and psychotherapists who take a learning or behavior theory approach to counseling or psychotherapy.

Allport's second image of the nature of man sees him as a reactive being in depth. Rather than man being conceived as a being reacting to his environment, he is seen as reacting to his innate drives, motives and needs and influenced by their past frustrations and satisfactions. Its concepts include repression, regression, resistance, abreaction, reaction formation, and recall and recovery of the past. This is the view of depth psychology, including psychoanalysis.

These two images are similar in basic respects. Both see man as reacting to forces or stimuli—in the one case from within, in the other from without. In the one case man is a victim of his environment; in the other, of his innate needs and drives. They may thus be combined to constitute a single model of man as a reactive being.

In contrast to this image is a second (Allport's third) model. Allport designates this as man as a being in the process of becoming. This model sees man as personal, conscious, and future oriented. It includes such concepts as tentativeness and commitment. This is the model of existentialism.

These two models appear to underlie differing approaches to counseling or psychotherapy, with behavior therapy, learning theory approaches, and psychoanalysis in one group, and client-centered and existential approaches in the other.

THE COUNSELING PROCESS

The therapy process is viewed differently by the various approaches. Psychoanalysis stresses insight in relation to the past, achieved by skillful interpretation. For Kelly (1955) therapy is the process of loosening old constructs and reconditioning personal constructs. For Ellis (1962) it is convincing the client that he has been functioning irrationally, and teaching him a more rational structure by which to live. The client-centered approach conceives of the counseling process as the experiencing, in a psychologically safe relationship, of feelings that have been too threatening for the client to experience freely and fully. Behavior therapy views counseling as eliminating undesirable behavior through desensitization, extinction, and reconditioning. Existentialists see it as the subjective encounter of two individuals in an affective relationship.

The writer, in his review of various theories (Patterson, in press), proposed a continuum varying from highly rational approaches at one end to strongly affective approaches at the other. In the rational approach, the counseling process tends to be planned, objective, and impersonal. In the affective approach, it is emphasized as being warm, personal, and spontaneous. One emphasizes reason and problem solving; the other affect and experiencing. Although there is probably no pure form of each approach, this distinction appears to be one that is supported by an examination of the various approaches. In fact, it appears that there may be two divergent trends in counseling; one toward a more cognitive approach and one toward a more affective approach, so that there may be a bimodal distribution, or a dichotomy in the making.

Another differentiation of approaches in terms of process is the insight-action dichotomy of London (1964). London includes under the insight therapies client-centered therapy and existential analysis, as well as the various schools of psychoanalysis. Although there are differences among the insight approaches, London sees these differences as insignificant in comparison to their commonalities. There are two commonalities that stand out, and dwarf other likenesses as well as differences. These are:

1. The single allowable instrument of the therapy is talk, and the therapeutic sessions are deliberately conducted in such a way that, from start to finish, the patient, client, analysand, or counselee does most of the talking and most of the deciding of what will be talked about.
2. The therapist operates with a conservative bias against communicating to the patient important or detailed information about his own life, that is to say, the therapist tends to hide his personal life from the patient (London, 1964, p. 45).

Techniques such as free association or permissiveness lead to exposure of the repressed or unconscious material, which is then responded to with reflection, empathic understanding, or interpretation by the therapist, leading to insight by the client.

Action therapies, or behavior therapies, on the other hand, are not concerned with verbalizations, or talk, but with behavior, actions, or symptoms. The action therapist operates on behavior, and "he cares not a whit what the patient does or does not say about himself or even know about himself except insofar as such *behaviors* have concrete and demonstrable value for producing change." Two characteristics of action therapists, according to London, are:

1. The therapist assumes a much greater influence over the detailed conduct of the treatment sessions, and possibly

over the outside life of the patient, than Insight therapists would.

2. The therapist is much more responsible for the outcome of treatment, that is, for whatever changes take place in the patient, than are Insight therapists (London, 1964, p. 78).

Ullmann and Krasner (1965) propose essentially the same dichotomy in their distinction between evocative or expressive therapies and behavior therapy, although they recognize that there are overlappings in techniques. While learning theory concepts are present in expressive therapy, in behavior therapy they are systematically applied.

In terms of the rational-affective dichotomy, both insight and action therapies may be considered as rational approaches. In insight therapy, the process or approach is rational in terms of the theory of personality and its disorders, and the techniques tend to be rational discussions of problems. In action therapy the approach is also rational in terms of its underlying theory of the causation of behavior and its disorders as faulty learning, which must be corrected by the application of specific techniques rather than by consideration of affects or feelings in a personal relationship. Thus, there would appear to be need for another category, to include those approaches that minimize a rational, logical, cause-effect approach to problems and their solutions, but which emphasize feelings, attitudes, and emotions and their treatment or modification by understanding, accepting, and empathizing with the client in a close personal relationship.

GOALS AND PURPOSES

If we examine the goals of different approaches, we find an amazing range and variety. Some therapists speak of personality reorganization, others of curing a disease or illness, others of adjustment to the environment, society, or the culture. Still others are concerned with the development of independence and responsibility or with assisting the client to use his potentialities or to actualize himself. Still others are concerned with helping the client feel better, or with removing disturbing symptoms.

The rational therapies may emphasize the solution of problems, the making of decisions, or the learning of problem-solving behavior. The affective approaches may emphasize the development of self-esteem, congruence between the self or self-concept and the ideal self, self-acceptance, or the achievement of a sense of meaning in life.

If London's dichotomy is used, the insight therapies have as their goal self-understanding, in terms of the motives, needs, and drives that have led to disturbed behavior or symptoms. Such understanding may or may not lead to, or be accompanied by, changed behavior. In psychoanalysis, what was id becomes ego, the unconscious or repressed becomes conscious, awareness of the historical causes of present behavior becomes insight. Action therapy has as its goal the removal of symptoms, as simply and as quickly as possible. The goal is clear, simple, and specific, and does not depend upon the client's insight or understanding of the origins of his symptoms.

To the insight therapist, symptoms are literally that—indications of an underlying disturbance or problem, which needs to be understood to be solved. However, for the action therapist the symptom *is* the disturbance or problem, and he tries

> more directly to eliminate the symptom so that the patient will feel better, and it makes no difference to him what the patient does or does not understand about anything. . . . He shapes behavior (in the latter case), not tampering with "selves" or "souls" or even "personalities." And if he can, by argument, seduction, threat, or even skillful violence (as a surgeon does), excise the symptom's painful barb, then he has done enough, but not too much (London, 1964, pp. 36, 37).

There are thus obviously many differences among various approaches to counseling or psychotherapy, in methods or techniques, goals or purposes, and philosophy. Sundland and Barker (1962) studied the differences in orientation in a group of 139 psychotherapists who were members of the American Psychological Association, using a Therapist Orientation Questionnaire containing 16 subscales. These scales included, among others: Frequency of Activity, Type of Activity, Emotional Tenor of the Relationship, Spontaneity, Planning, Conceptualization of the

Relationship, Goals of Therapy, Theory of Personal Growth, Theory of Neurosis, Theory of Motivation, and Criteria for Success. The therapists distributed themselves over the range of scores from strongly agree to strongly disagree on most of the scales. When the therapists were classified into three groups—Freudians, Sullivanians, and Rogerians—the three groups differed significantly on nine of the 16 scales, with the Sullivanians being in the middle position in eight of these comparisons.

The Freudian group, compared to the Rogerian group, believed that the therapist should be more impersonal, plan his therapy, have definite goals, inhibit his spontaneity, use interpretation, conceptualize the case, and recognize the importance of unconscious motivation. These results support those of Strupp (1955). Only one difference was found between therapists grouped by levels of experience.

A factor analysis of the 16 scales yielded six factors. A general factor cut across most of the scales, providing a major single continuum upon which therapists vary. One end is labeled "analytic" (not simply "psychoanalytic") and the other is designated as "experiential" by Sundland and Barker. The "analytic" therapist emphasizes conceptualizing, planning therapy, unconscious processes, and restriction of spontaneity. The "experiential" therapist emphasizes nonverbal, nonrationalized experiencing, the personality of the therapist, and therapist spontaneity. More therapists tended toward the "analytic" approach than toward the "experiencing" approach.

Wallach and Strupp (1964) obtained similar results from factor analysis of the ratings of two groups of therapists on a scale of Usual Therapeutic Practices. The major factor was called the maintenance of personal distance. Four groupings of therapists— Orthodox Freudians, Psychoanalytic General, Sullivanian, and Client-centered—were compared, with the first group being highest in the personal distance factor, the second group next highest, and the remaining two about equal, but lower than the first two.

McNair and Lorr (1964) studied the reported techniques of 192 male and 73 female psychotherapists (67 psychiatrists, 103 psychologists, and 95 social workers) in 44 Veterans Administration mental hygiene clinics, using an instrument developed on the basis of the Sundland and Barker Therapist Orientation Scale.

They hypothesized three dimensions to be measured by the AID scales: (A) psychoanalytically oriented techniques, (I) impersonal versus personal approaches to the patient, and (D) directive, active therapeutic methods. All three dimensions emerged in the factor analysis of the 49 scales included in the analysis.

High scores of the A factor represent traditional psycho-analytic techniques. High scores on the I factor represent a detached objective, impersonal approach, while low scores represent emphasis on therapist personally ard the therapist-patient relation-ship. High scores on the D factor indicate therapist setting of goals and planning of treatment, leading of the interview, and acceptance of social adjustment as a major goal. Low scores indicate therapist lack of direction of the interview and belief in patient determination of therapy goals. While the three factors are intercorrelated, McNair and Lorr consider them independent.

These studies support the existence of differences among therapists. The Sundland and Barker study provides evidence for the rational-affective continuum or dichotomy. The McNair and Lorr study also supports this ordering or classifying of approaches or techniques. McNair and Lorr also found a factor (D), which may indicate support for London's dichotomy. These studies would not support London's classification of client-centered and existential approaches with psychoanalysis in a homogeneous insight therapy group. However, none of these studies included behavior therapists. The results would, no doubt, have been different if any of them had. With the advent of behavior therapy, a new dimension has been added to psychotherapy or counseling, and it is the difference between this approach and all other approaches that now seems to present the major problem for the future.

It is here that the greatest differences in philosophy, methods, and goals appear. The behavior therapists are apparently interested in specific, immediate, concrete results. To obtain them, the therapist takes responsibility for the process, and controls and manipulates the situation. He may disavow any ethical implications of his control by contending that he is a technician in the service of the client, who determines what the goals of the process should be.

The relationship therapist is concerned about more general, long-range goals. He gives the client the responsibility for the direction and the pace of the counseling process. While he may be very active, his activity is not the directing, manipulative activity of the behavior therapist, but the activity of empathizing with and understanding the client and communicating that understanding. Paradoxically, however, he may not accept the specific goals of the client, but may impose his own goals of self-understanding, self-realization, or self-actualization on the client. However, implicit, if not explicit, in this goal is greater freedom for the client in his specific behavior. By choosing the goal of maximum future freedom for the client, a goal that is presumably that of our society, he resolves the value issue of imposing his own specific goals on the client.

CONVERGENCES

With all the differences among approaches, are there no commonalities or similarities among all, or even some, of the major systems? There have been a number of attempts to discover or define common elements (see Patterson, 1959, chap. 12). The search for common elements is stimulated by the observed fact that all approaches report successes; in fact, with the exception of the claims of the behavior therapists, the rate of success claimed is approximately the same, that is, about two thirds of those treated. It is reasoned that although the approaches may appear to be different, there must be common elements, unless there are different ways of achieving success or results. It is also possible that the same results are not achieved, but that different approaches lead to different results; that is, the criteria for success are different among the various approaches. It is also possible, as some behaviorists point out, that the common rate of success is the result of either spontaneous recovery, with no approach being effective, or of the so-called placebo effect, which shall be considered later.

PHILOSOPHY AND CONCEPTS

It would seem to be difficult to find a common philosophy, or even a single common concept, among the many points of view that exist. As has been indicated above, concepts relating to the nature of man and the nature of emotional disturbances vary considerably. There would seem to be little if anything in common between a concept of man as determined by his environment, or by his internal needs and drives, on the one hand, and the concept of man as a person capable of making choices and free to do so, on the other; or between the concept of man as essentially an organism to be manipulated by rewards and punishment, on the one hand, and as having the potential for growth and development in the process of self-actualization, on the other.

Nevertheless, as minimal as it may appear, there is agreement in regarding man as capable of changing, or at least of being changed. He is not hopelessly predetermined, but at any stage may still be pliable. A learning theory approach actually may assume that man is infinitely susceptible to change. Skinner (1958) expresses this as follows:

> It is dangerous to assert that an organism of a given species or age cannot solve a given problem. As a result of careful scheduling, pigeons, rats, and monkeys have done things in the last five years which members of their species have never done before. It is not that their forebears were incapable of such behavior; nature had simply never arranged effective sequences of schedules.

And, regarding the possibility of molding personality, he states:

> Give me the specifications, and I'll give you the man (Skinner, 1948, p. 243).

Other approaches may not be so optimistic about the change-ability of personality or behavior, but clearly they assume this is possible or there would be no point of engaging in counseling or psychotherapy.

There is at least one other common element, and that is the recognition that neurosis, disturbance, maladjustment, conflict, the presence of an unsolved problem, and so on is (a) unpleasant and painful for the client, and (b) such a state of affairs is undesirable and warrants attempts to change it.

A third possible common element is the recognition of the influence of the future, or of anticipations, hopes, or expectations related to the future, on present behavior. This is an element that appears to tie together approaches as different as operant conditioning and existentialism. In other words, the recognition that behavior is not entirely "caused" by the past, but is also influenced by future consequences or expectation of consequences, seems to be accepted by most points of view. Lindsley (1963) states it as follows, referring to operant conditioning: "The discovery that such [voluntary] behavior is subject to control by its consequences makes it unnecessary to explain behavior in terms of hypothetical antecedents." May (1958), presenting the existentialist position, writes: "The future, in contrast to the present or past, is the dominant mode for human beings."

THE COUNSELING PROCESS

In individual counseling or psychotherapy, it would appear that all approaches utilize the private interview, in which verbal interaction is the major component. The techniques of conditioning, which are a major aspect of behavior therapy, may be used outside the interview situation, of course, but the point here is that behavior therapy utilizes the interview. It is also true that the methods and techniques of other approaches may be applied in other situations than the counseling interview.

The most widely known studies of commonalities among schools of psychotherapy in terms of process are those of Fiedler (1950a, 1950b, 1951). Fiedler found that therapists from different schools agreed upon the nature of the ideal therapeutic relationship, and that factor analysis yielded one common factor of goodness of therapeutic relationships. How, then, are these results to be interpreted in view of the studies referred to above, which found important differences? The solution seems to lie in the nature of the instruments used in the studies. Sundland and Barker developed their instrument by eliminating items upon which therapists agreed. Fiedler, on the other hand, appears to have assembled a group of items on which therapists agree. Sundland and Barker point out that items that they discarded because they did not result in a distribution of responses were similar to items in Fiedler's studies. These items were concerned with empathy. There appears to be evidence, therefore, that therapists agree upon the importance of empathy and understanding.

The behavior therapists seem to deny or minimize the presence and importance of empathy. Nevertheless, it would appear that a minimum of empathic understanding is necessary for the continuation of the interaction of the counselor and the client, as well as being a factor in effecting change, as will be demonstrated later. That is, it appears that a relationship characterized at least to some extent by interest, acceptance, and understanding is basic to influencing others therapeutically. Other factors may direct change along the lines the therapist desires, but the relationship makes possible any change.

Thus, in addition to the common element of the interview, there appear to be a number of other aspects of the counseling process that most, if not all, approaches share. Among these are certain characteristics of the counselor or therapist and of the client or patient. The first characteristic of the therapist is a genuine interest in and concern for the client; a strong desire to help him, to influence or change him. Not only do counselors or therapists accept the possibility and desirability of client change, but they are also genuinely and strongly interested in being the agent of change in their clients. If they were not, they would not be engaged in counseling or psychotherapy.

Furthermore, all counselors or therapists expect their clients to change. This expectation may vary in degree: in some instances approaching a highly optimistic or even enthusiastic expectation, while in others, only minimal. However, it is always present. There is always an attitude of hope and expectation of change. Again, without this expectation, they would not continue to work with clients.

A factor that may not be independent of or separate from those already discussed is an acceptance of or respect for the client as a person, an individual, which is present in spite of his problems and difficulties or his unlikeable characteristics. In other words, it is not conditioned upon his evidencing behavior that the counselor feels is desirable, good, healthy, and so on. This does not preclude, therefore, disagreement with the attitudes, beliefs, and behavior of the client; it does not mean approval of them. It is a respect or even liking for him in spite of his unlikeable characteristics. It is the unconditional positive regard of client-centered therapy. It would appear that this must exist, at least to a minimal degree, or a counselor could not continue a relationship with the client. Counselors do not continue to work with clients where this condition does not exist, so that clients are selected on this basis.

Another element that appears to be common to all approaches is given various designations. In the client-centered approach it is referred to as therapist genuineness or self-congruence. Others refer to it as sincerity, honesty, or openness. The existentialists use the term authenticity. Some approaches do not refer specifically to this characteristic (for example, Ellis), but it is apparent in their discussions, and particularly in their protocols, that this element is present.

There is a final characteristic that unites therapists of widely differing approaches. This is the fact that each therapist believes in, or has confidence in, the theory and method that he uses. Again, if he did not feel it was the best method or approach, he would not use it, but would adopt a different one. It might be hypothesized that success (or at least reports of success) bears a strong relationship to the degree of confidence the therapist has in his approach. The failure or inability of the therapist to commit himself to an approach apparently limits his effectiveness and makes of him a technician, or technique-oriented. A common aspect thus appears to be commitment to a particular method or approach.

Most, if not all, approaches, therefore, seem to include a relationship that on the part of the counselor or therapist is characterized by a belief in the possibility of client change; an expectation that the client will change; interest in and concern for the client, including a desire to help, influence, or change him; sincerity and honesty in the process; and confidence in the approach used to achieve client change.

It is necessary to add one other point. This is that the crucial aspect of the therapist's impact or contribution is not his actual personality or behavior, nor even his intent, in the relationship. It is the client's perception of the therapist that determines the therapist's characteristics and contribution. Thus the client's characteristics, his attitudes and set, are important aspects of the relationship.

There are apparent some common aspects of individuals who come to counselors or therapists for help. In the first place, as indicated above, they "hurt"—they are suffering, or are unhappy, because of conflicts, symptoms, unfulfilled desires or aspirations, feeling of failure or inadequacy, or lack of meaning in their lives. They are thus motivated to change. Clients who are referred may not always be aware of their "hurt," or, if they are, may not feel the need for help or want it from a counselor or therapist. It may, of course, be maintained that everyone "hurts" in some respect and thus could benefit from counseling.

Second, clients also believe that change is possible, and they expect to change, to be helped. Frank (1961; Rosenthal and Frank, 1956) has emphasized the universality of this factor in clients. Cartwright and Cartwright (1958) indicate that this is a complex factor; there may be belief that improvement will occur, belief in the therapist as the major source of help, belief in the techniques or procedures as the major source of help, or belief in himself (the client) as the major source of help. These writers feel that it is only the last belief that leads to improvement in a positive linear manner. The other beliefs are probably present to some extent in all clients, however. The client must feel that the counselor is interested, concerned, and wants to help him. This appears to be a complex factor involving a complex of attitudes on the client. Clients must have some trust and confidence in the counselor and his methods or they would not enter counseling.

Third, the client must be active in, or participate in, the process. He is not a passive recipient, as is the physically ill patient being treated by a physician. All learning (behavior change) appears to require activity (whether motor, verbal, or thinking) on the part of the learner. This kind of behavior in counseling or psychotherapy includes self-analysis or self-exploration. Truax and Carkhuff (1965) refer to it also as intrapersonal exploration or self-disclosure. Jourard (1964) and Mowrer (1964) also speak of self-disclosure. It appears that the client as well as the counselor must be genuine, open, and honest in the process. Thus, all approaches appear to deal with clients who are in need of help, recognize this need, believe they can change, believe that the counselor can help them change, and engage in some activity in the attempt to change.

All approaches thus appear to involve a relationship between a counselor and a client, each of whom contributes to the relationship certain characteristics that lead to client change.

GOALS AND OBJECTIVES

It may be more difficult to find commonalities among goals than among concepts and techniques. The differences may not be as great as they at first appear, however. The behavior therapists, though they emphasize the removal of symptoms as an objective goal, also appear to recognize a broader goal. They seem to expect the client to feel better, to function better in life and its various aspects, to achieve at a higher level—in short, to live up to his potential. Salter (1961, p. 24), for example, speaks of freeing the individual by "unbraking" him. There would seem to be at least a similarity here to the concept of self-actualization, which is accepted in one or another form, in varying terminology, by most other approaches. The conditioning therapists also appear to see increasing freedom and expressiveness as desirable results of therapy. This would seem to be similar to the spontaneity and openness to experience of Rogers. There also seems to be general acceptance of the desirability of responsibility and independence as outcomes of counseling or psychotherapy.

Although a concept such as self-actualization may be criticized as being subjective, vague, and abstract (Ford and Urban, 1963, pp. 438–440), it would seem to be possible to reach agreement on what it denotes in terms of actual behavior. Perhaps, with adequate definitions of terms, a statement of the goals of psychotherapy that includes the concepts mentioned above might be developed and be acceptable to various groups of counselors and therapists. Possibly such a statement might be similar to Rogers' (1963) description of the fully functioning person.

Thus, there appears to be a great deal in common among the various and diverse approaches to counseling or psychotherapy. To some extent, the various theories or points of view represent different ways of describing or explaining the same phenomena. There may be relatively little overlap in some cases—the elephant's tail is quite different from his trunk or ears, even though they are the same elephant. In a sense, then, all theories are correct, or have elements of truth. It is only reasonable to believe that formulations based upon the long experience and observation of competent men should have some validity, and some commonality. Differences are, in part, related to the use of different emphases, to different perceptions of the same events, to differences in comprehensiveness of formulation.

To some extent, differences may appear greater than those that actually exist. This may be due, in part, to the use of different terminology to refer to the same or similar concepts. A study of the various points of view reveals many concepts that are essentially the same but carry different labels. Differences may also be exaggerated by the propensity to emphasize differences rather than similarities.

The question now to be examined is whether it is possible to develop a tentative integration of the common aspects that appear to exist, and to propose, in very general form, an approach to counseling or psychotherapy that will incorporate, or not be inconsistent with, the major theories proposed.

AN ATTEMPT AT INTEGRATION

Although there are many differences, there also appear to be many similarities among widely differing approaches to counseling or psychotherapy. Perhaps the greatest divergence is between the behavior therapies on the one hand, and the existentialist approaches (including client-centered therapy) on the other. In spite of the similarities or agreements noted above, it appears that these points of view are perceived by their adherents and by others as inconsistent and contradictory. The behavior therapies appear to be objective, impersonal, technique-oriented, mechanical. The existential approaches may be seen as subjective, personal, and not concerned with technique. Is it possible to reconcile these apparently inconsistent approaches? Rogers (1961, p. 85), recognizing these divergent trends not only in psychotherapy but also in psychology, states that they "seem irreconcilable because we have not yet developed the larger frame of reference that would contain them both."

A possible reconciliation is suggested. It derives from a consideration of the different models of man delineated by Allport. Allport (1962) writes: "The trouble with our current theories of learning is not so much that they are wrong, but that they are partial." It may be said, then, that the trouble with the behavior therapy or conditioning approach is not that it is wrong, but that it is incomplete as a description or theory of the nature of man and of his behavior and its modification. It is a "nothing but" approach.

There can be no question about the existence of conditioning, about man as a reactive being who can be conditioned and reconditioned. However, man is more than this; he is also a being in the process of becoming. He is not merely a mechanism, or organism, who is controlled by objective stimuli in his environment. He is also a being who lives, or exists, who thinks and feels and who develops relationships with other beings. Man lives not by objective stimuli alone, but in the subtle and complex interrelationships he develops with others. He becomes disturbed or disordered in these relationships, and he changes and improves in such relationships. This is a "something more" approach.

The essential nature or characteristic of counseling or psychotherapy, therefore, is that it is a relationship. It is a complex relationship, with various aspects. It is not simply a cognitive, intellectually impersonal relationship, but an affective, experiential, highly personal relationship. It is not necessarily irrational, but it has nonrational aspects. The nature of man's ties to his fellow man is essentially affective.

Evidence seems to be accumulating that the effective element in counseling is the nature of the relationship established by the counselor. Goldstein (1962, p. 105), reviewing the literature on therapist-patient expectancies in psychotherapy, concludes: "There can no longer be any doubt as to the primary status which must be accorded the therapeutic relationship in the overall therapeutic transaction." The behavior therapists appear to be unconcerned about, or to minimize, the relationship. However, as indicated in the discussion of the approaches of Salter and Wolpe, it appears that the relationship is of greater significance in their methods than they admit. It should be apparent that the characteristics of the counselor or therapist and of the client discussed above are manifested in, or manifest themselves in, a relationship.

The counseling relationship always involves, or includes, conditioning aspects. The accepting, understanding, nonthreatening atmosphere offers the opportunity for the extinction of anxiety, or for desensitization of threatening stimuli. In this relationship, where external threat is minimized, anxiety-arousing ideas and words, images, and feelings are free to appear. Moreover, they appear in a sequence in terms of the kind of hierarchy that Wolpe establishes: that is, from least anxiety arousing to more anxiety arousing. Thus, in any nonthreatening therapy relationship, desensitization occurs in the manner achieved by Wolpe (1958). The relationship, by minimizing externally induced anxiety, makes it possible for the client to experience and bring out his internally induced anxieties, or anxiety-arousing experiences, at the time and rate at which he can face and handle them in the accepting relationship.

In addition, operant conditioning serves to reinforce the production of verbalizations that the therapist believes are therapeutic, or necessary for therapy to occur. The therapist rewards these verbalizations by his interest and attention, or by explicit praise and approval. At the beginning of therapy, negative elements may be rewarded—for example, the expression of problems, conflicts, fears and anxieties, negative self-references, and so on. As therapy progresses, the therapist may reinforce positive elements— for example, problem-solving efforts, positive thoughts, attitudes and feelings, and positive self-references. The therapist expects progress of this kind and is sensitive to its expression in the client.

The question to be faced, to quote Jourard (1961, p. 14), is: "What conditions foster output of a kind of operant behavior in the *therapist* that we call 'patient-growth-fostering'? That is, what conditions serve to increase the rate at which the *therapist* will emit behavior which, in turn, serves as a stimulus which evokes growth-conducive behavior in the *patient?*"

Conditioning principles have thus contributed to an understanding of the nature of the therapeutic process and the therapy relationship. However, the conditioning that occurs is not the mechanical conditioning of a rat in a Skinner box. The conditioning is an aspect of, takes place in, and is influenced by, the relationship. There is considerable evidence that the rate and extent of conditioning is influenced by the personality and attitudes of the experimenter and his relationship to the subject (Ullmann and Krasner, 1965). This relationship involves characteristics of the client—his interest, motivations, thoughts, attitudes, perceptions and expectations—as well as those of the counselor. It also is affected by the situation or setting in which the relationship occurs—what are called the demand characteristics in a research experiment. As Ullmann and Krasner (1965, p. 43) note, "both the subject's and the examiner's expectancies, sets, and so forth have a major effect on the individual's response to the situation," and "the best results are obtained when the patient and the therapist form a good interpersonal relationship." The relationship, therefore, cannot be ignored, even in behavior therapy.

Krasner (1962, p. 69) points out that Skinner classified attention as a general reinforcer. The most powerful influencers of behavior—or, in conditioning terms, reinforcers—are the respect, interest, concern, and attention of the therapist. The demonstration by research of the effects of these generalized reinforcers supports the importance of the relationship in counseling or psychotherapy.

There is a further point emphasizing the importance of the relationship. Many, if not most, of the problems or difficulties of clients involve interpersonal relationships. It is being increasingly recognized that good interpersonal relationships are characterized by honesty, openness, sincerity, and spontaneity. Psychotherapy is an interpersonal relationship having these characteristics. It is therefore a place where the client can learn good interpersonal relationships. In fact, therapy would be limited if it tried to influence the client's interpersonal relationships by providing a different kind of relationship. If it attempted to influence interpersonal relationships by avoiding establishing a therapeutic relationship, it would seem to be inefficient. Teaching, or conditioning, individual behavior in a mechanical manner would not appear to offer much hope of generalization to personal relationships outside of therapy.

London (1964) sees Mowrer as offering a solution to the inadequacies of insight therapy on the one hand and action therapy on the other. However, Mowrer's (1964) approach, though not yet systematically developed or presented, is a relationship therapy. Mowrer, recognizing that personality is a product of interpersonal relationships, emphasizes the therapeutic value of openness and self-disclosure in interpersonal relationships. However, although he feels that this may begin in a relationship with an individual therapist, he states that it is seldom that more that one or two interviews are necessary. He feels that the client should move quickly from the group of two to the larger group of significant others in his life (to use Sullivan's phrase) or to the primary groups in his life (to use a sociological term).

There is thus no basic or necessary contradiction between behavior therapy and relationship therapy. One emphasizes shaping or changing of specific aspects of behavior by specific rewards or reinforcers. The other emphasizes more general behavior changes (including attitudes and feelings) using generalized reinforcers. Both utilize the principles of learning: one rather narrowly, emphasizing conditioning; the other more broadly, emphasizing what might be called a social learning approach (Murray, 1963). The behavior therapists are, as Ullmann and Krasner (1965, p. 37) point out, systematic in their application of specific learning concepts. However, it might also be said that many relationship therapists are also systematic in the application of generalized reinforcers.

The conditioning or behavior therapy approach is supported by research evidence, including laboratory or experimental research. The relationship approach is also supported by research, including some of the research on conditioning. It is interesting, and significant, that both groups are coming to the same conclusions—one from laboratory work in conditioning, the other from experience and research in counseling or psychotherapy. It is important, however, that behavior therapists come to recognize the complexity and the social or relationship aspects of the learning process, and also that relationship therapists be aware of the conditioning that is also an aspect of counseling or psychotherapy. However, the total process, although it may be learning, is a complex one, involving various kinds of learning, and not simply operant or classical conditioning. It includes perceptual, cognitive, and affective aspects, is greater than providing a laboratory conditioning relationship, or even a rational, problem-solving relationship in an interview.

There is an important implication of the complexity of the process and the importance of the therapist's interest, concern, and understanding. The process cannot be mechanized, routinized, simplified, or controlled in the sense of programming or of objective, planned manipulation of rewards in terms of expressing interest, concern, and so on. This is because the therapist's behavior is only effective if it is sincere and spontaneous, not when it is a contrived technique. The therapist is most effective when he is a person—when he is, as the client-centered approach terms it, genuine in the relationship. While the behavior therapists strive for effectiveness by attempting to reduce treatment to the essentials of technique, it would appear that to be most effective, the therapist must be a real, human person. The most effective influence is another person offering a genuine, human relationship.

Jourard's (1961, pp. 15–16) comments are relevant here:

I believe we are on the brink of discovering that when an experienced therapist eschews technique, and just is *himself* in the presence of his patient, then he is in fact accomplishing the following things:

1. He is actually providing a condition which elicits real-self-being, that is, spontaneous, uncontrived self-disclosure in his patient. This is analogous with priming the pump, or showing the rat how the lever works.

2. He is providing a powerful reinforcement to real-self-being in his patient. Real-self-being begets real-self-being.

3. By *spontaneously* responding to the patient's output, the therapist not only fosters real-self-being in the patient, but he is also extinguishing many of the sickness-fostering responses emitted by the patient.

4. He is avoiding the therapy-defeating behavior of contrivance, seeming, and impersonal manipulation of himself and his patient. Rather, he is providing the patient with a role-model of honest, healthy behavior.

The evidence seems to point to the establishment of a particular kind of relationship as the crucial element in counseling or psychotherapy. It is a relationship characterized not so much by what techniques the therapist uses as what he is; not so much by what he does as the way that he does it. Rogers (1961, p. 269) notes that "some of the recent studies suggest that a warmly human and genuine therapist, interested only in understanding the moment-by-moment feelings of this person who is coming into being in the relationship with him, is the most effective therapist. Certainly there is nothing to indicate that the coldly intellectual, analytical, factually-minded therapist is effective." Much of what therapists do is superfluous or unrelated to their effectiveness; in fact, it is likely that much of their success is unrelated to what they do, or even occurs in spite of what they do, as long as they offer the relationship that it appears therapists of very differing persuasions do provide. To some extent at least, even the most extreme behaviorists provide this.

TWO QUESTIONS

The conclusion that the essence of counseling or psychotherapy consists of a genuine human relationship characterized by interest, concern, empathic understanding, and genuineness on the part of the therapist leads to two questions.

1. What is there unique about this relationship? How does it differ from all good human relationships? If the answer is, as should be obvious, that there is nothing unique or different, then what is there special about the practice of counseling or psychotherapy? Fiedler (1950a) concluded from his studies that "a good therapeutic relationship is very much like any good interpersonal relationship."

This view may be opposed by those who feel that it deprives counselors or therapists of unique powers; who fear that "it leaves the practitioner without a speciality" (Mowrer, 1964, p. 235). However, it should not be surprising that the characteristics of psychotherapy should be the characteristics of good human relationships. Nor does it follow that if they are not limited to counseling or psychotherapy they are not relevant or specific. The essence of emotional disturbances is disturbed human relationships. The individual has become estranged from others, has become detached from the community of men. His relationships with others have become ruptured or have been placed on an insecure, false, or untenable basis. He needs to reestablish good relationships with others.

Often, however, he cannot do this alone, for several reasons. He may not be able to change his behavior, which contributes to the poor relationships. He may not know what behaviors are involved. Others may not provide him the opportunity to change, or even if he changes they may not recognize, accept, or believe in the permanence of the change. Their behavior, stimulated in part at least by his own behavior, contributes to the vicious circle of poor relationships. The situation is not conducive to change; the individual is or feels threatened by others, and reacts in turn to threaten them.

There is a need, then, for someone who can accept the disturbed individual, with all his disturbed, irritating, threatening behavior, and offer him a nonthreatening relationship in which he can respond in an open, nonthreatening way. Therapy offers the opportunity for learning how to relate to others in a different, more effective way. It utilizes or embodies the principles of good human relationships, which although they appear to be simple are not widely practiced outside of therapy. If such relationships were practiced generally, there would presumably be no emotionally disturbed people, except those whose disturbances were of organic origins. Perhaps the difficulty of providing such relationships within the confines of the patterns of many human interrelationships is the basis for the therapist's avoiding relationships with clients outside the therapy relationship. While there is merit in Schofield's (1964) analysis of psychotherapy as the purchase of friendship, therapy is, however, more than the offering of friendship, at least in the usual sense of the word. While viewing psychotherapy as something dark and mysterious classifies the therapist with magicians and witchdoctors, viewing it as bought friendship places him in the same category as taxidancers, gigolos, and call girls.

2. The characteristics of counseling or psychotherapy that have been developed above have frequently been considered nonspecific elements. It is often assumed that they are not related to the specific nature of the disturbance present in clients, and that, while they may be considered as necessary conditions, they are not sufficient. Further, such characteristics as attention, interest, concern, trust, belief, faith, and expectation are part of what is designated as the placebo effect in the treatment of physical diseases. While it is not usual to insist that these effects be eliminated from counseling or psychotherapy, it is generally accepted that these factors, as nonspecific, are not sufficient and that other methods or techniques must be included to deal with the specific aspects of the disturbance. It is generally argued that any method or technique must produce greater effects than those obtained by placebo elements in order to be considered useful.

The placebo effect is a psychological effect. Where the interest or concern is with determining the physical or physiological effect of a drug or medication on a known physical disease or disturbance, it is reasonable to consider this effect as extraneous and nonspecific. Even here, however, it is of interest to recognize and study the effects of such psychological factors on physical functioning.

However, this concept may not be applicable in counseling or psychotherapy. Here, the disorder or disturbance is psychological. Should it not be logical that the specific treatment for a psychological condition should be psychological? Should it not be reasonable to suggest that the specific treatment for disturbed human relationships is the providing of a good relationship? Is the placebo effect, as Rosenthal and Frank (1956) state, "a nonspecific form of psychotherapy"?

It has long been known that any new form of treatment of emotional disturbance, from electric shock to tranquilizers, meets with great success when it is introduced, but that its success declines with time. This is because, when it is first used, it is expected to be successful—there is hope and expectation on the part of both the therapist and the patient. Patients become the object of increased interest and attention. However, as time goes on, as the procedure becomes routine, as doubts or questions arise because it is not always successful, its effectiveness decreases. Its early success was the result, in whole or in part, of the placebo effect. It is only reasonable, again, that in evaluating the results of an experimental treatment, this effect should be considered nonspecific. We might also look at the apparent success of behavior therapy in the same way, however. How much of its success is the heightening of the placebo effect? Should it not be required that this effect be eliminated in order to evaluate the real effect of conditioning?

It is strange that, with all the evidence of the power of the placebo effect, it has not been recognized as the most effective approach to the treatment of psychological problems. As Krasner and Ullmann (1965, p. 230) put it: "Whereas the problem had previously been conceptualized in terms of eliminating the 'placebo effects,' it would seem reasonable to maximize placebo effects in the treatment situation to increase the likelihood of client change. The evidence is growing that 'placebo effect' is a euphemism for examiner influence variables."

NECESSARY AND SUFFICIENT CONDITIONS
FOR PSYCHOTHERAPY

Are there any necessary and sufficient conditions of psychotherapy, and if there are, what are they? Ellis (1959), criticizing the necessary and sufficient conditions proposed by Rogers (1957), concludes that there are no necessary conditions, but that there are a number of sufficient conditions. With the wide variety of approaches and methods in counseling or psychotherapy—all of them claiming success with some apparent justification—this would appear to be a reasonable position to take.

However, if there is a common element in all methods and approaches, it would also be reasonable to conclude that this would be the necessary and sufficient condition of psychotherapy. The attempt has been made to show that this common element is the relationship between the client and the therapist. This relationship is a complex one, and it is possible that it is not understood completely; thus, we are unable to specify all its aspects. At least some of its aspects are known, however, and they include those enumerated above. They have been demonstrated to be sufficient conditions for therapeutic personality change (Truax, 1963, and Carkhuff, 1964, 1965).

In addition to the research on psychotherapy, there is considerable evidence of the positive influences these conditions have on behavior when they are incorporated into the programs of institutions ranging from industry to schools to mental hospitals. The effects of the use of environmental treatment in the form of the therapeutic milieu in mental hospitals seem to be evident and to come essentially from the change in human relationships between staff and patients. These are essentially the conditions postulated by Rogers. Whether they are necessary as well as sufficient conditions is not so easily demonstrated. If these conditions are necessary as well as sufficient, then it must be shown that therapeutic personality change not only occurs when they are present, but that it does not occur when they are absent. It can, of course, be demonstrated that changes in behavior can be obtained when they are not present, as in simple conditioning, which may not involve the presence of another person; or in instances of coercion, by the use of threat or physical force, including punishment. However, it can be questioned whether such changes are therapeutic.

There is some evidence from research on psychotherapy that in the absence of these conditions in psychotherapy, positive change does not occur. Truax (1963) found that while the (schizophrenic) patients of therapists evidencing high conditions of accurate empathy, unconditional positive regard, and self-congruence improved, patients of therapists evidencing low levels of these conditions showed negative personality change. Similar results have been found with clients in college counseling centers, according to Truax. There also appears to be considerable evidence that the absence of these conditions in other situations leads to psychological disturbance. This evidence includes studies on the influence of schizophrenogenic mothers, the effects of the double bind, the effects of an institutional environment lacking in human attention on infants and children, the results of sensory isolation, and the effects of imprisonment.

Thus, there appears to be evidence that the elements of the therapeutic relationship described here are common to all approaches to counseling or psychotherapy, and that where they are absent, positive change or development does not occur. There appears, then, to be a basis for considering them the necessary and sufficient conditions for psychotherapeutic change.

XII TECHNIQUES OF COUNSELING

Lloyd H. Lofquist

The word counseling has become a very general, and rather meaningless term. It needs a modifier to specify the class of client problems on which the major focus is to be placed. The Vocational Rehabilitation Administration traineeship programs in which many students are enrolled, and the vocational rehabilitation responsibilities of the public and private agencies that provide employment for many counselors, suggest that the word "vocational" could be an appropriate modifier. The additional word "educational" can be assumed to be implicit in this modifier. Vocational counseling, as a term, permits the specification of the major class of problems with which counseling will deal. These are problems of educational-vocational planning and of appropriate vocational choice. The focus is *not* primarily on psychopathology, or on personality re-structuring, or on psychotherapy, or on "better adjustment to all phases of living." The vocational counselor focuses primarily on vocational problems. He is not a clinical psychologist, or a cross-trained, cross-fertilized "clinselor." He is working instead with relatively "normal" individuals, who are capable of rational communication, and whom he hopes to assist in learning about what they have to offer the world of work, what they need from it, and what it offers as feasible alternatives to them.

It should be noted at this point that statements have *not* been made to the effect that these clients will be without personal problems or that psychotherapeutic benefits will not accrue to them. The modifier *does*, however, put the primary focus of activity on vocational problems. To some, this will sound simple and un-dynamic. The techniques of vocational counseling are, however, by no means simple or unchallenging. They call for development of a very complex technology and requires every bit of effective counselor-client communication that can be mustered.

In dealing with techniques, the focus will be less on "business as usual"—there is ample literature on that—and more on techniques that may be used effectively in the future—with all its complications related to manpower problems. Before dealing with techniques, however, it is necessary to do some additional conceptualizing and defining.

Having modified "counseling" to read "vocational counseling," with the focus on a class of client problems centered on vocational planning and choice, it is necessary to specify some goals at the end of the process. This needs to be done so that we can establish, and measure, defined outcomes. The outcome measures will make possible an evaluation of the effectiveness of counseling and its component techniques.

We might specify, as the outcome farthest out in time, tenure in a job, or tenure in a related class of jobs. Tenure results when an individual comes to terms with his work environment; that is, when the individual achieves what can be called work adjustment. Tenure, obviously, can be measured rather directly. Work adjustment can be measured by its two indicators: job satisfactoriness and job satisfaction.

In vocational counseling, then, the focusing is on vocational problems and seeking to facilitate educational-vocational choices that will result in the outcomes of work adjustment and job tenure that this makes possible. These are the specific ends of a vocational counseling activity or process, that is, the client-problem class and the outcomes.

Assuming that a client has vocational planning and choice problems, he must now somehow be moved to a point, or in a direction, where he will achieve the outcome of work adjustment. It has been shown from experience, and the literature, that a relationship is needed that will enable the counselor and client to work together. It is also know that certain "stages," which are part of the counseling process, are sometimes identified as rapport, acceptance, understanding, and participation. We might measure these "stages" by, for example, counting task-oriented words or statements, calculating talk ratios, or noting other problem-relevant kinds of client behavior. We may also note the achievement of some intermediate goals in the counseling process, and these can be measured as well. Vocational choices, acceptance into a training program, grades in training courses, obtaining job placement—are all examples of intermediate goals.

To move a client along in a vocational-counseling process, the counselor has at his disposal certain counselor-action variables. He can, for example, provide a climate, advise a client what to do, selectively reinforce desired behaviors, use suggestion, or structure and manipulate environmental conditions. Again, there is a literature available on these kinds of counselor-action variables, and they do not need further emphasis here.

It is feasible, then, to observe the movement of a client with vocational-planning problems through some measurable "stages" to intermediate goals such as vocational choice, with more distant outcomes such as work adjustment and tenure in mind. Also, there are ways of influencing, or facilitating, client movement. It is elementary to state that the next big problem is that of knowing what vocational choices are the desirable ones for the client. Which choices hold the most promise for work adjustment? What choices would be best for him to make? Solving this problem is not an easy task.

A counselor would surely and quickly react to the challenge that this problem poses by stating, correctly, that there is a considerable technology that can be utilized to describe each unique client and to describe jobs. He uses psychological tests, interview-obtained data, school records, and reports of other professionals to describe the individual. There are job descriptions, worker-trait data, and labor-market information to describe the world in which he can work. There is also available a respectable technology to aid the counselor in describing individuals and in describing jobs. What system, or systems, then, is used to compare the two sets of descriptive information? How does a counselor establish, for the many and the unique individuals requiring his services, which, among the thousands of jobs, are the "good" choices—the choices for which he would predict ultimate work adjustment? How can he conceptualize work adjustment in such a way that both individual differences in job requirements and rewards can be accommodated?

In the typical practice of vocational counseling, many counselors have not faced up to this problem. As a matter of fact, it may be fairly accurate to say that in practice, vocational counselors frequently feel forced to take some isolated bits of hard data on a client, to combine these with some soft hunches, to add a little bit of occupational data, to allow all of these to become rather well mixed up, and to pass the mixture through a stored apperceptive mass of one counselor's experience with clients, and then to have an insightful experience that a specific job or cluster of jobs seems fairly reasonable for this person. Having arrived at this insightful counselor decision, it can usually be buttressed by such statements as: "This is what George feels he really wants to do," or, "It so happens that the Fisby Company has just such a job opening for one of our clients."

It might be said that in the counselor's frustration at not having a readily available system for describing men and jobs in the same terms, and for matching men and jobs, he resorts to a rather unsophisticated set of procedures. Perhaps it is the frustration in this area of techniques for combining data to make sophisticated predictions that has led to so much dependence on the relationship aspects of counseling. It has led the counselor also to rationalize, perhaps, when strong emphases are placed on such things as the counselee's ability to choose properly, or on the good decision being one for which the client is willing to take the responsibility.

Unless the relationship between people and work can be conceptualized, a counselor's experience in recognizing and in identifying "good" vocational decisions may be severely limited. It is necessary to know something about the "goodness" of such decisions in order to know what a counselor wishes to facilitate in the counseling process.

In the Work Adjustment Project at the University of Minnesota, the researchers think about people and work in the following ways:

People differ in their work-relevant personality characteristics; that is, they have unique work personalities. They differ in what they can do, not ordinarily on the basis of whether or not they have an ability but rather in terms of how much of each kind of an ability they have. They also differ in their preferences for different kinds of stimulus conditions under which they will respond; that is, they have preferences that express needs for certain stimulus conditions.

Psychological tests provide the best available means for the description of an individual's unique personality. They can be used as aids in choosing occupations; they contribute to predictions of success or failure. In this sense, they provide an individual with a means of arriving at better-informed choices.

Although an individual goes through work-relevant experiences and takes many psychological tests as he progresses through schools, the relevance for work of his experiences is rarely called to his attention, and the tests he takes are given for reasons not specifically or directly related to work. In other words, he develops personality traits that have relevance for work, and some of these are measured, but he ordinarily has little organized knowledge of their nature and amount. It is suggested that it is *not* usually true that "the individual knows himself best" when occupational choices are involved. The individual needs the help of a professional person to know his unique personality structure and its relevance for different occupational possibilities.

When vocational counselors are available, they can be helpful. Unfortunately, their technology for practice is somewhat limited. The psychometric instruments available need improvement. Even more limiting is the fact that research studies on prediction have been directed largely to predicting success in education and/or training for an occupation. Predictions relate to grade point averages or to success in occupational training, but do not relate clearly to a longer-term objective such as career success. Most limiting in our technology is the general absence of systems for combining all the relevant "person data" with all the relevant "occupational data" to predict career success.

This state of affairs appears to have resulted from an overemphasis on purely educational and training goals, an arrested progress in the development of vocational psychology, and a paucity of interest in theories of work. It is necessary to accelerate activity in vocational psychology and, as Brayfield (1961) has said, to "commit ourselves to the development, as an enterprise of the highest priority, of a psychology of occupational behavior."

There is a need to provide more substantial underpinnings for the practice of vocational counseling. We must be able to describe individuals more completely in work-relevant terms. We must be able to describe occupations more completely in terms that relate to the individual and his work-relevant problems. There is a need for systematic ways of relating characteristics of individuals to information about jobs. Also, vocational counselors must be provided with techniques that will enable them to make predictions concerning such matters as occupational success, job satisfaction, and work adjustment. Only with such underpinnings, from a revitalized vocational psychology, can there be expert vocational counselors who can put some guts into the vocational counseling process.

There is a need for a psychology of work that investigates psychological principles as they relate to work behavior—the application of psychological concepts to understanding the nature and the eventual solution of work problems.

Theoretical frameworks are needed to enable us to conceptualize the development of the individual as a person ready for work, as a working person, as a person adjusting to work, and as a person experiencing the effects of having chosen certain specific occupations. In addition, the theoretical frameworks should enable us to conceptualize work in such a way that the impact of physical and/or social trauma and changes can be accounted for, for example, in disability, displacement by automation, and retirement.

Super (1957, 1960, 1962), in his career development studies and in his activity in the measurement of work values, is contributing to our knowledge in vocational psychology. Roe (1956) is obviously interested in such an enterprise. At Minnesota, there has been developed a Theory of Work Adjustment (Dawis, *et al.,* 1964) as another contribution to vocational psychology. This theory is premised on the development in individuals of a stable work personality. Briefly, this development can be described as follows:

As an individual responds, specific reinforcers in the environment (that is, conditions that maintain responding) become associated with specific responses of the individual. The broad classes of responses generally utilized by the individual develop into his "set of abilities," while experiences with classes of environmental stimulus conditions, which occur frequently in the reinforcement of his responding, develop into his "set of needs." Because of differing social-educational requirements, the individual experiences differential utilization of his abilities, resulting in a unique set of more specific abilities at varying strengths. Similarly, the individual's experience with differing social-educational reinforcer systems results in some reinforcers becoming more effective than others. As a consequence, his unique set of needs becomes differentiated, with some needs operating at higher strengths than others.

As the individual persists in a particular environment, with its relatively fixed sets of reinforcers and requirements, his sets of needs and abilities become more specific and more stable, until changes in successive measurements of abilities and needs are negligible. With this stabilization of the work personality, it is hypothesized that an individual's work adjustment and tenure for specific jobs can be predicted from knowledge of the correspondence between his abilities and job requirements, on the one hand, and between his needs (preferences for stimulus conditions) and the job reinforcer system, on the other.

Work adjustment, in the Theory of Work Adjustment, is the outcome of the interaction between an individual and his work environment, and is defined in terms of two concepts—satisfactoriness and satisfaction. Satisfactoriness is defined as the evaluation of the individual's work behavior principally in terms of quality and quantity of task performance and/or performance outcomes. Satisfaction is defined as the individual's evaluation of stimulus conditions in the work environment with reference to their effectiveness in reinforcing his behavior. The theory proposes that satisfactoriness is a function of the correspondence between an individual's set of abilities and the ability requirements of the work environment, and that satisfaction is a function of the correspondence between the reinforcer system of the work environment and the individual's set of needs.

Some instruments have been developed to measure the work-adjustment indicators, that is, satisfactoriness and satisfaction. Other instruments were developed to measure the work relevant needs of an individual, and, in the existing technology, some ability measures were found, like the General Aptitude Test Battery. With such instruments, and with the conceptualization of work adjustment to guide the research, it was found that we can begin to describe men and jobs in the same terms. By studying differing amounts of measured satisfactoriness and measured satisfaction, it becomes feasible to establish the limits of correspondence needed to predict tenure and work adjustment, that is, to establish the amount of matching of work personalities and work environments necessary to predict success. We can, in other words, begin to sort out the jobs for which adjustment can be predicted and to identify the kinds of information we wish to communicate to a client in the relationship of counseling. We also begin to see ways in which large amounts of relevant data can be machine processed for most efficient use with individual clients.

All of this lengthy discussion has implications for vocational counseling techniques and procedures. The Theory of Work Adjustment suggests first that the appropriate focus is *not* on changing the counselee to fit the world of work. Perhaps some minimum change is feasible in a relatively short counseling relationship. The theory would suggest, however, that relatively little change (except for persons with very limited reinforcement histories) is likely. The appropriate emphasis for vocational counseling, then, assuming large numbers of our population have relatively "normal" personalities and rather broad reinforcement histories, is placed on finding, in the realities of the world of work, appropriate situations in which a counselee (with a stabilized work personality) can utilize his skills and satisfy his needs. For example, instead of working to reduce client dependency (in a client who is not immobilized by the presence of this trait) or instead of seeking to increase problem solving ability (in a client with a long history of behavioral experience with problem solving), the counselor seeks to help the counselee to find appropriate work environments to which he can adjust with his established work personality. He takes the "normal" counselee as he is, and tries to help him to use his work personality, not change its characteristics.

Using the Theory of Work Adjustment as the basis for conceptualizing vocational counseling, the following specific techniques and procedures are suggested:

(1) Information to enable the counselor to estimate the counselee's needs should be obtained to facilitate management of the initial stages of counseling.

Some knowledge of counselee need structure will help the counselor to structure his plan for establishing a continuing relationship. For example, if data indicate a strong dependency need, the counselor would take a more active role in leading the interview.

At the present state of practice, the counselor must infer counselee need structure from such data sources as school cumulative records, referral information from agency workers, available test results, other records, and correspondence with the counselee. The important considerations are: that the counselor have a systematic conceptualization of needs; that he view data in terms of this conceptualization; and that he test the inferred need structure in his initial interviews with the counselee. When the technology of counseling is improved, perhaps the counselor will have available to him a referral instrument designed to include those data shown by research to be significantly related to measured needs. With such an instrument he should be able to infer some needs with more confidence than others, depending upon the kinds of data available for a specific counselee. In the absence of such data, the referral instrument might provide the basis for the initial interview, that is, be used as an intake instrument.

Some research (Warnken and Siess, 1965) indicates that it is feasible to develop such an instrument. Given a systematic conceptualization of needs, and an instrument to measure needs, it would appear feasible to select items for a referral instrument, utilizing an approach similar to that used in developing weighted application blanks (England, 1961). There is, of course, no reason why counselors must wait upon the completion of such research and the validation of such an instrument. As an interim measure, it should be desirable to examine the data accessible to him, to select and group data from the counselee histories likely to be related to needs, and to design a referral instrument that facilitates the assessment of needs from these data. He should verify assessments based on such an instrument against actual need measurements taken later in the counseling process.

(2) In the first interviews, the counselee should be encouraged to express fully his vocational and other problems, his aspirations, and his understanding of his possibilities for working with his problems and/or his aspirations. This procedure should provide some verification of the counselor's initial estimate of the counselee's needs. It also should provide reference points against which subsequent measurements may be evaluated to ascertain the extent of the counselee's knowledge of his work personality and of his potentialities in the world of work. This type of information helps to identify for the counselor the optimal beginning steps in the coun-

seling process and defines the areas of information in which he must communicate most effectively with this counselee.

(3) The counselor should obtain extensive personal-history data from the counselee, including educational, social, and work-history information. These data are needed to provide a context within which the initial referral data and the counselee's statements of his problems and aspirations can be viewed. These data will serve also as a background for subsequent psychometric evaluation. Because personal history data reflect an individual's reinforcement history, the counselor, in the course of gathering these data, will be able to improve his initial estimates of counselee needs. He will also gain information about the general skill levels of the counselee, which will aid him in choosing the appropriate instruments for use in psychometric evaluation.

(4) The counselor should obtain data that will establish the counselee's present levels of skills and needs. The most accurate and most dependable means for obtaining these data are provided by psychometric evaluation. Using testing procedures, the counselor samples the broad range of measurable skills and needs so that he can describe the counselee's unique work personality. The counselor's earlier estimates of his counselee's needs will guide the manner in which he introduces and carries out this psychometric evaluation. While personal history data are useful in establishing the counselee's skills and needs, psychometric data are preferable because work environments are more readily and more frequently described in psychometric terms. The counselor will find personal history data useful in corroborating test results. Discrepancies between personal history and test-derived data will point to areas requiring further description of the work personality.

In the present state of vocational psychology, the counselor has available to him instruments to measure a wide variety of skills. However, his choice of instruments is limited by the extent to which they have also been used to describe various work environments. In some cases—for example, in the development and standardization of multifactor tests such as the General Aptitude Test Battery (USES, 1956) and the Differential Aptitude Tests (Bennett, *et al.*, 1947–1959)—the individual and the environment (work and/or educational) have been measured, using the same set of dimensions.

In the area of need measurement (as needs are defined in the theory of work adjustment) the counselor does not have as wide a selection of instruments. Some beginnings have been made in the measurement of work-relevant needs (Super, 1962, Weiss, *et al.*, 1964) and in the description of the work environment on the same dimensions (Weiss, *et al.*, 1965). In the interim, the counselor must infer the work-relevant need patterns of the counselee from personality measurements, using established instruments (such as the Minnesota Multiphasic Personality Inventory, the Edwards Personal Preference Schedule, and the Allport-Vernon Lindzey Study of Values). In order to relate these inferred patterns to the work environment, he must utilize what is available in the way of information on job reinforcer systems (for example, in the temperament ratings found in the *Worker Trait Requirements for 4,000 Jobs,* the *Dictionary of Occupational Titles,* or in other published job descriptions). Much is yet to be done in the discovery, definition, and measurement of skill and need dimensions that will account for individual differences in responding to the full range of job requirements and reinforcer systems. This is the research area that should be given the highest priority in vocational psychology.

(5) The counselor should determine a number of feasible occupational possibilities for the counselee. He does this by collating his extensive psychometric information about the counselee with similar information about the available work environments. One way in which the counselor can accomplish this task is by determining the following:

a. Which jobs, across levels and field of work, are similar in skill requirements and reinforcement patterns to the counselee's established skills and needs? In other words, the counselor must examine information on the Occupational Ability Patterns (OAP's) and on the Occupational Reinforcement Patterns (ORP's) for a representative number of jobs.

b. Which jobs (in terms of their OAP's and ORP's) meet optimal matching ranges for the counselee's work personality (in terms of his skill and needs)?

If this task of matching men and jobs is to be carried out in the most effective manner, more work must be done to further the development of OAP and ORP job descriptions. This information, to be most useful to the counselor, must be organized so that fields and levels of work are represented and so that the job groupings are based on similarities in OAP and ORP characteristics regardless of field and level classifications. Furthermore, improved techniques for determining degrees of matching that will predict satisfactoriness and satisfaction for specific jobs must be developed. The validation of the Theory of Work Adjustment requires the development of such techniques.

(6) Utilizing his knowledge of the counselee's reinforcement history, the counselor should attempt to bring about job choices for which the skill and need correspondences with work environment characteristics are such that work adjustment can be predicted. The counselor may seek to facilitate counselee selection of appropriate jobs by the use of such techniques as selective reinforcement, suggestion, selective use of occupational information, and placement of the counselee in work-relevant situations that are reinforcing to him. It is understood that these techniques are aimed at facilitating job choice, which will insure work adjustment with its attendant satisfaction for the counselee and satisfactoriness for the employer and society.

(7) The counselor should, as a matter of course, follow up on the outcomes of his predictions concerning each counselee's work adjustment. This should reinforce the counselor and provide for a source of data to be used in evaluating and improving his predictions.

The procedures described above constitute the basic and minimum requirements for vocational counseling based on the Theory of Work Adjustment. It is recognized that the practice of vocational counseling in different settings and with different counselee populations will require the addition of specialized knowledges and techniques to this basic set of procedures. The vocational rehabilitation counselor must concern himself with the effects of disabling conditions (that is, illnesses or injuries). In addition to knowledges and techniques for the basic counseling procedures, he should have specialized knowledge of medical information in order to communicate with medical and related specialists. He should also be well informed about the plans for medical treatment and about the physician's recommendations for counselee activity. He also will want to have specialized knowledges of the training and rehabilitation facilities that are available to disabled individuals.

While the vocational rehabilitation counselor is expected to have this overlay of specialized information, the Theory of Work Adjustment requires that he assess the *impact* of disabling conditions on the counselee, using work-adjustment measures (that is, in terms of skill-ability losses and associated changes in need-value patterns) rather than view his counselee as belonging to a medical category with stereotypical expectations for him as a member of that group. In order to make this psychometric assessment, he must be able to reconstruct the counselee's work personality prior to the disabling condition, using the types of data generally available in school, agency, and industrial records. Though the focus here is on vocational rehabilitation counseling for work adjustment, it is recognized that these counselors also need knowledges and skills to work with the initial emotional impact of the disabling condition on counselees. Even at this stage of rehabilitation counseling, knowledge of the work personality prior to the disabling condition would appear to be essential in objectively determining the actual impact and in assessing the counselee's subjective reactions.

A new and urgent need relates to counselor procedures that may be desirable for adoption in the very near future, in the face of acute manpower shortages of professional personnel. First, a little background to recall the acuteness of the manpower problem, then, some possible approaches to resolving it. Much of the legislative effort in the "Great Society" program is directed toward such goals as employment for the "hard core" unemployed, equal opportunity for work, training minority group members for work, raising individual work levels, increasing work opportunities in disadvantageous labor market areas, relocating workers to more viable labor markets, counseling youth for work, helping individuals to adjust to leaving the labor force for retirement, and providing general and special education that will, among other things, facilitate productive and satisfying employment.

Prior to the current massive efforts to assure a better society, there were, of course, a number of other programs with similar work-adjustment kinds of goals. Examples are provided by such activities as the vocational rehabilitation programs, the counseling and training programs for returning servicemen and disabled veterans, the program for training school counselors to work in our secondary schools, and the federal-state employment service program to provide counseling and placement for any citizen. These examples make the obvious point that there is a great deal of legislation in effect that specifies or implies long-range goals in the general category of adjustment to work.

Often the legislation itself, and surely the discussion that shapes it and that assures its passage, correctly points out the importance of work to complete the satisfaction of, and to insure the dignity of, any man. In addition, man's worth as a producing economic unit, and man's ability after placement to repay the cost of specific legislation in a short span of years, are considered. The arguments for social legislation to facilitate work adjustment, and the social and economic benefits likely to accompany it, are compelling for both the legislative branch and the public. When such legislation is passed and funded, there is an urgent demand for agencies and administrators to start service programs immediately. Substantial results are expected by the end of the fiscal year.

The kinds of programs that are being discussed, however, either specify or imply that the individuals to be served will be assisted in making their adjustments to work and their choices of jobs by professional counselors educated to serve as vocational experts. Some programs include job titles and generally-worded descriptions for the counselors who are to be employed. Little attention is given, however, to specific job duties that will insure utilization of the existing technology in vocational psychology. In most cases, no consideration is given to the likelihood of filling the newly created positions with qualified professional manpower.

It is both interesting and alarming to note that of all the examples of social programs directed toward work adjustment mentioned above, only the vocational-rehabilitation, veterans-rehabilitation and secondary-school-counselor programs have been concerned enough with the supply of qualified personnel to have also initiated and maintained educational programs of high quality to insure practice that will meet professional standards in vocational counseling. Even these programs, however, can no longer meet staffing needs. Expansion of service programs, plus competition from new programs, makes the number of graduating vocational counselors in the foreseeable future look very inadequate indeed.

The need for specially educated vocational counselors has far outrun the present and the anticipated supply. It is a fact that we cannot adequately staff the recently legislated programs. Harried administrators, however, must get programs underway. They are sometimes urged to hire less qualified staff and to train them later. They are also often urged to forget about the "old technology" and to "innovate." They take these actions; get programs underway; find it difficult to arrange further training for staff; and, perhaps, find it less than easy to "innovate." In any case, these approaches are distressing to vocational psychologists and to counselor educators, who work with the knowledge that there is an established technology for practice and that there is a need to train additional qualified practitioners. The amazing opportunities now possible, to clients and behavioral scientists alike, should not ignore existing technology, avoid orderly conceptualization, be entrusted to unprepared staff, or rely on hollow exhortations to innovate. With these dissatisfactions in mind, one feels bold enough to offer suggestions for meeting manpower needs. The suggestions are based on the conceptualization of adjustment to work and on the desire to advance the technology this conceptualization suggests.

It would appear that additional and new emphases are needed at three different levels of education in the broad field of vocational psychology. Counseling functions need to be job analyzed and described with a new focus on levels of functioning. Parts of both the vocational-counseling and agency-administration technologies need to be "mechanized" and "simplified" to facilitate their use by personnel educated to function at different levels of competence. The following will illustrate possible specific steps that can be taken to implement these generally stated suggestions.

More individuals must be educated to the Ph.D. level of competence *in vocational psychology* and in its applied special area of *vocational-counseling psychology*. Such education in *vocational psychology* should be aimed primarily at producing high-level research workers to improve the technology of work adjustment and to translate research findings into applied procedures of utility to professional personnel educated to less technical levels of work competence. Education at the Ph.D. level in *vocational counseling psychology* should have as its goal the expansion of high level manpower available to teach vocational counseling in our graduate schools and to direct agency programs and agency staff development and training. Social legislation to facilitate work adjustment should provide for the establishment of faculties and student-stipend programs in these areas and at this level of education. Such action appears necessary if the technology is to be expanded.

Continuing educational programs at the master's degree level in vocational counseling need to be expanded in agencies where they exist (for example, the Vocational Rehabilitation Administration) and provided for in agencies where they do not exist (for example, in the war-on-poverty programs and the federal-state employment service system). Perhaps there is a basis for a common training in technology that has implications for practice across the special areas within vocational counseling psychology (for example, rehabilitation, employment-service, and school counseling). Since the total manpower needs for practicing vocational counselors appear unlikely to be met even by expanding the master's-level programs, the primary aims of these educational programs should be seen as providing counselor supervisors as well as counselors who will work with more limited caseloads of clients, for whom diagnosis, treatment, and communication problems are particularly difficult.

A third level of education can probably be successfully undertaken in the form of short-term training at colleges and universities, with an emphasis on technological applications. This would be followed up by continuing in-service training programs within the service agencies themselves. Such training should be directed toward practitioners at the sub-master's degree level, who will utilize the technology developed and interpreted by vocational psychologists and who will be supervised in both applications and caseload management by the M.A.-level supervising vocational counselors. To make continuous progress in a viable program of in-service training, and to insure upward mobility (as a career incentive), individuals hired to be trained and to practice at this level should, whenever possible, have the abilities that will enable them to pursue graduate level education at a later date, if this is desired.

These three levels of education must be viewed as interdependent in terms of goals and balance, and must be seen as operating across all major agencies that deal in programs oriented toward work adjustment. This requires improved agency-university cooperation. Some serious attention is being given to this area (McGowan, 1965). It also requires considerable coordination of activity in the several independent major agencies. Perhaps this is the point in time where it is necessary to suggest that a commissioner of vocational counseling, chosen in consultation with the professional communities in vocational psychology and counseling psychology and the practicing agencies, and with authority to function across agencies, be appointed. This last suggestion arises from the current state of confusion that characterizes our approaches to meeting public needs through vocational counseling.

Agencies are understaffed and, in many cases, have underqualified personnel. Agencies compete with one another for qualified staff only to find them in very short supply. Colleges and universities, in the midst of facing the demands of a markedly expanded student population, find it difficult to give faculty time to expanding graduate-level educational programs and to in-service training programs when these are requested by agencies. Agencies and universities alike appear on the surface to be uncooperative. Both the hiring of substandard personnel by the agencies, and the lack of ability to educate more fully trained personnel by the universities, are deplored. Professional organizations are concerned about the effects of new social legislation on the accepted standards for professional preparation (for example, the master's level as a minimum for practicing vocational-educational counselors). It is obvious that simple acts of writing job titles into legislation and then providing funds to hire professional personnel will not solve our current problems. Defining levels of desired education and supporting these levels constitute one part of an approach that may have desirable results.

To effectively employ a levels-of-education approach, and to improve services to clients, it is necessary to do a careful job analysis of vocational counseling functions and to group functions by levels. Most counseling psychologists should agree that there are several job requirements that they meet frequently that *do not* call upon skills and knowledges provided by their high level of education (at either the master's or the Ph.D. degree levels). Coupled with job analysis activity, it would appear desirable to simplify and to organize the tools available and the methods of using them. Some tools and procedures now employed only by highly trained personnel can be "mechanized" and made effectively applicable by less trained persons. The following are illustrations of some of the ways in which vocational counseling could be "simplified" and "mechanized" to utilize personnel educated for different levels of competence.

Agencies should set up systems for procuring relevant advance referral information on clients to be seen for service in an agency. Such information can be obtained from typical referral sources, from the clients themselves, and from social institutions known typically to have served the agencies' clients (for example, schools, the employment service). The relevance of such information for screening and for client assignment to personnel in the agency would be determined by research-competent vocational psychologists. Structured devices can be prepared that will specify the minimum information needed. Different combinations of information would indicate such things as whether or not an agency can be of service, what services are likely to be most effective, what level of counseling difficulty is likely, what extent of agency involvement is necessary, and how the client is likely to react in his first contacts with the agency.

Using such a system, an M.A.-level supervisor or an agency-office supervisor can specify in advance the data to be checked, the hypotheses to be explored, the likely courses of action, and, in many cases, the rather simple actions necessary to resolve problems. With the advance referral information and supervisor specifications for likely actions, clients can be seen for initial interviews by an intake interviewer. There would appear to be no reason why these intake interviewers would require training beyond the bachelor's-degree level if they function under competent supervision and in the context of systematic review. Sensitive and reliable individuals with some in-service training in effective interpersonal relations should be able to meet the job requirements. Intake interviewers should be able to describe agency functions, answer requests for relatively simple information, refer inappropriate clients to other agencies, and arrange referrals within the agency to higher professional staff levels.

Another level of professional personnel at the sub-master's

level, but with considerable in-service training (conducted by Ph.D.-
and M.A.-level persons), should be able to do much of what the
trained master's-level vocational counselor now does. To make
this possible, our techniques must be translated into forms that
make applications simpler, and perhaps even more effective, than
they are at the present time. It is also necessary to insure continuous
supervision of the procedures by counselors educated to the level
of present standards (the master's degree, usually two years of
graduate work.) A brief description of a program of testing carried
out by the Minnesota Work Adjustment Project with the Minnesota
Division of Vocational Rehabilitation may illustrate how this
"mechanization" and "simplification" could be carried out. The
project is set up primarily to gather research data, but has
implications for counselor functioning and for counselor in-service
training.

In the work adjustment program, all clients referred to the
state agency are tested by psychometrists on a predetermined
battery of the most relevant tests. This battery can, of course, be
supplemented by additional testing later in the counseling process.
The client takes the General Aptitude Test Battery (GATB), the
Minnesota Vocational Interest Inventory (MVII), the Strong Vocational Interest Blank (SVIB), the Minnesota Importance Questionnaire (MIQ), and the Minnesota Multiphasic Personality Inventory
(MMPI). To illustrate both "mechanization" and the process of
focusing counseling in directions that utilize accepted tools and
procedures, only the GATB results will be discussed here.

The GATB is scored on a computer and processed, for each
individual, through a computer program that prints out raw scores,
standard scores, and percentiles for each subtest. The program also
prints out the Occupational Ability Patterns (OAP's) for which
this individual qualifies. This leads the counselor to a list of possible
jobs for each OAP for which the individual meets minimal ability
requirements. In addition, the program prints out the page and
line numbers that correspond to job titles in the *Worker Trait
Requirements for 4,000 Jobs* (WTR) for all of the listed jobs for
which the individual's abilities qualify him. This leads the counselor
to additional essential information contained on each specified line
of the WTR. For example, he will be able to consider such other
information as that pertaining to levels of education (general and

special), interests, temperaments, and physical requirements that are deemed by experts (job analysts) to be desirable for job success. Additional machine sortings can be made for these kinds of information.

Information presented in this way should not demean the job of the vocational counselor. Instead it should save time in testing, scoring, interpretation, and the location of the most relevant resource information. Also, methods like this ought to facilitate the use of relevant but simply presented data on clients by less-skilled persons working under supervision. At the same time, perhaps higher levels of skill will be utilized by master's-level personnel in supervision, in training—as planning with several subordinate counselors—and in working with the most difficult clients in the agency's population.

The work by Gilbert (1964), using programmed instruction techniques in test interpretation to clients, provides an illustration of another kind of simplification and mechanization that may add to the sophistication of our total technology in vocational counseling. It is entirely possible that counselor time can be saved in test interpretation activity, to be used in more critical parts of the process; that programmed interpretation can be presented in the counseling process by less skilled personnel (after the experts, that is, the vocational psychologists, have programmed the material); and that clients will receive, through this process, a better understanding of their assets and liabilities than is now likely.

These examples point to the possibility of changing our traditional counseling procedures so that better use can be made of professional personnel at different levels of education. If we also improve our technology at the level of research in vocational psychology, and if we are guided in doing this by conceptualizations like the Theory of Work Adjustment, we may also become more effective as experts in facilitating the work adjustment of individuals.

"Mechanization" and "simplification" can also be effectively employed at the administrative level in an agency. Recently, to cite one example, Weiss, Potter, and McGuire (1965), working with the Minnesota Work Adjustment Project, established a computer program system for the state services for the blind in Minnesota. After giving attention to the data to be included and the data-reporting structure, a program was set up that prints out data on the status of case actions at regular intervals. This enables supervisors and counselors to keep up with the demands of heavy caseloads and appears to motivate efficient case handling as well as appropriate data gathering. The program also prints out total agency report data whenever this is desired. An annual report is printed out in a few minutes and requires only the dictation of the verbal context in which one wishes to present the data.

The use of such administrative technology in combination with simplified data processing and data presentation techniques in counseling should facilitate better agency use of manpower skills in a tight professional labor market. It is hoped that these suggestions may stimulate additional activity to define and to "simplify" vocational counseling and to improve the technology of vocational psychology. In any event, talking about them during a period of change and some unrest in counseling psychology can be therapeutic for the profession.

DISCUSSION QUESTIONS

1. What are the differences and similarities between counseling and psychotherapy? In view of the position taken that the counseling relationship is the critical variable, is it important for the counselor to be aware of whether he is doing counseling or psychotherapy?

2. Vocational behavior is regarded by some writers as differentiable from other behaviors, and consequently worthy of study on its own merits. To what degree is it possible to isolate vocational behavior from total behavior so as to make it a focus of rehabilitation counseling?

3. Research conducted at the University of Minnesota resulted in the formulation of the concept of a "normal" work personality. Can such a personality be achieved by emotionally or intellectually disabled persons? Is it necessary to attain a "normal" work personality in order to become vocationally rehabilitated?

4. Will computerized operations result in more effective informa-

tion gathering and diagnosis in rehabilitation? Will mechanization really free counselors for more creative tasks?

5. Some counselors seem to function almost instinctively, on a
   pragmatic basis, without an explicit personality theory. Is this
   undesirable? Why?

6. If all counseling theory were to be unified into a single,
   generally acceptable system, would this result in a standardized
   orthodoxy of counseling method? If this occurred, how could
   individuality of counseling practice be preserved?

7. Is it possible for a rehabilitation counselor to adopt a particular
   theory of personality and counseling and yet retain an open
   mind about various ways of perceiving clients? If it is possible,
   how can counselors achieve such "open" attitudes?

8. Since various counseling orientations have much in common,
   would it be desirable for most rehabilitation counselors to be
   "eclectics," drawing upon the various orientations as the need
   arose? On the other hand, what are the limitations of "eclecticism"?

9. Since much of present-day rehabilitation counseling consists
   of coordinative and administrative activities in fulfillment of
   legislative and procedural requirements, is it possible for the
   client to see his counselor as a person who allows him to make
   his own decisions?

10. A treatment process may seek to modify the client and/or the
    environment. Vocationally-oriented counselors tend to place
    greater stress upon developing a suitable environment for the
    client in which his assets will be maximized and his limitations
    minimized. Is this largely environmental approach a suitable
    model for vocational rehabilitation, or would a therapeutic
    model that modifies behavior be preferable?

PART FIVE

PROFESSIONAL CONSIDERATIONS

INTRODUCTION TO PART FIVE

Young professions almost always pass through an identity crisis. Rehabilitation counseling is no exception. Since 1955, conference after conference has addressed itself to the problem of defining the rehabilitation counseling profession and charting its future development. Today, more than a decade after the passage of Public Law 565 and the initiation of widespread counselor training, the field still perversely resists neat categorization. The rehabilitation counselor remains an enigma. Whitehouse and Muthard accept the challenge of penetrating the enigma and developing a model for the profession.

The two papers in this section summarize the current state of the profession of rehabilitation counseling from two vantage points. Using certain recognized yardsticks of a profession, Whitehouse measures rehabilitation counseling against a philosophical criterion and suggests that progress toward professionalization is apparent. Viewing the counselor as a therapist, he reaches hopefully toward a model that would insure a large measure of freedom for the counselor and the client to individualize the rehabilitation process and to select interventions that seem to both participants to offer the greatest promise of growth.

On the other hand, Muthard emphasizes the historical and social context of rehabilitation counseling as a profession and also finds the situation promising. Reviewing the literature, he concludes that it is still emerging from a complex matrix of social forces and that although much remains to be done, it is already a profession that has achieved considerable public acceptance.

Although the optimism expressed by these two authors has different roots, it is consistent and pervasive. Characterized by a profound concern for the individual and an explicit responsibility to society, rehabilitation counseling has achieved in a generation what has taken centuries in other fields. Yet, at the same time, there is an awareness of a considerable gap between professional practice and ideals. At times it may seem as though self-interest, petty factionalism, and personal ambition dominate an agency, a service, or a community. Anyone engaged in community organization who has attempted to interest rehabilitation workers in undertaking an especially difficult new service (for example, to the homebound) becomes aware of resistances that are sometimes based upon unprofessional considerations.

Over the long run, the rehabilitation movement has shown a remarkable resiliency. Every few years, if not annually, new legislation is proposed by rehabilitation leaders. Such legislation is characterized not merely by "tinkering" with established concepts but, more often than not, embodies substantial alterations in services and innovative approaches that promote improved professionalism. As we study the flow of new rehabilitation statutes from the federal and state governments, we are impressed with the unique capacity of organized rehabilitation to develop from within. Although the most significant alterations in professionalization have occurred in training and research, those that deal with improved service to clients are equally important. The Vocational Rehabilitation Act amendments of 1968, following closely on the heels of other vital amendments of earlier years, offer numerous new opportunities for rehabilitation counselors to be of greater service to their clients.

The unsettled state of rehabilitation counseling as an emerging profession and the improvements that are appearing almost daily in legislation and practice are the opposite sides of the same coin. Those who deplore the transitional and unstable status of the profession should recognize that the danger in early crystallization of a young field is that of hardening of the innovative arteries. By staying "loose," at the risk of appearing less professional than some of the more established fields, rehabilitation counseling pays a price. It suffers in prestige, in the security it offers to its practitioners, and in the establishment of a "science." Nonetheless, the gains are substantial. Despite a considerable bureaucracy and an entrenched establishment, rehabilitation counseling responds with remarkable alacrity to new challenges.

Will the introduction of firmer standards, more systematic

approaches, and better defined counselor functions reduce the responsiveness of rehabilitation to rapid changes that are taking place in the social context in which it operates? Both Whitehouse and Muthard see the advantages and dangers of early institutionalization of this profession. Perhaps, the answer lies somewhere in the region between freedom to innovate and individualize, on the one hand, and the assumption of responsibility for externally imposed standards, on the other. The next decade may not see a resolution of this dilemma but it may result in a more rational balance between the two contending forces and a narrowing of the gap between practice and ideal.

XIII   SOME PROFESSIONAL CONCEPTS

Frederick Whitehouse

A profession may be inspected from a number of formal aspects. There are its intellectual, ethical, social, legal, educational, and training features. It may be viewed as an organized and structured body of knowledge in a philosophical framework, a particular subdivision of the broader tree of human knowledge; a vocation in which the practitioner commits himself to some noble purpose and follows explicit and implicit principles of conduct; an occupation that may require certain qualifications for certification and licensure by state regulation; a special combine of individuals in the field that sets up standards and declares those who qualify as approved practitioners; a union of those who profess a particular practice that serves to protect and enhance its members; and finally a group that, by adhering to certain community demands and expectations, is permitted to provide such services with their approval.

These criteria are frequently discussed, and sometimes exclusively so, since usually only slight attention is given to what a professional is and what professionalism entails. Yet these less specific and less definable aspects are the most important of all, especially in the fields that encompass human therapeutic services. For the academic requirements, the qualifying experience and the ornamentation of investiture are secondary to what a professional really is. A person may achieve entrance into the profession and yet never achieve the status of a true professional.

An aphorism states: "It is easier to become a father than to be one." Having acquired the knowledge, and being aware of the rules of the game, how does one play it well? The answer defies specificity and concreteness of interpretation, since it is a highly individual and personal issue. It warrants a neverending review, even though its form of expression cannot be circumscribed for anyone. With

245

these acknowledged limitations, we shall endeavor to discuss what appear to be some guiding principles as reference points, or merely as reflective considerations for a personal philosophy about our profession.

THE QUALITY OF COMMITMENT

When a person enters a profession, he engages in a way of life. The nature of this passage and the personal dedication it requires is tied to the substance and purposes of the profession. Rehabilitation counseling penetrates deeply into the stream of humanity. Consequently, it carries a responsibility that should not be entered upon unless the person entering recognizes the kind of commitment it requires and accepts its demands. Perhaps the first principle, then, is the quality of commitment he must make. It is not realized overnight, but as a seed it grows as our comprehension of its importance develops.

The hours freely given; the discomfort and frustration borne with good grace; the anxiety of honest, but uncertain decisions; the promotion of courage when a great deal is required; the devotion to continued learning; the dedication to ideals; the empathetic strain on emotions; the lack of capricious freedom that others enjoy but that costs us too much in time; the extraordinary patience that must be endured with clients but that is easy compared with the patience we must have with a society that injures, rejects, punishes, and denies our clients—these are some of the facets of being a professional that ought to be recognized.

To some, the words "sacrifice" and "self-discipline" may seem the banners of compulsive neurotic, guilty people, and they might shy away from them. They also appear to be words that come from "old-time religion." Furthermore, we may fear these words, as they may imply a demand upon ourselves we are unwilling to make, or afraid to become involved with. However, they are important steps toward maturity that a professional vitally needs if he is to help others.

If we are not afraid of these concepts and give them a chance to flourish, we gradually appreciate their worth. Sacrifice may be self-denial, but not in the sense of denial of self-identification. The insight that sacrifice is not a loss, but a gain; that self-discipline is not restrictive, but a winning of greater freedom; and that by serving others we serve ourselves in the best possible way, may come about only through trial. Any worthy accomplishment in art or life comes through self-discipline, and its reward is greater maturity, greater control over our lives, and a greater awareness of life's dimensions. Knowledge is power, but self-mastery is more powerful.

It doesn't mean that we forego enjoyment and entertainment. It may cause some displacement of what we consider pleasurable. We may be more bored than ever at the trivial talk of the cocktail party, of the superficiality of many social gatherings, and of the vapidity of much present-day diversion. Often we shall resent people and circumstances that waste our precious time. It doesn't mean we don't take a son to the football game, but it may occasion working late that night, if we do.

Our investment, however, has exceptional returns. The satisfaction that the educator receives in teaching an individual to develop in mind and body; the gratification that a physician receives in treating and restoring; the fulfillment it may bring to the counselor to find the client growing in achievement; the sense of contribution that is felt upon placing a client in a job; the stimulation of other intelligent people with whom we work, and the challenge that the human problem represents, are some of the rewards gained.

The rehabilitation counselor becomes involved with problems as intricate as those faced by the physicist, as soul-tearing as those faced by the clergymen, as practical as those faced by the businessman. Yet, while the field demands fortitude, working in it generates superior strength. Although not true of all clients, the patient suffering of some, their courage in the face of disaster, their spirit and motivation to achieve, will support faith in ourselves and the importance of our work.

Since a degree of personal immunity is inevitably developed as minor protection against the emotional blows, we must resist at all costs the insidious onset of callousness and indifference that is destructive not only to the client but eventually to ourselves. By education and training, the rehabilitation counselor develops greater sensitivity to the injustice and cruelty that is so characteristic of our society. However, he must avoid succumbing to this burden by not reacting resentfully and cynically, and by channeling his anger into crusades for human betterment.

RESPONSIBILITY TO THE CLIENT

A review of the issue of responsibility may be profitable. A serious commitment is the price required for the privilege of being a professional. Unfortunately, most young people entering a profession assume that the greater the obligation, the more burdensome it is. Under such a misapprehension, it sometimes takes them a long time to realize that reponsibility is, in fact, uplifting. It is not oppressive, but gloriously exhilarating. One is not bowed down with the weight of duty, but raised and inspired by the challenge. A vocation filled, is sustaining; a profession engaged in, is fortifying; a duty observed is gratifying; and a spending, instead of hoarding of our talents, multiplies their worth.

PROFESSIONAL INTEGRITY

The nonprofessional has the naïve opinion that when one engages in a vocation, "one never thinks of oneself," and that "everyone and everything should come before we consider ourselves." This is at best a distortion and at worst a denial of the quality of the compact.

We must maintain and develop a sense of self-integrity. If this is not firmly established, our obligations are not seen clearly, our focus becomes unbalanced, and our services to others will deteriorate. As Shakespeare said: "This above all: to thine own self be true, . . . Thou canst not then be false to any man."

Integrity does not come without toil, nor when the mantle of the profession is put upon our shoulders. Furthermore, with its achievement, we cannot simply maintain what we have as if it were an ornament in a display case. Integrity is constantly developed, improved, polished; it grows, it requires cultivation by use and refinement. Nor can it be hidden. It must be put on the line and meet challenge. It decays when denied expression. It becomes a mocking ghost that whispers too loudly to be ignored when one attempts to escape its promises. True, some confuse rigidity and inflexibility with integrity. Actually they are at opposite poles, since such an individual as a pretender and hypocrite is worse than the unprincipled. This real quality again defies concrete specification. However, it is suggested that perhaps it rises and grows by obtaining satisfaction from one's work, by a recognition of the incompleteness of one's knowledge, by sensitivity to ethical considerations, and by greater clarity about one's own motivations.

NEED FOR SATISFACTION

To discuss each facet in turn: the issue of satisfaction in one's work is extremely important. If we do not obtain it, our unhappiness inevitably is transferred to our clients and harms them. It manifests itself in our overt actions and sometimes very subtly in our nonverbal transactions, and usually in both ways. However it may be expressed, the message burdens our clients and others with whom we deal. If we are unsatisfied, we should seek another field or some level of the field in which the operations may give us sufficient return.

However, young entrants to rehabilitation counseling must be aware that it takes time to learn how to obtain satisfaction constructively and even how to recognize satisfaction. Like the highly romantic couple who enter marriage expecting the aura of fantasy to continue, we must learn to accept and adjust to the realities. Often a rehabilitation counselor with a self image as some kind of savior can be disappointed when the society doesn't throw flowers in his path. He may indeed earn accolades, but not be given them. It isn't easy to realize that what we think of ourselves is more important than what society does.

WORKING WITH INCOMPLETE KNOWLEDGE

In rehabilitation counseling, we face a vast array of medical, social, psychological, educational, vocational, and specialized rehabilitation information for sampling. This threat to our ego, this certification to our ignorance, must be faced and dealt with. We should accept the fact that never again can we say to ourselves: "I'm well informed," or "My knowledge is adequate." For the more knowledge a person acquires, the greater will be his feeling that he knows very little. This humble position prompted Diogenes to say of Socrates: "He declared that he knew nothing except the fact of his ignorance."

Furthermore, throughout our professional career we shall continue to be faced with this dilemma. Our responsibility is to deal with a human being in a total way. We are expected to be concerned about his medical, social, psychological, economic, vocational, and even spiritual needs. We must be careful, considerate, patient, ethical, scientific, realistic, efficient, and, of course, legal.

You may say, "Surely my training cannot begin to prepare me to fill these expectations. I cannot be certain whether this job placement might not deteriorate the client's condition or even lead to premature death. My reliance upon medical opinion cannot be absolute. I need to know much more about the job and about other factors in his life that stress him.

"I don't really know how successful or happy my client will be on his job, or whether it is the best opportunity for him. I don't know whether his family will be supportive of him. I know I didn't give them enough attention. Why can't I become a better counselor? Perhaps, I should spend more time at counseling, but I don't see how I may."

As professionals, we are not alone in this frustration. One might compare the general practitioner of medicine with the rehabilitation counselor, who is the "general practitioner of rehabilitation." Society expects far more of both professions than they can possibly deliver. Both must do the best they can under the most trying circumstances for an ethical conscience. If we are afraid of challenge, if we cannot sustain such conflict, if this takes too much strength, it is best we leave. One would suspect that a fair number of physicians in the public health field have been driven there by this conflict. It is no disgrace to find challenge or conflict intolerable. Some of us are built differently. On the other hand, this issue is parallel to the general ambiguities of our lives, for as Samuel Butler said: "Life is the art of drawing sufficient conclusions from insufficient premises."

The practical time limitations of all professional training in an era of rapidly expanding knowledge force compromises that focus upon the job training aspects, which are the tools and techniques of the profession. The scope of the rehabilitation counselor, as with other therapeutic professionals, lies beyond training. Consequently, there is no intellectual relaxation after formal education, but equally hard work learning more about the field and about its changing complexion, since much information will rapidly become obsolete in the face of extraordinary scientific developments. Principles, however, are slower to change, and most will be valid for a lifetime. Yet all will be modified, and we should be prepared to remain open to alterations brought about by experience and social reform.

The knowledge available today, the degree of therapeutic commitment required, and the necessary specialization of professional practice, demand an unrelenting study by all professionals. It is, furthermore, about time that our society set up the regulatory machinery to guarantee at least a minimum standard of continuing professional development for all disciplines by the institution of continued training and reexamination measures.

None of us will live long enough to achieve the proficiency about which we dream. This combination of conscientiousness, of scientific discipline, and of public and private responsibility exacts a high price for the privilege of service. Yet, its return in personal satisfaction makes professional practice the most rewarding vocation on earth. Actually, this is why we seek a profession. Our courage and ambitions are high, and our concern for human welfare is paramount. We can and will strive, and we will scramble to achieve. About 2,000 years ago the philosopher Seneca said: "A great pilot can sail even when his canvas is rent; if his ship be dismantled, he can yet put in trim what remains of her hull and hold her to her course."

ETHICAL CONSIDERATIONS

The "profess" in a profession is a basic acknowledgment of one's personal and professional ethics. A professional cannot but seek the highest ethical standards. By this we are not referring to mere adherence to a legal obligation, which is a minimum standard, nor to the typical, reciprocal, protective codes by which one extends professional courtesy to other professionals. For example, one would not openly criticize another professional nor act covertly to bypass his actions. We mean ethical standards based upon the protection of and guarantees to the client that arise from assumptions about the dignity and rights of man; that are based upon the individual's right to choose and be responsible for his own destiny.

Such generalizations cannot remain sterile. They require application to each and every client.

Ethical principles are fine. They read well on paper and move us when passionately spoken. However, the real issue is our reaction to them: our comprehension of their meaning and the attitudes and feelings we have about them. Also related is how we interpret and apply them in practice. They need to be, in other words, a part of our living and not a reference page in a text. Their real expression lies not merely in performing what is demanded of us but in what we demand of ourselves. Codes of ethics in any profession are typically arid standards. They serve as a minimum basic guarantee to those served, as guides to the neophytes in the field, and perhaps as some means for the outsider to understand the profession.

However, they are only indicators, sign posts, or simple prescriptions, and we may only begin to understand their potential value by observational samples of a competent professional's behavior. True understanding requires practice as a professional.

One obligation frequently bypassed is the need to speak when we observe injustice to the client. Injustice may consist of many different evils, but the net result is harm to the client. Our ethical feeling may require us to cry out in spite of the consequences to ourselves. An honest opinion should not become dishonest silence. This is never an easy position, because such stands are frequently felt by others to be professionally treasonable or socially disruptive. Misgivings about such protests are natural. Yet it is well to remember that there is no escape in the long run, because we cannot hide from ourselves. Playing safe may lessen risk, but such a violation of trust will take greater toll in the certain erosion of our self-esteem.

In our profession we need no oath of allegiance, no sword touched to our shoulders, no anointing of our foreheads to certify the excellence expected of us. It is, in fact, a higher level of expectation than the formal pledge or investiture, because so much is left to the quality of our consciences.

OBLIGATION TO REVIEW ONE'S OWN MOTIVATIONS

Do we ever really know why we have selected rehabilitation counseling as a profession? Can we learn what combination of reasons and circumstances, of unconscious needs, of rationalized thoughts provoked the gravitational-like pull toward this human service? By what amalgam of intellectual interest, emotional yearnings, compassionate feelings and challenging expectations were we brought to this decision? We may never fully know. Part of it unfolds as we practice, although it may be a lifetime of disclosure. A professional career is frequently a kind of inner need or compulsion for creative activity that we are convinced has important value. We may believe it is an idealistic conviction that our service to humanity transcends personal comfort, that our devotion to our work is the finest expression of our being. In spite of such altruistic assumptions, we must constantly be on our guard that they don't blind us to our own possible distortions.

The truth is that we must examine ourselves almost as much as we examine the client. Clients may remind us of the teacher we disliked in the 6th grade, of our father who put on the same expression when he was angry, of a neighbor who took advantage of us. The client's morals or personal appearance may be shocking or distasteful; his heart disease reminds us of our fears—Didn't our mother die of heart disease? However, there is no need to catalog the many threats that could be found, for there may be something represented in every client we meet. Forgiving enemies is an obvious issue; we might find that "forgiving" innocent clients is so subtle that it requires frequent self-inspection.

Unfortunately, the professional has a more covert opportunity to vent his aggressions on the client. Society can easily see the policeman who swings his club without sufficient justification, or the mother who punishes a child because of her own frustrations. However, the professional has more subtle poisons at his command that may kill the spirit of the recalcitrant or rebellious client. Unnecessary withdrawal of approval, denial of favors that might easily be given, incomplete statements that worry, vague hints at consequences, inhibition of warmth, nonreaction to disclosures of fear and concern—there are countless ways, and unfortunately we may do many of them unconsciously. Sometimes the clues are the clients' actions: they may be reacting to us.

Perhaps three brief quotations on individual performance will serve to sum up this section on personal responsibility. Anne Roe said in the *Psychology of Occupations:* "All that a man can be, he must be." A British physician, Pickering, said in speaking of a good researcher: "He is obsessed by his ignorance and by his desire to know." Francis Bacon speaks of qualities that may be a guide to us: ". . . the desire to seek, the patience to doubt, the fondness to meditate, the slowness to assert, the readiness to reconsider, the carefulness to dispose and set in order . . . and to hate every kind of imposture."

RESPONSIBILITY FOR PROFESSIONAL STANDARDS

A. CLINICAL FREEDOM

The professional must seek and establish clinical freedom, since it involves a serious commission and an implied compact with the client. By clinical freedom is meant the right and responsibility to deal professionally with a client without interference and with every reasonable opportunity for independent decision. This does not mean that the performance cannot be otherwise analyzed or evaluated. Also, obviously, trainees and new entrants require close supervision until the privilege is earned by competent performance.

If the professional is not trained well enough, or cannot exercise the proper ethical standards commensurate with this critical function, he should not be in the professional field, and the educator and administrator are violating their responsibility if they permit poorly prepared individuals to enter the high office of interpersonal engagement. If clinical freedom cannot be accepted or permitted, then the occupation is no longer professional. Competent people will not accept positions with such restrictions. Those who do enter will soon leave to locate elsewhere, and this happens frequently. Usually other reasons than the truth are given by both employer and employee, because such fictions require no explanation.

ACCEPTANCE OF PROFESSIONAL LIMITATIONS

Theoretically, all scientific fields are boundless, and our profession, because it deals with man—the most complicated and intriguing subject of all—demands openmindedness to knowledge and, more particularly, to the frames of reference that are the cognate disciplines allied to our field. Recognition of where we stand in relation to other bodies of knowledge and other professions must be grasped, and this information begins with knowing who they are and what information or service they may offer to the client and to us.

One could not list the totality of related therapeutic professions, contributing professions, and other expert bodies of knowledge that conceivably might be employed for some clients during the course of their rehabilitation. In fact, the rehabilitation counselor is restricted only by his imagination in the variety of people and special services that may be employed.

The profession is a relatively new one, and its development and evolution are still in progress. We stand related to our field, to the more generic principles of rehabilitation, to the whole social welfare complex, and indeed to the total scientific endeavor. As a specialized part of the whole related scheme of human knowledge, the profession is a growing, expanding field, creating new information and initiating new ideas. Since it will grow in complexity, it will, as other professions, divide into new specializations.

The specific principles of the profession are derived and applied from broader principles that we put into practice, commensurate with our particular framework of knowledge and abilities. All of the disciplines in the field of rehabilitation have common generic principles of rehabilitation as well as their own specific ones related to their frameworks and competencies.

While we break down knowledge into logical pockets for convenience, it is necessary that we do not draw lines that impose such arbitrary boundaries on ourselves and our clients. Every profession has the responsibility to utilize whatever may be learned from others, as well as to use other disciplines appropriately.

Rehabilitation counseling faces, as others do, what may be called "professional nationalism": The tendency to take on the mantle of the profession is a universal characteristic. This hood may cover our eyes as well as our hearts, with a resulting narrowness of outlook and spirit. This is not to disparage the pride, the confidence, and the special orientation that serve to identify a person with the profession. Such things are a source of strength, and a personally satisfying medium for self-expression, which is desirable. However, we cannot permit this grandeur to stifle our thinking, to constrict our imagination, to make us fearful to break out of its usual routine, or to become trapped in its cozy, temporary answers.

How easy it is to say we must recognize our limitations. This is what we keep telling one another. Obviously it is difficult to achieve, because it requires superior knowledge and a personal security. Yet, usually the more we learn about other professions, the easier it is to temper our own narrowness. Observing the limitations of other professions may also console us.

THE LIFE PROCESS CONTINUUM

Another aspect of this relatedness is an appreciation of what may be termed the "life process continuum." One of the most important facets of a therapeutic profession is to locate its position within the life continuum of professional services: that is, it is valuable for us to study and review what happens or doesn't happen to the client *before* he comes to us, and to review what happens to clients *beyond* our services. This will not only give us a better perspective of where our clients may be at the time we see them and what may await them in the future, but it also gives us a wonderful opportunity of reporting back to previous service areas and telling them our problems and how they might improve or alter their services to avoid prospective candidates for us, or what they might do to make our job more successful.

The special educator and others, such as physicians and nurses, should be known to us, and we need to exchange with them. Furthermore, in thinking ahead, it should give us the impetus to incorporate into our clinical schemes the kinds of planning that will tend to preserve our client's physical, mental, social, and vocational integrity as long as possible. We should, in a similar fashion, be asking those who deal with the aged person, what kinds of problems they face and what is needed, so that our performance may make their work more successful. To make a generalization: any time we have contact with a client at whatever stage of his life, we should be sensitive to his whole life process so that we may offer the kind of service that will tend to secure the best long-term result.

Therefore, since our professional field, in spite of its broad-ness, is unavoidably narrow, we need to keep incorporating new information and to use other professions and services continually as part of our obligation.

RESPONSIBILITY TO SUPERIORS

In every professional field there are individuals who contribute different types of services than those of the clinician, who is primarily engaged in a personal relationship with the client. It is essential that the roles and obligations of these various positions be examined, since there is a tendency to oversimplify the issues.

The rehabilitation counselor will undoubtedly experience some conflict between his desire for excellence of performance, as he may view it, and the pressure of administrative demand for production. Frequently, this gap is discouragingly wide. First of all, it is an easy answer to castigate the administrator. However, let us consider the issue. He is, as is the counselor, responsible for certain functions. Such functions are never completely, or even mostly, determined by administrators themselves. The process is basically fashioned by the social sensitivity of a society that has seen fit to commit itself only to a limited extent, partly because the society is not as perceptive as it should be, but partly also because our voices have not been heard in the proper forums. Yes, counselors should resist and challenge certain, but not all, administrative strictures, and their efforts should also be directed at the basic source of the problem to correct what they think should be remedied. They can speak in public, they can discuss it privately, they can write letters to the newspaper and to congressmen. Professional articles can be published and ideas presented on radio and television. The political field may also be engaged as well as other persons in positions of power.

In addition, a major responsibility of the administrator himself is to see that a high standard of professionalism is maintained. Sometimes this obligation is neglected. Frequently it is translated almost solely into various educational upgrading measures, which although worthwhile, are only one aspect of professional needs. The maintenance of professional, clinical freedom, of high ethical standards, of careful and judicious work performances, and of respect for individual opinions and the establishment of appropriate opportunities for discussion of views without threat or recrimination, are some means of guarantee for a professional staff.

On the other hand, the main responsibility lies with the individual professional. He cannot expect to be honored by his agency's administration unless he exhibits, promotes, and fights for high standards. He demands this of himself first; he earns the right by his own performance. Indeed, there are very few if any prizes in life that are not paid for, that are not strained, sweated, and worked for. Fortunately, these efforts usually bring their deserved rewards. However, one need never think he is a martyr if he doesn't get what he hopes for, because he yet achieves greater strength by the struggle, which make other ventures more likely to succeed.

The good professional is idealistic, but he doesn't permit this idealism to bind his actions. There is a personal balance with which idealism can be treasured and sustained, while yet permitting some compromise. We must admit that our idealism is never perfect, nor even perfectly clear to us, and that others also have ideals that are equally worthy, even if they have some conflict with ours. How much right any man has to pursue an ideal of his own without deviance or compromise, no one can answer. It is a matter of individual conscience and recognition of external realities. There are many administrators whose vision and devotion equal or exceed those of the rehabilitation counselor. Such individuals do not expect silence; most would welcome a partnership in the pursuit of excellence and justice for the clients of all concerned.

RESPONSIBILITY TO SOCIETY

Frequently we find the professional who believes that he can accomplish his mission by not permitting the external affairs of society to delay him or to intrude upon his client focus. Not only is this seen as a right, but some conceive of this withdrawal as a legitimate duty. After all, such noninvolvement "gives us more time with our clients." However, it would seem that this is a forfeiture of a broader responsibility. Whether we are in a profession or not, we exist in a society that needs the assistance and advice of all who enjoy its benefits. An educated person whom society has trained owes his fellow men his active concern. Furthermore, he owes it to himself and his profession, because if he is not broadly enough informed, both his work and his clients may be hurt by community decisions in which his voice was not heard.

Let us consider two hypothetical case histories, which may illustrate this thesis. A child was born early this morning while we slept, who may be our client when he reaches middle age. Whether we shall ever actually see him or not, or if we do, whether we shall help him, may depend upon what we do for him in the intervening years. For, in a broad view of our responsibility, he became our client today. As the community molds him, he will be affected by the method, rules, provisions, and availability of education, health, and welfare services in which we are participants. Whether he comes to us at all: as a good candidate for rehabilitation, or as a poorly educated, deprived individual, whose diseased condition could have been avoided or alleviated by early detection and preventive measures, we now, at this time, have a responsibility to correct society's indifference, neglect, and lack of foresight.

We should not be selling the public the idea that we have magic. We in rehabilitation, in a misguided, but well-intentional effort, have been sinners by our promises. We should be admitting that our limitations cannot rectify, cannot cope with nor rehabilitate many individuals who come to us too late, at least in part because society and its health and welfare services have not entered the process soon enough.

John B. Carter, a man of forty-two, had a so-called "silent" heart attack, something that occurs in from 20 to 30 per cent of cases, after dinner last evening. He didn't realize he had heart disease, nor had a heart attack, and he still doesn't, since this kind of attack occurs apparently without pain. He will not see his doctor because he seldom goes, and would go only if a situation appeared serious. He is supporting a large family and, to use his words: "What with my wife and children's illnesses, it's expensive enough." If he went to his physician, there would be good chance that his condition would not be detected unless an electrocardiogram was done. His doctor may even be resentful at his coming without any real complaint, because the doctor doesn't wish to "waste his time on well people." He is too busy anyway to give substantial physical examinations with a waiting room full of patients.

We cannot duck this and say it was inevitable; that we cannot be responsible for the lack of concern for personal health on the part of an individual; for the absence of sophistication of the physician; for the clutter of people in his office, many of whom don't really need physical attention; and for the inadequacy of our health and welfare schemes, since these things are also our concern as educated, privileged, informed, insightful members of society. We, too, have a role: in preventive actions, in public health in medical and social services, and in community planning and organization, and this is also part of our mission.

Ivory towers no longer exist; a professional becomes a citizen of the world and its affairs even though it may be a painful position and a challenging one. Consequently, in the larger dimension of responsibility, the rehabilitation counselor needs to be involved and active in human affairs. Our profession can change society's values; can help give direction, focus, and emphasis, and can arouse sensitivity on the part of the public to human enhancement rather than satellite entertainment.

CONCLUSION

What is the justification for the investment of the one treasured life we have? Is the game worth the effort? Does it bring us happiness? The answer lies in the recognition that the investment of our selves yields a profit beyond price: a reward far above what we contribute. If we do not achieve this realization, we are missing the very best part of our professional endeavor.

Albert Einstein said: "To make a goal of comfort or happiness has never appealed to me. . . . The ideas which have always shone before me and filled me with the joy of living are goodness, beauty and truth."

Every man must determine for himself what he calls happiness. For in some men's estimation, we may never be happy. We may enjoy our work immensely and gain much satisfaction from its deep contact with human problems, but the result is a state called "divine discontent." This to some of us is happiness. It is a motivating force arising from knowledge and insight, which compels us to wish to improve what we find. It becomes something we cannot suppress or tolerate denial of, but must continue to enhance as a trust that men of similar purpose have given to our temporary keeping.

In some ways our profession is more complicated than that of a physicist, more influential than a politician, more freedom stimulating than the liberator, more life giving than a physician's treatment, and more soul saving than a clergyman's counsel. We do more than light candles for others to see, we help them find their own candles to kindle their hope of fulfillment.

A profession should make us more human, not less so; more loving, not less so; more dedicated, not less so; and we default on our professional birthright unless we can reach out to others and communicate this feeling of concern for the common bond among us all.

It is the food upon which our spirit feeds. It is the sustenance that helps motivate our clients to get well, or, rather, our fellow human beings to get well. We must give them this above all, and we must try even when they seem unable to accept it or profit by it. We fail others when we fail ourselves, and when we succeed with ourselves, we inevitably succeed with others.

Robert Oppenheimer, the eminent physicist said: "The world alters when we walk in." Not only has our presence on earth changed the world, but the decision we made to become a rehabilitation counselor is, perhaps, more serious and far ranging than we may realize. Not only shall our own life be changed, but the lives of the clients whom we serve will also be transformed. This will affect the lives of their children and the community and, to some extent, all mankind; indeed, the future of mankind.

THE CONCEPT OF OBSERVATION

The importance of observation is seldom sufficiently stressed. In some therapeutic professions it is almost a lost art. Yet, there appear to be unconscious impressions, subtle semiconscious cues, nonverbal manifestations, and, more apparent, perceptual information by critical examination, which come to us by association with the client. Observation then is no mere visual accounting of the client's actions, and it is more than a categorical assessment of his performances.

The therapeutic sciences today appear to suffer from a pendulum swing toward what is conceived to be a more scientific role—having come from an era of therapeutic inspection, when mere observation was almost the only tool available. Consequently, in the past, observation was stressed, particularly in medicine, and a skill was developed that was highly effective even though it was subjective and little concrete evidence could be offered to justify personal opinion. This "clinical impression" was accepted as legitimate. However, with the increase in instrumentation and a new generation of practitioners, as well as the assumption that the use of technology made one more scientific, the old "art" of observation was played down and even questioned. However, the best clinicians still revere observation, and it remains a vital part of clinical judgment.

We need hardly review the errors psychology has made with the misuse of tests, particularly intelligence tests. It was more than a professional mistake, for clients suffered from the decisions. Psychologists believe that the profession becomes a science as it achieves objective measurement. While this assumption is generally correct, it frequently traps them into mechanistic operations and colors associations with clients that cause the psychologists to miss other factors that are important to understanding the client.

The subject of testing is too large to be treated adequately here. Perhaps, however, the experience of the writer may tend to show a process that some may go through, leading to a greater appreciation of observation.

When one begins to study testing, it appears to be a wonderful tool. One picks a test or two and gives it to a subject, and one immediately knows all about him. This, or something like it, is a first stage.

However, with increased experience comes disillusionment. Somehow the magic disappears as the many pitfalls are recognized. Faith in the tests themselves is shaken. One finds that some are overpromoted by the vested interests of the author and the company that produces them. Even a feeling of victimization by a fraudulent practice troubles one. This is the second stage.

With continuing experience, one begins to reassess one's attitude and to gain perspective. Testing *is* useful when the test is carefully selected and the information achieved not overgeneralized, when the subject is prepared and understands the reasons for testing and, most importantly, when all such information is placed in conjunction with all other facts about the individual and assembled into a coherent picture. This clinical evaluation is the third stage.

However, this level is not sufficiently refined for handicapped clients. For the typical tests are not too appropriate, results are less valid, comparisons less secure, evaluation much more difficult, and errors of judgment more critical.

Before arriving at the fourth stage, one looks with envy, as most social scientists do, at what is usually regarded as the highly scientific and objective medical tools of measurement and assessment. How nice it would be to have this degree of preciseness in our psychological and vocational tools. However, again comes disillusionment as one finds that the same parallels exist. Medical instrumentation is far from perfect; equipment is possibly faulty; misinterpretation is frequent; a high level of sophistication is required to assess the findings; and, finally, many of the measuring devices are subject to the emotional and psychological condition of the patient, the implications of the setting, and the conditions under which the test is made. In addition, the assessor is not only subject to a routine observer error, but his own psychological condition tends to influence the patient as well as himself. Furthermore, there are other biochemical conditions of the body, often undetected, that can seriously alter the measurement. From a psychometric viewpoint, one becomes conscious that the problem is a more universal therapeutic issue.

Out of this experience comes further recognition of the illusiveness of man. Like Heisenberg's "Principle of Uncertainty" in physics, in which one cannot measure both the speed and position of an electron but only one or the other, it appears that when we hold a client in our office we cannot fully know him even though there may be some clues, for he is a different man with his family, at his job, and in the aloneness of his spirit. The short behavior samples we take are at best somewhat indicative but not necessarily prognostic in a changing client in a changing world.

One significant example in the medical field can be cited. A group of experts on hypertension were asked how many blood pressure readings should be taken to provide a good baseline. The largest number of the group said "twelve." There are two aspects that should be noted: the need for multiple measures, even of a single device, and the issue of getting a base over a time period.

Consequently, the fifth stage at which one arrives is the need, particularly with handicapped clients, to improve evaluation by a multiplicity of life samples, informal as well as formal, and under a wide variety of settings in which the client is in one way or another coping with life. This means observation in our office, at his home, at the workshop or rehabilitation center, at his training, in a recreational program, in the company of his wife and family, among his friends, at his work if he is employed, and other life-altering and life-revealing contexts.

Being verbal people ourselves, we usually can understand the articulate client and often do not feel as compelled to subject him to the kind of practical performance we seek from the less-verbal client. However, we can be fooled by a client who "talks a good game." Any such suspicion should be checked by observing some applied performance.

When the rehabilitation counselor is dealing with the inarticulate client, the culturally deprived, the experientially bereft. the emotionally disturbed, and others, he requires supplementary knowledge of the client's behavior that only real life samples can offer. Yet, even this will be no guarantee, since some of these performances will also be poor and not necessarily indicative of incapacity but of lack of qualified *experience* in the particular behavior sample that we have observed.

True, not all of these observational opportunities are readily available, but any increase in such samples would add to our understanding. The development of rehabilitation programs, of prevocational work evaluation and personal adjustment programs, of job sample testing and shop tryouts, are all examples of the circumstances of evaluation that utilize observational techniques and expose the client to new ways of learning and meeting realities that we have called a "living period evaluation."

THE CONCEPT OF THERAPY

The rehabilitation counselor is primarily a *therapist* who employs counseling as one of his major therapies and who understands and uses a great variety of therapeutic measures for his client. Any tool or technique of the profession is intended as a means of therapy in a broad sense. Frequently, many therapeutic professionals do not know the means and measures that could be utilized by them or by others for the benefit of their clients. Sometimes also they are not sensitive to the modifications that could be made of their own tools, which would lead to increased effectiveness. Furthermore, they are seldom sufficiently aware that the most important and critical means of achieving therapeutic goals is the counselor himself and that technique is not only secondary but can also be either useless or even antitherapeutic if he does not play his part properly.

An attempt to discuss a subject fundamentally is always faced with semantic issues, and tolerance by the reader is necessary. The concepts of therapy, counseling, and interpersonal communication are all involved with one another and are often the same things from different aspects.

Certainly, the fabric of rehabilitation is woven with the threads of many therapies and therapeutic measures and techniques. This tapestry presents a complex structure centered around the theme of purposeful activities leading to client development. Regardless of the colors used or the width of the threads, it is one unified picture.

PHILOSOPHY OF THERAPY

An effort to report the essentials of therapy begins with an examination of a philosophy of therapy. We need to do this in order to approach any prospective therapeutic measure with some recognition of the assumptions so that we may understand what it is, why we might use it, what we would be doing, how we might apply it, who may benefit, what might take place, how to measure it, when to modify it, and how it can be individualized, not only for the client but also for the therapist.

Such an understanding helps us to evaluate new methods as they arise and assess their relevance and use. It also gives us the opportunity to create new therapeutic ideas, means, or procedures that may be profitable and that can meet new and extraordinary circumstances.

WHAT IS THERAPY?

What is therapy? The word comes from the Greek *therapeia* and means a tending, a nurture, a service for the sick. One could define it as "a beneficial means, measure or instrument of a professional service directed to human need, which engages as far as possible the active interest and cooperation of the patient and therapist."

The objective is to evoke a favorable physical and/or mental response from the client. Therapy cannot have a uniform, prescribed method of application. As far as possible it must be a flexible, individually-tailored measure. It is a means by which the active participation of the client results in a synergistic gain: that is, it is greater than the mere sum of the client's and therapist's actions. It is a truism in medicine that "patients don't get better unless they want to." A given therapy can be useless, or even dangerous to the client's best interest, if he is uncooperative and rebels or over-reacts to its application or to the therapist.

WHAT CAN BE THERAPEUTIC?

Perhaps a more revealing question is: "What can be thera-peutic? It would seem that almost anything under the sun can be therapeutic to some extent for some people, with certain needs, at a particular moment in time, with the proper therapist, and with the conviction by the client that he wishes to be helped and trusts the procedure. The client may benefit from a word, a touch of the hand, the sound of music, the photograph of a happy occasion, or a placebo. As to the latter, there is a great deal of evidence that a patient's confidence in his doctor not only enhances real drug therapy but also that achieved by placebos. In fact, there are patients who benefit more from a placebo, when they have rapport with the therapist and a faith in the procedure, than others do with the actual drug; and if the real drug is given without patient support or trust, it may be worse than no action.

Most, and probably all therapies rest upon the quality of communication between therapist and client, so much so that one can use what amounts to the wrong therapy, as in a sense a placebo is, and yet obtain good results if the relationship is interpersonally responsive. Consequently, we need to recognize the symbolic nature of a therapeutic offering: therapy is an indication of concern, of acceptance, and of love for the client. It is a mode of believing in him, a faith in his response. We may choose our therapy wisely, and administer it according to prescribed conditions, but unless we arouse and exchange intangible feelings of rapport with the client, it may be a useless procedure.

A client improves under a therapist in whom he has confidence and trust. The counselor, social worker, physician, or nurse may become a therapeutic facilitator more powerful than words, drugs, or measures. If we learn this, our effectiveness will be related to our ability to utilize this insight.

THERAPEUTIC PRACTICE

This naturally brings us to the question of how best to use a therapy. One factor is the readiness of the client as well as the therapist. Who the therapist is may also be crucial. Under some circumstances the client may see the physician's ministrations as more powerful and effective, and in some instances the client will be more receptive to the rehabilitation counselor, social worker, or nurse. It may also depend upon what the particular therapy is, and whether the client sees the rehabilitation counselor as more appropriate in the role of therapist than the physician or any other therapist. This means, for example, that employment advice given by the well meaning physician can be not only a waste of time, but it can also force the client into unsophisticated solutions that aren't helpful and that he wouldn't conclude with the counselor.

PERSONALITY AND COMPETENCE OF THERAPIST

The personality of the therapist is important to the therapeutic procedure. In psychology or psychiatry, for example, we find the therapist selecting for himself the kind of therapeutic method most agreeable to his personality. The writer remembers hearing a lecture on psychodrama while in a state of mixed feelings about the relative value of the different approaches to counseling. The presentation was by Moreno, the pioneer in this field. It was far more a *performance* than a lecture. This therapist's histrionic and persuasive ability was so evident that one could easily see how suitable psychodrama was for him and how evocative it could be for his clients, but how equally poor it might be for another good therapist with a different personality and differing beliefs in therapeutic measures.

We cannot help everyone equally well. Perhaps there are some clients whom we cannot help at all. In any setting in which there are several counselors or therapists, it would be wise to try to match the counselor with the client. In psychiatry, a patient may not be accepted because of some incompatibility and is referred to another therapist initially or at some stage in the psychotherapeutic process, because of a possible interpersonal conflict.

Recent studies have shown, in the case of schizophrenics, that psychotherapy with the wrong therapist not only inhibits progress with the client but, unfortunately, actually depreciates his level of adjustment by the experience. The possible explanation for this is that the client has had his agonizing problems revived and has failed again.

SELECTION OF THERAPIST

In considering the question of which therapist to use for a particular client, one could include in this assessment not only the personality of the therapist and whether his therapeutic practice was suited to him but also the desire of the therapist to help the client. Some of us do not work as well as others with old people, young people, aggressive, complaining, or dependent people, or individuals with certain physical or mental impairments because of our feeling about the disability or our lack of special knowledge or experience. True, one cannot have a large number of any given therapeutic personnel at hand, but if a choice of therapist can be made, it may be highly desirable. Furthermore, the therapist should be conscious of his possible emotional and psychological blocks to certain kinds of people. The assumption that any good therapist can be equally capable with all people is foolish. Humanly, this doesn't work out any more than do marriages of incompatible people. It is evident that professional training, which can neither be comprehensive nor psychoanalytically cleansing, and the less-than-perfect screening of applicants for such training are at least partly at fault. It is also apparent that some individuals have been trained in the wrong profession, and others may be using a therapeutic method not suitable to their personality. These derelictions ought to be corrected by the profession, or in time society will take over the responsibility. They must be corrected most of all because it is unethical to decrease the client's chances for good treatment.

CLIENT READINESS AND SETTING

The client should be prepared for the therapy carefully: the appropriate time and occasion need to be chosen. The introduction to the therapist and the initiation of therapy must take the client's present state and background into consideration. How the therapy is described and its purpose stated, the role that the client is expected to play, and the goal to be achieved or hoped for, are all important in the planning. The environment and general surroundings may augment or detract. For example, this is why work therapy is not really effective in a hospital with its "pajama atmosphere." It is better when done in realistic work settings with therapists who are practically oriented to work and to the transmission of its values. This is also why the client's home instead of the hospital might be a better environment for a particular client and a special type of therapeutic endeavor.

We must then gauge the client's predisposition to a therapeutic process by understanding his physical, mental, social, and vocational propensities; by his image of the therapist's role, as well as his own perceived contribution and readiness. If we can learn the client's attitude toward his incapacity and what value, use, or loss it has for him, we may be able to specify our most appropriate method. If we do not take his situation into account, he may resist physically and mentally. For example, although we do not know the actual dimensions, he does have a degree of control over the various conscious, unconscious, and even autonomic responses of his body that may assist or lessen his favorable response.

Consequently, it isn't as much the therapeutic means or method as it is *what therapist* and *what client*. Moreover, the therapist must also gain emotionally as well as intellectually from the encounter, or he may transmit his lack of faith and disappointment with the affair to the client consciously and openly, or unconsciously and covertly, and thereby harm the client's progress. The real question is: With whom can the particular client develop the kind of empathetic relationship that will be profitable both to him and his therapist? On some occasions the setting and the circumstances can be altered as a general means of facilitating the therapy milieu.

THERAPEUTIC STRATEGY

An important factor in a therapeutic program is the therapeutic strategy. Often when therapy fails, it is not necessarily due to the medium used, but to the absence of fit in a structured projected design. We tend to think in a simple direct line and seldom see that a necessary adjunct to treatment is planning to cover errors of omission and commission, emergencies, unforeseen circumstances and changes in the client, and other contingencies.

In the physical sciences, if there is insufficient feedback correction, an entropy or disorganization begins to worsen, since perfect planning per se is beyond human capacity. We need to set up our model with the kind of organization that will tend to preserve its integrity. The design must allow for a continual check and measurement of results, and have substitutive, alternative actions or modifications ready to meet emergencies or failure in the process. Consequently, all therapeutic programming ought to be contrived in a logical, developmental sequence with alternative choices prepared ahead of time and opportunistic and emergency measures anticipated and inserted in the scheme. The struggle for a human life or human happiness is not inconsequential, and unless we organize a good clinical system our clients may move beyond the point of return.

Obviously, we can handle critical situations far better if we are prepared to anticipate them and have a projected therapeutic framework as a reference point for rapid application. Even so, the human mind cannot compete with the theoretically unlimited contingencies of a situation. Therefore, the assistance of the so-called "Electronic Brain" will undoubtedly play an increasing role in future treatment as an important assistive tool to the professional.

THERAPEUTIC MODULATION

Related to strategy is a flexibility of plan, which may be called *therapeutic modulation*. While it may be applied elsewhere, one may observe its relevance particularly in a rehabilitation center with a comprehensive team. In such a setting the exchange of opinions, the coordination of individual therapeutic plans, and the opportunity to devise a master plan that may deliver the needed therapy at the right time and in the proper sequence and with a variance of stress, produce maximum flexibility. This flexibility as an ebb and flow modulation of therapy is a quality that fluctuates coordinately with the client's changing needs and progress and permits alterations in emphasis.

One of the irrational decisions that occur in treatment is the assumption that a certain sequence of therapy ought to be followed. Frequently we find the assumption that therapy should begin with medical treatment or with therapeutic counseling or with something else. Often this decision is related to a professional who sees his discipline as the natural starting point. Of course, priority of attention varies with each client, and in most cases it would be some combination of therapies given concurrently.

Finally, we need to be careful lest we tend to use other therapeutic disciplines only when a crisis occurs, on what might be called on *ad hoc* basis. We need to consider their possible use from the very beginning. The phrase one often hears is that "we refer when indicated." Unfortunately, unless we are sensitive to the need it may never occur to us to refer. It is easy to make the decision that a bleeding client needs a physician or that one who insists he is Napoleon requires psychiatric attention. In reality, many mistakes will inevitably be made, because therapy essentially requires an expert who has been trained and experienced in the particular area to detect if and when help may be needed and to plan avoidance of pitfalls. Frequently, the specialist says: "Why wasn't the client referred sooner?" Perhaps the solution is better too soon than too late.

ESSENTIALS OF THERAPY

One may postulate a number of essentials of therapy and the therapeutic process that are not necessarily discrete and that do not necessarily apply equally to all therapies:

(1) A desire, a need, on the part of the client for improvement or benefit—either recognized or unconscious—as part of his "readiness";

(2) the importance of the client's understanding the purposes of the therapy;

(3) the necessity for the client to believe in the efficacy of the therapy offered;

(4) the need for the client to achieve a self-engagement, an involvement with the process and to make a self-contribution to it;

(5) the importance of the client's developing a rapport with the therapist and the setting;

(6) the belief by the client that he is improving (demonstration by some evidence or yardstick may be important);

(7) the need to create client opportunities for expressive release, either actually or symbolically, either physically and/or mentally;

(8) the importance of matching the personality and compatibility of the client and therapist;

(9) the need to select the most appropriate therapy or therapies and to time the application to the appropriate moment, with the most suitable emphasis or stress;

(10) the necessity for the therapist to believe in, and have confidence in, his therapy;

(11) a desire on the part of the therapist to serve this particular client;

(12) the ability of the therapist to achieve empathy with the client, to transmit it, and to continue a responsive exchange;

(13) the value of individualizing, altering, changing, or modifying the therapy to suit the particular client, commensurate with the client's progress or emergent needs;

(14) the need for awareness on the part of the therapist to the particular conditions or situations that may be therapeutic for the client and that may contribute to or be supportive of the major therapies; and

(15) the value of therapist's satisfaction in the process, since absence of this may detract from his performance and also may be transmitted in one way or another to the client, thereby harming his progress. Ideally, this return for investment should be an emotional and intellectual combine. The therapist needs a feeling of gratification as well as of solution to the intellectual challenge. Some therapists experience chiefly one or the other. The best experience both, or can be satisfied with either.

CONCLUSION

It has been a fascinating experience to see the large number of therapeutic means that have arisen. Each new approach presents its method and no doubt legitimately claims success. One could indeed be puzzled because in some instances the approach offered is apparently incompatible with other, older methods. Some of us become converts; some of us retain our love for our present system. Undoubtedly, however, each new successful method is essentially composed of the elements of many earlier proposals.

Do we not suspect that any constructive process that may be devised by man can be therapeutic if he uses it with concern, selectively, and in accordance with his own personality? Does this not open to us a glorious opportunity for the employment of our own creativity to construct new and untried means for aid to our clients, or, perhaps, to mold the clay of our present therapeutic idol into a more suitable model in which we can participate with our clients? Is not the effectiveness of this dependent upon our own breadth, our eclecticism, our clinical freedom, and our sensitivity to human need to contrive the unique method for each client? Does not all this tie in with rehabilitation and its emphasis upon totality and individuality of the human being called our client? Rehabilitation has certainly shattered the graven images nurtured by each profession that its models alone are the true faith.

XIV THE STATUS OF THE PROFESSION [1]

John E. Muthard

In thinking about what to say on the profession of rehabilitation counseling, the conclusion was reached that there was little new to be said. The best hope, if one may use the analogy of wine-making, is to try for a blend of the old and the new, of the fact, fancy, and philosophy that have surrounded this topic, in the hope that the blend will not only please the palate and warm the inner man but also make one feel a bit lightheaded. With this sense of lightheadedness, one can enjoy the slightly euphoric mood of being a worthy person in a worthy calling.

In the discussion that follows, an attempt will be made to describe the rehabilitation counselor as he is. To do this, the paper will present his origins, his training, and the nature of his work. Secondly, the paper will be about rehabilitation counseling as an emerging profession, the extent to which professional attributes can be ascribed to rehabilitation counseling, and some of the problems and issues associated with attaining professional status.

Some personal opinions will also be given about some of the things to be done if the promises and responsibilities that are associated with the aspirations for professional status are to be met. Finally, the future of the work to which rehabilitation professionals are committed, as practitioners, administrators, or teachers, will be discussed. An attempt will be made to examine some of the problems and issues that are now confronting the profession and that can be expected to remain for some years to come, as well as those about which one can only conjecture.

SOME HISTORICAL PERSPECTIVES

Others have chronicled the story of vocational rehabilitation's origins. This, then, is only a reminder that the legislation for and administration of vocational rehabilitation programs in the post-World War I period influenced and continues to influence counselor practices. It can be seen in the counselor who uses training as his prime rehabilitation resource for most clients, and sees his client moving in a stereotyped pattern through a process developed in the early 1920's. The long history of small, underpaid staffs, trying, with limited financial resources, to help large numbers of people cope with complicated rehabilitation problems nurtured a constricted, production-line practice of rehabilitation that is still influential. The rewards of demonstrating that rehabilitation was good business long fostered the view that rehabilitation clients should be good business risks.

It is well to remember that rehabilitation counselors had no association they could call their own until 1958. Many were members of the National Rehabilitation Association. However, this organization, although wielding substantial legislative force after employing an executive secretary in 1942, offered counselors only a limited forum for their ideas. It was not until the two existing rehabilitation counselor associations were formed in 1958 that counselors had a corporate identity. More will be said about these associations later.

Despite its short history as an occupation claiming a professional association, one should be mindful of the labors and vicissitudes of rehabilitation counseling's occupational forebears. Without significant help from universities, without established training programs, and without a focus for their professional aspirations, they worked unstintingly to meet their clients' needs.

One of the harbingers of modern approaches to rehabilitation was the Veterans Administration program during the post World War II period. The services and professional training programs fostered by VA provided a working model, high standards, a basic counselor curriculum, and, in 1954, proved to be the major supplier of teaching personnel for the new VRA training programs. Various authors have detailed the dramatic changes that followed the enactment of the Vocational Rehabilitation Act of 1954, including the prodigious growth in clients served, counselors trained and employed, and opportunities for research that anticipated the needs of the years ahead. This paper will focus on the counselor, his work, and his future.

WHO IS HE AND WHERE DO WE FIND HIM?

Before discussing the varied titles and settings for rehabilitation counseling, it might be useful to see how Jaques (1959) described the general aims of rehabilitation counseling: ". . . to help the disabled person through the client-counselor relationship to make the best use of his personal and environmental resources in order to achieve the optimal occupational adjustment—this being an integral part of the individual's adjustment in all areas of life."

Today, the job titles ascribed to counselors are not as varied or exotic as those found by Warren (1959). However, even though there is a national net of programs preparing rehabilitation counselors, and two associations with a total membership of 4,000,[2] the job titles used in state agencies and rehabilitation facilities do vary. In the current study of rehabilitation counselor roles and functions, the job descriptions submitted by state vocational rehabilitation agencies, general and blind, and by a large sample of rehabilitation facilities, indicate that the most common title today is "rehabilitation counselor." Others, such as "vocational rehabilitation counselor," "vocational counselor," and "counselor" are also fairly common. Although the sample of job descriptions included 23 different labels, there is a trend toward using "rehabilitation counselor" or variations of it as the official title, and a trend away from titles that describe the counselor as agent, supervisor, or specialist. Eighty per cent of the sample used one of the four titles just mentioned. Such findings are a sign that rehabilitation counseling is establishing a unique identity.

Though it is as true today as at the time of Warren's survey that rehabilitation counselors are found in many different settings, they are for the most part employed by three major types of facility —blind and general state agencies of the federal-state rehabilitation program; rehabilitation facilities such as rehabilitation centers, mental hospitals, halfway houses, sheltered workshops, and the Jewish Vocational Services; and the two programs of the Veterans Administration. Certainly there is diversity within these broad classes, and rehabilitation counselors do work for other institutions, such as schools, prisons, universities, workmen's compensation boards, and so on. However, these last settings account for only a small part of the total.

To get an impression of the major habitats of this hard-to-classify animal, some data from Sussman (1965) were examined. In preparing for their rehabilitation counselor career study, the Western Reserve University staff developed a national register of rehabilitation counselors in the spring of 1965. Table 1 shows the distribution they found.

Table 1—Total Study Population [3]

Category	Number	Per cent
VA	363	*8*
Benefits	166	4
Hospitals	197	4
Private agencies	586	*13*
General	499	11
Blind	87	2
BVR (Bureau of Vocational Rehabilitation)	3,610	*79*
Supervisors	780	16
Counselors	2,830	63
Total	*4,559*	

The confusion—or variation—associated with the counselor's job title has its counterpart in the papers that describe what the counselor is reported to do, expected to do, or should do. A bibliography of articles describing the rehabilitation counselor's roles and function published in the last ten years would take at least several pages. There is that well-known series of papers that describes the counselor's work from the point of view of a state agency supervisor (Johnson, 1957), rehabilitation counselor educator (McGowan, 1957), and, of course, counselor (Clements, 1957). A paper can be found to suit any theoretical bias. If one likes the client-centered view, there is Anderson (1958) or Patterson (1957). If one favors a more pragmatic and eclectic view, there is Lofquist (1959). One can find papers asserting that placement is a prime responsibility of the rehabilitation counselor, and others that would relegate this task to specialists.

Patterson (1957) avows that a rehabilitation counselor is a counselor and not a coordinator, while others insist that his role requires that he facilitate, expedite, and arrange services for the client. There are papers that assert that rehabilitation counselors of the future must be specialists, although many hold to the ideal of the generalist. There are also those who call for increased numbers of counselors with special backgrounds in mental retardation and mental health. It appears to be a favorite pastime of this fraternity to write about what people in this job should do.

Before describing research that examines the work of the rehabilitation counselor, a sense of humility can be drawn from the great expectations the Charlottesville Workshop (Hall and Warren, 1956) conferees had for them. Listed below are the 24 knowledges and skills the conferees thought the rehabilitation counselor needed. These include not only those competencies expected of counselors everywhere but also substantial medical information, knowledge of human anatomy and physiology, and the ability to interpret a medical report. In addition, he needs a sound understanding of community resources and their use, social legislation, occupational analysis, labor market, and so on. Their list of desirable personal traits for the ideal counselor describes a model that can only be approached by living man.

Table 2—Knowledge and Skills Needed by the Rehabilitation Counselor [4]

Successful rehabilitation of the disabled requires rehabilitation counselors to have professional competence.

Rehabilitation counseling has a professional scope that is concerned with all areas of the adjustment of the disabled.

The rehabilitation counselor demonstrates his competence as he applies his knowledge and skills to a great variety of operational problems. The knowledge and skills needed by the rehabilitation counselor in the performance of his functions include:

(1) An understanding of human growth and development; the effect of childhood and adolescent experiences upon adult behavior;

(2) an understanding of human anatomy and physiology; the effects of disease or injury on body structure, functions, behavior, and personality;

(3) an understanding of mental and emotional conditions affecting social and vocational adjustment; their nature, course, and probable cause;

(4) the ability to detect and identify the manifestations of disability—mental or physical—and to understand their relationships to vocational and social adjustment;

(5) a familiarity with medical information, therapies, prosthesis, services, and equipment designed to remove or minimize the effects of disability;

(6) the ability to use accepted methods and techniques of individual case study, recording, evaluation, and reporting, and to adapt procedures to the practices of employing agencies;

(7) the ability to establish and maintain a satisfactory counseling relationship;

(8) the ability to use methods and techniques of vocational and personal counseling to assist the client in achieving an understanding of his problems and potentialities and in planning constructively for his own rehabilitation;

(9) the ability to analyze occupations in terms of skills, physical demands, training requirements, and working conditions;

(10) an understanding of relationships of aptitudes, skills, interests, and educational background of the handicapped person to occupational requirements;

(11) an understanding of community organizations and of the facilities and procedures, policies, and limitations under which their services are made available to applicants;

(12) the ability to make use of available community services and resources in meeting problems of disabled persons and to maintain effective relationships with such sources;

(13) the ability to analyze the rehabilitation needs of a community and to organize resources to meet these needs;

(14) an understanding of the relationship of administrative policies and procedures to the counselor's work;

(15) the ability to organize his work to make the most economical use of his time;

(16) the ability to analyze reports furnishing medical, psychological, or social data and to interpret the relationship of such data to the needs of the client;

(17) the ability to carry on basic study and research growing out of his rehabilitation practices and to interpret and apply the findings;

(18) the ability to use consultative services both within and outside the rehabilitation agency staff;

(19) the ability to utilize national, regional, and state reports concerning industrial, occupational, and labor market trends; and to analyze specific community job information and opportunities;

(20) the ability to collect occupational information and use it effectively in counseling;

(21) the ability to orient employers to the employment of disabled persons;

(22) an understanding of federal, state, and local laws pertaining to rehabilitation and of related social legislation;

(23) an understanding of agency policies, practices, and standards as they apply to the counselor's work; and

(24) the ability to interpret agency policy, laws, and regulations to clients and others.

THE REHABILITATION COUNSELOR'S JOB: RESEARCH REPORTS

In this section there will be summarized the research that has systematically examined what the rehabilitation counselor does and how he spends his time. These have influenced the training programs considerably. In addition, a brief description will be made of the several major projects now under way to further study the counselor and his work.

COUNSELOR TASKS, SUBROLES, AND ACTIVITIES.

A pioneer and still influential investigation of the rehabilitation counselor's job duties is Rusalem's (1951) dissertation done at Columbia University. He divided the list of 179 functions he developed into nine major categories. These categories, which are listed on page 282, are still impressive as a fair outline of the counselor's functions. The counselors reported regularly performing a wide

Table 3—Rusalem's Nine Major Categories [5]

Medical diagnosis
Social and vocational diagnosis
Case finding
Counseling
Restoration
Training
Placement
Follow-up
Miscellaneous activities

range of activities in each of the nine areas. Approximately 90 per cent of Rusalem's respondents reported doing two thirds of the 179 functions listed, either regularly or occasionally. Certainly, Rusalem's study showed that in 1950 a rehabilitation counselor performed a wide range of tasks, even as he does today.

In another significant study of the rehabilitation counselor, Jaques (1959) applied the critical incidents technique—a job analysis procedure that focuses upon the critically effective or ineffective behavior of the worker—to study 404 rehabilitation counselors in various settings. We can see from Tables 4 and 5 that the two types of incidents most often cited as critical were the creation of a therapeutic climate and the quality of interaction between counselor and client. From the counselors' reports, she found that the ability to create a therapeutic climate has relatively more impact on client movement in effective than in ineffective incidents. The counselor's ineffective evaluative behavior was frequently mentioned as a deterrent to client movement.

In interpreting Jaques' findings it is imperative to remember that the original questionnaires requested counselors to describe incidents where they were most effective and least effective in *counseling* a client. These instructions may have focused the attention of counselors on events within the counseling interview rather than upon counselor acts outside the interview. That is, there is probably no justification in saying these are the critical incidents for the total role of the counselor. Rather, they should be thought of as incidents related to the core counseling role.

One gross way of examining the job of the rehabilitation

Table 4—Number and Per Cent of Effective Behaviors Classified in 7 Subroles According to Counselor Type *

Roles	I DVR Counselor N = 289		II [a] Counselor Other N = 63		III DVR Supervisor N = 52	
	No.	%	No.	%	No.	%
I₁. Creation of therapeutic climate	295	38.35	49	37.98	41	29.08
II₂. Structuring: arranging	69	8.98	3	2.33	17	12.05
II. Structuring: Defining limits	75	9.75	9	6.98	17	12.05
III. Information gathering	40	5.21	4	3.10	7	4.96
IV. Evaluating	39	5.08	12	9.31	10	7.10
V. Information giving	83	10.79	20	15.50	14	9.93
VI. Interacting	168	21.84	32	24.80	35	24.83
Total	769	100.00	129	100.00	141	100.00

[a] Type IV counselor data combined with Type II counselor data.
* Jaques, Marceline E., *Critical Counseling Behavior in Rehabilitation Settings* (Iowa City, Iowa: State University of Iowa, 1959), pp. 59–60.

Table 5—Number and Per Cent of Ineffective Behaviors Classified in 7 Sub-roles According to Counselor Type

Roles	I DVR Counselor N = 289		II [a] Counselor Other N = 63		III DVR Supervisor N = 52	
	No.	%	No.	%	No.	%
I₁. Creation of therapeutic climate	150	21.37	42	30.65	31	30.10
II₂. Structuring: arranging	70	9.97	3	2.19	6	5.83
II. Structuring: defining limits	72	10.25	6	4.38	9	8.74
III. Information gathering	66	9.40	13	9.49	12	11.65
IV. Evaluating	157	22.37	37	27.01	13	12.62
V. Information giving	45	6.41	12	8.76	5	4.85
VI. Interacting	142	20.23	24	17.52	27	26.21
Total	702	100.00	137	100.00	103	100.00

[a] Type IV counselor data combined with Type II counselor data.

counselor is to see what he devotes his time to during a given week. In Table 6 there are summary tables for this type of information, from papers by Miller, Muthard, and Barillas (1965) and the 1965 Guidance Training and Placement (GTP) Workshop. Rusalem's (1951) counselors used a different category system to report their use of time, but apparently spent about the same amount of time in counseling interviews. The three sets of findings suggest that state agency rehabilitation counselors, sampled at widely different times and in quite different settings, spend about a third of their time in counseling. Lest this seem cause for alarm, Bob Walker, who is assistant director of the Minneapolis Rehabilitation Center, reports that despite the best efforts of his counseling staff to increase the proportion of time spent with clients, it is almost impossible for them to get beyond the 40 per cent level. The counselor in university settings, who is usually regarded as the prototype of the counseling counselor, has difficulty devoting as much as 50 per cent of his time to the counseling function.

Rehabilitation counselors, along with their counterparts in many settings, are plagued with tasks that do not involve or require their professional talents. They are often assigned work roles and duties that might readily be done by persons without specialized training or experience. Thus, they often feel frustrated in meeting the many demands for counseling help. Measures can probably be taken to increase the proportion of time spent in counseling by rehabilitation counselors. However, within the present patterns of service, 40 to 50 per cent would seem to be close to the upper limit of the time one can expect the counselor to work in the counseling function.

STUDIES OF REHABILITATION COUNSELOR IN PROCESS

If one of the marks of an occupation that is striving for professional status is its willingness to study itself, then rehabilitation counseling may be coming of age. There is movement from the level of describing what the rehabilitation counselor is, does, and should do to studies designed to better understand rehabilitation counseling as an occupation and to provide a foundation for enhancing its stature as a profession.

The Regional Rehabilitation Research Institute at the University of Wisconsin is doing core research on the professional

Table 6—Weekly Time Distribution for Rehabilitation Counselor Activities

Activity	GTP STUDY * N = 139			IOWA STUDY † N = 30		
	% Time	Mean Hours	S.D. Hours	% Time	Mean Hours	S.D. Hours
1. Clerical work	8.83	3.53	2.86	7.0	2.8	1.52
2. Counseling and guidance	33.60	13.44	3.71	27.0	10.8	2.65
3. Overall planning of work	5.88	2.35	1.49	4.7	1.9	1.25
4. Professional growth activities	5.60	2.24	1.81	6.5	2.6	1.70
5. Public relations and program	7.98	3.19	1.91	6.75	2.7	2.65
6. Recording	10.57	4.23	2.36	18.5	7.4	3.30
7. Reporting	5.10	2.04	1.52	3.8	1.5	1.05
8. Resource development	5.97	2.39	1.93	2.25	0.9	0.85
9. Traveling				11.0	4.4	1.95
10. Placement work				4.75	1.9	1.85
11. Other	15.60	6.24	2.79	7.75	3.1	1.75

* Miller, L. A., Muthard, J. E., and Barillas, M. G., 1965.
† Office of Vocational Rehabilitation, 1956.
1. The category OASI Disability Determination was dropped from the GTP data.

functions of the rehabilitation counselor. As a first step in their research, they interviewed every counselor in Region Five. Counselors were asked to describe the problems associated with each of their many functions and to give recommendations for resolving their problems. They were also asked to discuss such problems as professional development, counselor recruitment, and public relations. Doctor Wright and his associates plan to issue a number of reports describing this research.

A second major project is being conducted by Dr. Marvin Sussman and his sociology associates at Western Reserve University. Although his research program will ultimately study a wide range of occupations in the rehabilitation field, he is studying the rehabilitation counselor first. He aims "(a) to determine the concepts of professionalism held by rehabilitation counselors; (b) to describe their career contingencies; (c) to determine changes in role concept, career plans, commitment, mobility and the like as a consequence of experience and learning of the job of rehabilitation counseling; (d) to determine how the rehabilitation counselor integrates his roles with those of physicians and psychologists in private and public agencies and hospital settings." This project has already published four working papers: *Professionalism and Rehabilitation Counseling: an Annotated Bibliography* (Sussman, 1965c), *Professional Associations and Memberships in Rehabilitation Counseling* (Sussman, 1965b), *Profile of the 1965 Student Rehabilitation Counselor* (Sussman, Haug, and Trela, 1966), and *The Practitioners: Rehabilitation Counselors in Three Work Settings* (Sussman and Haug, 1967).

The third project developed from the concern of the American Rehabilitation Counseling Association of the American Personnel and Guidance Association (APGA) and the training and research staff of VRA for a sound base upon which to establish training and professional standards. Begun in September, 1965, it will examine the present roles and functions of the rehabilitation counselor and relate these findings to professional standards and educational programs for rehabilitation counselors. In addition, the research staff will attempt to determine factors in the counselor's personality, work roles, and functions and in the organizational system of his agency that contribute to the role strain or conflict experienced by the rehabilitation counselor. This three-year study moved into its data collection phase in the fall of 1966, and is nearing completion.

Two other projects have important implications for the recruitment and placement of rehabilitation counselors. In 1966 The National Rehabilitation Counseling Association initiated a five-year program, underwritten by VRA, to facilitate the recruitment and placement of rehabilitation counselors. Also, the State University of New York at Buffalo with the aid of a VRA grant produced a film describing the work of the rehabilitation counselor.

Apparently, there has been and continues to be considerable interest in the rehabilitation counselor's work. A significant corrollary of the rehabilitation counselor research—counselor performance evaluation—will now be considered.

COUNSELOR EVALUATION

Since many writers regard autonomy and self-control as significant characteristics of a profession, it may sound anomalous to describe performance evaluation research. Research directed toward developing and testing various evaluative procedures is a necessary foundation for improving the effectiveness of the rehabilitation counselor and the rehabilitation counseling process. Whether we are concerned with counselor selection, training, utilization, performance, the use of rehabilitation specialists with graduate training or with training different from that of the rehabilitation counselor, or the development of new patterns of service and the like, thought must be given to criteria.

Prior to constructing a rehabilitation counselor performance rating scale based upon the Jaques categories (1959), those at Iowa thought it desirable to study evaluation practices used by state agencies: how presently used and available criteria related to each other, and how counselors, supervisors, administrators, and educators differ in their views of what a good rehabilitation counselor should do. Since more complete descriptions of these studies are available elsewhere (Muthard and Miller, 1966), only the relevant parts will be highlighted.

Findings from the survey of state-federal agency practices suggested two major criticisms. Since only half of the agencies were using standardized evaluation procedures, and only ten per cent of the traits listed on the Personnel Evaluation Questionnaire (PEQ) were rated by such forms, agencies needed to both develop and use systematic counselor rating procedures that covered the major aspects of the rehabilitation counselor's work. The lack of congruence between how important 29 PEQ traits were judged to be and the frequency with which they were required suggested that perhaps even more critical than standardized procedures was a need to clarify what should be measured.

In the study of the relationships among available performance criteria, cluster analysis showed two major clusters. The first of these was called "case management," since it included size of caseload, number of 12 closures, and number of 15 closures. The second was called "performance rating," since it included the three rating indices of the study. This study, along with the preliminary work on the Joint Liaison Committee (JLC) rating study and the findings of criteria studies for other complex occupations, strongly supports the need for multiple success criteria in rehabilitation counseling.

The differences between rehabilitation counselor educators and all other groups reacting to a set of 18 rehabilitation counseling incidents reaffirmed the admonition that the relevance and appropriateness of a criterion is a function of one's point of view. Educators as a group rated active, goal-oriented activity lower than did all other groups, including VA, JVS (Jewish Vocational Services), and trained DVR (Division of Vocational Rehabilitation), counselors. Whatever their rehabilitation setting, counselors and their supervisors appear to prefer active, facilitating and problem-solving roles more than do educators. Counselors who have their client's suitable employment as a ready index of success may be less tolerant of permissive, insight-developing counselor responses than are educators, who are prone to judge their effectiveness by how well their students conduct themselves in the counseling interview. In other words, counselors and administrators may focus more upon achieving agency goals, while educators are concerned more with the counseling process.

Although some type of rating procedure is needed as an intermediate type criteria for rehabilitation counselor performance, a satisfactory research based procedure has yet to be developed. Miller's (1963) Structured Case Review Blank (SCRB) required the supervisor to review the counselor's cases systematically and to assess his effectiveness in meeting various client needs. Unfortunately, it lacks utility for staff development, since the SCRB ratings were intercorrelated to a marked degree, with the range extending from 0.56 to 0.88, and the median intercorrelation being 0.75. Such ratings suggest the operation of a halo effect. However, they may also indicate that case records, at least in their present form, do not offer sufficient data to permit discriminating assessment of a counselor.

Through the Sub-Committee on Counselor Evaluation of the Joint Liaison Committee (JLC), agency administrators and counselor educators have continued to be interested in developing a satisfactory rating scale. An experimental rating scale has been developed and tested against such criteria as global ratings and rankings, agency records, and client satisfaction with the agency, his counselor, and his present job. Although it enables reliable rating of counselors over four factors, these ratings by supervisors do not appear to be related to the client evaluations of their counselor (Muthard and Miller, in press).

COUNSELOR PREPARATION

In the 1930's and 1940's, educators and vocational rehabilitation leaders expressed concern for the training of rehabilitation counselors. However, with few exceptions, the universities and colleges did not establish new curricula for this field until 1954.

Before moving on to developments following the enactment of Public Law 565, there should be some recognition of the pioneering efforts of Dr. Ronald Spaulding at New York University, who in 1941 set up the first curriculum in rehabilitation counseling in this country. Two other famous rehabilitation educators—Kenneth Hamilton at Ohio State University in 1944 and John Lee at Wayne State University in 1948—also developed special programs of study for rehabilitation counselors. It is significant that each of these programs was the outgrowth of work by dedicated men in different disciplines—vocational education, social work administration, and special education, repectively. This diversity was in keeping with the personnel practices of vocational rehabilitation agencies during that period. They were employing people from a wide range of backgrounds, who had experience in one of the helping professions and who had a genuine interest in aiding those whose disability created a handicapping condition.

The Vocational Rehabilitation Amendments of 1954 brought a complete change in the educational and professional picture for rehabilitation counselors. VRA, then the Office of Vocational Rehabilitation, moved immediately to encourage and support training programs in major universities and colleges over the country. As an initial step, it sponsored a conference, under the direction of the National Rehabilitation Association (NRA) and the National Vocational Guidance Association (NVGA), designed to supplement the more general document, *Counselor Preparation,* published by NVGA in 1949. As it turned out, the report of that conference— *Rehabilitation Counselor Preparation* (Hall and Warren, 1956)— influenced curricula development in the field substantially at that time, and it still does. It examined the work of the counselor as it existed in state and private agencies, the desirable knowledges and skills and the ideal personal characteristics needed of such workers, and then went on to outline the major subjects that should be included in such a curriculum. To obtain some idea as to how these recommendations compare with those suggested by Rusalem (1951), they are listed below.

Table 7—Recommended Subject Areas for the Preparation of the Rehabilitation Counselor

> An Introduction to Rehabilitation
> Legislative Aspects of Rehabilitation
> Human Development and Behavior
> Medical Aspects of Rehabilitation
> Cultural and Psychosocial Aspects of Disability
> Psychological Evaluation
> Counseling Techniques
> Occupational and Educational Information
> Community Resources
> Placement and Follow-up
> Research and Statistics
> Supervised Experience

Since Patterson (1958) has rather thoroughly reviewed the early literature on the preparation of rehabilitation counselors, this will not be discussed further. Rather, the growth of training programs, what should be incorporated in the curriculum, and what present curricula include, will be discussed.

By the fall of 1955, 26 universities and colleges either had begun programs or had secured planning grants from VRA. As is commonly known, this program continued to expand, until there were 39 programs in 1965–1966, and approximately 13 more schools initiated programs in 1966. It has grown from about 300 graduate students in 1956 to 1,400 in 1965, to more than 2,000 in 1966–1967, and an expected 3,800 in 1970. The VRA counselor education program, underwritten by two thirds of a million dollars in 1956, expanded to a program that authorized approximately $4,750,000 in fiscal 1966, with double that amount anticipated by 1970.

Although educators encourage and seek reactions from their students and graduates regarding the fitness of their curriculum for preparing the counselor to work in agencies and facilities, relatively little research has been done on this aspect. In the first and only published study of this type, Cantrell (1958) secured questionnaire data from rehabilitation counselors in state agencies, rehabilitation centers, and the vocational rehabilitation and education program of the Veterans Administration. Her summary findings indicated that with but two exceptions the counselors from the three different settings showed high agreement in their ranking of the importance of areas of study. These two showed the special significance of psychological testing in the VR and E (Vocational Rehabilitation and Education) program and, possibly, the academic origins of many of the practitioners in that agency.

The preeminent ranking given casework methods and the duties and responsibilities of the rehabilitation counselor by state vocational rehabilitation agency counselors reflects their concern for meeting client needs within the framework of agency procedures and practices. It was not unexpected that practitioners would give first place to skills and knowledges directly pertinent to their everyday practice, and place least importance on research, medical information, community resources, and rehabilitation concepts and legislation.

In 1962–1963, Division 17 of the American Psychological Association (APA, 1963) established an *ad hoc* committee on the role of psychology in the preparation of rehabilitation counselors.

It found that psychologists were heavily involved in rehabilitation counselor education. Three fourths of the program directors were members of APA, and another one sixth met APA's membership requirements but had not joined. Psychology was the major graduate field for 70 per cent of the group, with counseling psychology accounting for the largest share. Another 20 per cent had taken their degree in counseling and guidance.

The committee found that the extent to which psychology courses are required in rehabilitation counseling curricula does not differ by department affiliation. The typical program included about 75 per cent of primarily psychological coursework, and approximately 15 per cent of its coursework was somewhat psychological in nature. These findings were consistent with the earlier surveys by Patterson (1958).

Their recommendations for the curriculum in rehabilitation counseling presumed that rehabilitation counseling, like other fields of counseling, finds its basic tenets and rationale in the discipline of psychology. It asserted that the professional training of the rehabilitation counselor should be based upon psychological principles and knowledge. Admittedly, the outline was an ideal that most programs approached rather than met. As it stands, an undergraduate minor in psychology would be necessary to meet the ideal.

The Vocational Rehabilitation amendments through 1968 have created increased demands for rehabilitation services, not only within the state agency structure but also in rehabilitation facilities. Thus, Smits' (1964) estimate that there need to be 225–400 counselors per year for rehabilitation facilities alone is now a gross underestimate. Assuming that the greater funds available to rehabilitation resources will increase the demands for rehabilitation counselors in rehabilitation facilities by 50 per cent, the total demand for counselors for each of the next several years is approximately 2,000. The current manpower crisis, created by these rapidly expanding programs, cannot be met by the conventional procedures, either in state agencies or in the university teaching programs. The universities supplied only about one fourth of the need in fiscal 1967 and reached only 35 to 40 per cent of the total need in the following year.

The 1966 VRA report on counselor manpower suggests various novel approaches for adding counselor staff with B.A. degrees to state agencies and, at the same time, providing for graduate study in rehabilitation counseling. Such procedures as work-study plans, leaves of absence for a semester or summer session, extension work, and correspondence study would enable the working counselor to secure his M.A. From their position paper, the inference is that VRA believes that the fully qualified rehabilitation counselor should have an M.A. in rehabilitation counseling. It also provides for differentiating not only the job titles of rehabilitation workers with different amounts of preparation in rehabilitation counseling but also their career patterns and salary schedules. It seems to be a sound idea in that it assures that the competencies developed through graduate preparation will be retained as the standard and such preparation will be differentially rewarded.

The VRA guidelines and the Hansen paper (1965) in the McGowan report clearly suggest that the patterns of duties now performed by fully qualified counselors need to be examined to see whether the duties of the nonprofessional worker can be clustered to enable such workers to meet certain client needs within the vocational rehabilitation process. There are, of course, many possible ways of combining tasks needed to fulfill the rehabilitation of handicapped clients. Three patterns that have already been tested in an experimental study conducted by the Arkansas DVR (Division of Vocational Rehabilitation) (1961) include the use of an intake counselor aide, a physical restoration counselor aide, and a training and placement counselor aide. This latter cluster of duties is familiar to many in the form of the training officer within the VA rehabilitation program.

Universities need to implement new patterns for educating individuals interested in rehabilitation counselor careers, including many of those suggested by the VRA guidelines. For many institutions, the suggestions are not new, since the bulk of the school counselor population has been prepared by a wide range of training patterns. For the most part, the patterns suggested by the VRA guidelines make fewer demands upon the rehabilitation counseling student in training than do the methods that have enabled teachers interested in a counseling career to switch careers. As the report of the coordinators' meeting in 1963 (Joint Liaison Committee, 1964) shows, novel approaches have already been developed by many universities and colleges. In some cases, educators will need only to apply them to the local setting. In others, it may be necessary to press for modifications in graduate college requirements so that persons interested in rehabilitation counseling can become qualified within a work-study plan rather than solely through three or four consecutive semesters of graduate study.

The challenge to the state agencies may be even greater, since it requires that they no longer think of the counselor as a generalist who does all things for his client and works with clients with all types of disabilities and problems. This is no longer an efficient way to use a fully qualified counselor. Agencies need to use rehabilitation specialists who, although lacking graduate training, can be expected to provide certain services effectively.

PROFESSIONAL ASSOCIATIONS

One of the characteristics of occupations aspiring to professional status is the inevitable formation of an association to foster the interest of the practitioners in the profession. Although the establishment of associations to further the interest of an occupational group is hardly a distinguishing characteristic of professions, such associations are an integral part of the fabric of professional life.

In emerging professions such as rehabilitation counseling, the major impact of associations (Sussman, 1965a) is to establish standards for admission to professional membership. It follows that associations have an interest in standards of education and training. To promote the continuing education of their members, they publish journals and conduct national, regional, and state conventions. These activities are, in themselves, steps toward defining the place of the occupation in the social structure. Through their associations, the more mature professions have established standards of certification and licensure, which supply some assurance that practitioners meet minimal standards and also establish and perpetuate the autonomy of the profession.

The history of professional associations in rehabilitation counseling is brief, with many sharing in their development. Sussman (1965b) has summarized the major developments in the two rehabilitation counseling associations.

Since it is the larger group, the National Rehabilitation Counseling Association (NRCA), a division of NRA, will be described first. At the NRA meetings in Minneapolis in 1957, rehabilitation counselors, with the support of NRA leadership, initiated measures to establish a professional division for rehabilitation counselors within NRA. The desire of the counselor within the state vocational rehabilitation agency to have a voice in his own affairs, and the need for NRA to retain the loyalty of the critical core of its membership, were major determinants in the creation of NRCA. Officially established in 1958, NRCA proposed to advance the field of rehabilitation counseling by (1) increasing public understanding; (2) developing special training opportunities; (3) developing professional standards; and (4) encouraging research in the counseling field.

Until 1962, when the criteria for professional membership were set at the M.A. degree level in rehabilitation counseling or a related field, there were no academic requirements. To accommodate the many counselors who did not meet these requirements, a grandfather clause was set up, with January 1965 as the cutoff date. In 1965, NRCA established an executive office within NRA. At present it has approximately 3,000 members. NRCA publishes a quarterly newsletter (*NRCA News*) and at irregular intervals publishes NRCA professional bulletins.

The American Rehabilitation Counseling Association has its roots in two special-interest groups—counselors serving the physically handicapped and the mentally retarded—of the National Vocational Guidance Association. At the 1957 APGA Convention, steps were taken to form a division, and by the fall of that year, a tentative division had been established, with Salvatore Di Michael as its first president. In 1958, APGA formally gave it divisional status.

ARCA leadership has always asserted that the future of the field as a profession should be linked with APGA, which has a concern for counseling and guidance in all settings. They believe that the goals of continued professional development of the counselor, through the publications of the association and its annual meetings, can also be best secured within the APGA framework. Its constitution provides for fostering the rehabilitation of the handicapped by: (1) providing and encouraging professional relationships among rehabilitation counselors; (2) encouraging, promoting, and disseminating research in the field; (3) collaborating with other professional and national rehabilitation organizations; (4) establishing and maintaining standards of professional competence; and (5) providing leadership in developing the field of rehabilitation counseling. For professional membership, an M.A. in rehabilitation counseling or related areas is required. A grandfather clause was in effect until 1963. ARCA in 1968 had about 1,600 members. In 1967 it grew by 23 per cent.

ARCA members subscribe to the APGA code of ethics, but plan to supplement it to accommodate the unique ethical issues raised in rehabilitation settings. ARCA publishes the *Rehabilitation Counseling Bulletin,* a 48-page quarterly, which includes articles and research papers in the field and a 20-page section called "Digests for Rehabilitation Counselors." In 1966–1967 this was expanded to 56 pages per issue, and two supplementary issues are projected.

The impact of the American Psychological Association, as might readily be inferred from what has been said regarding training, has been primarily through the rehabilitation counselor educator group. Few counselors in state vocational rehabilitation agencies are members. Also, it is only within the Veterans Administration programs and in private rehabilitation facilities that APA membership is significant among practicing counselors. This appears to be directly related to the higher levels of training attained by counselors in these two settings and to the academic origins of the VA staff.

CRITERIA FOR PROFESSIONAL STATURE

Implicit in the title of this paper is the acceptance of rehabilitation counseling as a profession. Although the free use of the prestigious adjective "professional" might be used by any group of workers in an occupation requiring expertise to assert their right to such a designation, the rehabilitation field is not without descriptive criteria that characterize professions. The problem is in deciding which criteria to use. The criteria chosen seem to be a function of each proponent's frame of reference or purpose. Occupational sociologists such as Sussman (1965a) and Hughes (1958) have emphasized the distinguishing characteristics of a profession within the social fabric. Economists focus upon the existence of a corporate history.

Two relevant papers, which illustrate how criteria for a profession can be applied, look at the college student personnel worker and the rehabilitation counselor. Both the Wrenn and Darley (1949) and Obermann (1964) papers see the vocation they analyze as meeting many of basic criteria they set and being somewhat remiss on others.

To examine the extent to which rehabilitation counseling qualifies as a profession, the four qualities listed by Barber (1965) in a recent compendium on "The Professions in America" was chosen. By his definition, professional behavior has the following attributes:

(1) a high degree of generalized and systematic knowledge; (2) primary orientation to community interests, rather than to individual self-interest; (3) a high degree of self-control of behavior through codes of ethics internalized in the process of work socialization and voluntary associations organized and operated by the work specialists themselves; and (4) a system of reward (monetary and honorary) that is primarily a set of symbols of work achievement and thus ends in themselves, not means to some end of individual self-interest.

GENERALIZED AND SYSTEMATIC KNOWLEDGE

Most rehabilitation counseling students have little doubt that rehabilitation counseling requires a high degree of generalized and systematic knowledge. If the knowledge and skills recommended by the Charlottesville workshop can be mastered, we should be able to give a quick affirmation to this criterion. However, looking at the knowledge and skills required, it is clear that it is not knowledge uniquely developed by and for rehabilitation counseling that is referred to, but, instead, such disciplines as psychology, sociology and, to some extent, special education, medicine and labor and economics. Before seizing upon this point as evidence of the immaturity of rehabilitation counseling as a profession, we might well ask if it is not both necessary and desirable that rehabilitation counseling continue to draw heavily upon many behavioral and other sciences for its basic knowledge. It is clearly true for medicine, the prototype of professions, whose close association with the life sciences has enabled it to be markedly more effective in the 1960's than it was in the 1930's.

When we ask ourselves to what extent a similar liaison between the behavioral sciences and rehabilitation counseling exists, we can at best talk only of beginnings. As capabilities for meeting client needs improve, there will continue to be two developments that will affect the level of generalized and systematic knowledge. One of these will be research. We can anticipate that as the medical and vocational rehabilitation research and training centers and regional rehabilitation research institutes mature, they will provide a base for creating and testing new or, perhaps, unfamiliar concepts and approaches related to the problems faced by rehabilitation counselors. These university-based research facilities will, in combination with the expanding program of VRA-sponsored grant and programmatic research, assure a steady flow of knowledge and technology to the field. Thus far, this is more a promise than a fact. However, this state can be attributed to the brief period during which the VRA research programs have been operational.

The other development that is anticipated is the movement toward requiring the graduate student in rehabilitation counseling to come to graduate school with not only a broad general education but also basic preparation in the life sciences, including not only psychology and sociology but also human physiology, anthropology, and economics. This concept is already a reality at Penn State, where Ken Hylbert has established an undergraduate curriculum in the College of Liberal Arts that provides foundation preparation for either work or further study in the health professions. As college undergraduates and even high school students become aware of rehabilitation counseling as a career opportunity, more will come to graduate school with appropriate academic backgrounds.

Two other developments that may make possible the requirement of prerequisites for graduate training are the increasing numbers of students seeking graduate training and the increasing interest in careers that offer an opportunity not only for self expression and development but also for contributing to the well being of one's fellow man.

COMMUNITY INTEREST RATHER THAN INDIVIDUAL SELF INTEREST

From its beginnings, the occupation now called rehabilitation counselor has been a public concern, supported by legislation and public funds. Thus, even when the representative of the vocational rehabilitation agency was an agent and coordinator of services rather than a counselor, his actions served the community interests rather than his own interest. Although some psychologists have incorporated rehabilitation counseling into their private practice, this has been and probably will continue to be such a minute portion of rehabilitation counselor practice as to be of no significance. A prime characteristic of a profession has always been a personal relationship in which the confidence placed in the professional person by his clientele has required large individual responsibility from the practitioner. It is a relationship in which the *caveat emptor* of the marketplace is replaced by the admonition *credat emptor*. As Hughes (1958) and Sussman (1965a) state, it is a "relationship of mutual trust in which the client places his case fully and completely in the hands of the professional and in return the professional is given the freedom to act on the merits of the case without being judged except by his colleagues."

Whether professional status can be achieved depends largely on the profession's capacity to be worthy of the trust of the public. Embedded in the notion of worthiness is the assumption that a worthy practitioner is a competent practitioner, who has the knowledge and skill known in his domain of service and can render services in keeping with what is known at the time. Looking at some of the established professions, such as medicine and law, we can see that it was primarily by this standard that they could justifiably be called professions at the turn of the century.

There seems no reason to question whether rehabilitation counselors have a primary orientation toward community interests rather than to individual self-interest. One possible source of conflict that might arise would be the enactment of certification or licensure laws or regulations that interfere with the delivery of needed rehabilitation services to clients. With government and community agencies as the prime consumer of rehabilitation counselor services, this is not expected to occur.

CODES OF ETHICS

At this time, a separate code of ethics for rehabilitation counselors does not exist. The two professional associations have committees investigating the need for such a code and the possible form it might follow. Within the framework of APGA, there is a clear code of ethics for counselors, to which members of ARCA, as part of the parent body, subscribe. APGA has developed a set of statements and critical incidents that complement the ethical codes of APGA so that its membership have clear standards for the general problems they face as counselors. The ARCA Ethics Committee is considering parallel materials for the rehabilitation setting.

NRCA also has a committee that is actively examining this problem. NRCA and ARCA leadership think it desirable to develop a code of ethics that can be underwritten by both associations. Such agreement would seem to be in the interests of both rehabilitation clients and rehabilitation counselors.

SYSTEMS OF REWARD

A rehabilitation counselor clearly does not have the prestige associated with the traditional professions nor with those colleagues in related fields such as clinical psychology or college counseling. Granger's (1959) study showed that the rehabilitation counselor, as a psychological practitioner, rates very low in the status hierarchy of psychology. The public recognition of membership in an elite calling is not yet associated with rehabilitation counseling. On the other hand, the increased public concern for service to one's fellow man, as well as the more positive evaluation made of such work, presages public recognition.

The recent Porter and Saxon (1966) study shows that the economic well-being of rehabilitation counselors has improved substantially. An examination of the midpoint salaries listed for state agencies shows that the mean salary in 1965 was $6,909, compared to $5,798 in 1961. It is about $8,000 in 1968. This 19 per cent gain compares favorably with that of other professions employed primarily by public institutions. It is markedly better than the ten per cent gain among all wage earners for the same period.

THE FUTURE FOR REHABILITATION COUNSELORS

Whether the rehabilitation profession attains full professional status in the eyes of the public, other professions, and ourselves depends more upon extending the knowledge and competencies of practicing counselors than upon the ability to meet any other criteria for professional status. This goal can be seen as pivotal, because unless the rehabilitation counselor has something substantial to offer the client in his time of crisis and transition, and unless his services enable the community to meet its obligations to its disadvantaged citizens, the counselor cannot aspire to being a full professional man. To put one's fellow man before oneself, to have associations eager to further the interest of one's group, to have university training programs, and to work for the intrinsic satisfaction derived from knowing that one may aid others is not enough to make or sustain a profession. It is the obligation of all who are engaged in this broad endeavor called vocational rehabilitation to act as wisely as possible to ensure that more and more rehabilitation counselors measure up to high standards in their practices. This is a responsibility that must be accepted by the universities and colleges who prepare rehabilitation counselors, by the professional associations, by the rehabilitation agencies and facilities that employ them, and by the counselors themselves.

UNIVERSITIES' RESPONSIBILITIES

As the locus for the formal preparation of the rehabilitation counselor, universities have a great responsibility for providing the fundamental, generalized and systematic knowledge that is basic to the professional performance of the rehabilitation counselor. Recalling the earlier discussion of training, the universities can best meet this obligation by providing basic preparation in counseling, vocational psychology, rehabilitation, and other related areas. The universities must continue to prepare generalists in rehabilitation counseling, as opposed to individuals who are equipped to function within only one type of agency setting or with only one type of disability. Specialization must follow basic preparation.

Although the student's preparation for development in, identification with, and commitment to, rehabilitation counseling is a responsibility of his teachers, this does not mean that it is the universities' responsibility to produce finished rehabilitation counselors, fully equipped to take their places in the vocational rehabilitation picture. Rather, the universities can be seen as providing the fundamental training in the manner that Martin (1964) recommended. In comparing the two diametrically opposed courses being followed by professional schools, the satellite or trade-school approach and what he labels the university approach, Martin said: "The educator must disavow his interest in education for practice but avow an interest in education for growth in practice. Instead of education for practice, the student is given the opportunity to learn how to learn in the field of practice. The student is given the basic method needed to solve problems, the scientific method. He is taught to apply the information of current research in the basic disciplines to problems in his profession." His approach is in keeping with the view that to be a professional necessitates remaining abreast of new developments in the field.

It follows from this explanation that the university certainly has an obligation to contribute to the continuing education of rehabilitation counselors. This obligation is now being met in a wide variety of ways (JLC, 1964). However, much remains to be learned about how best to meet the needs of rehabilitation counselors.

Not the least of the universities' obligations is their role in the creation of new knowledge, their work in developing and testing new approaches, and their responsibility for providing scholars who can collate the flow of information from the social, biological, and medical sciences that are the bedrock of rehabilitation. It seems that one of the major needs in the rehabilitation field is a mode of operation that encourages and satisfactorily rewards capable people, who now invest their energies in more prestigious research papers, for turning their talents to the difficult but equally important task of preparing critical reports on the state of the art in various areas—people who can take the almost indigestible outpourings of rehabilitation-related disciplines and translate them into comprehensible overviews that can be mastered within reasonable periods of time.

The universities are partners with VRA in focusing university resources on research relevant to vocational rehabilitation. The associations in the rehabilitation field also have an obligation, through their publications, conventions, and standards, for promoting the high degree of generalized and specific knowledge critical to the profession. More must be done to make important new ideas and developments in rehabilitation available to the counselors through readily accessible journals and publications.

The ambitious counselor who, in addition to the basic association journals, regularly reads the *Rehabilitation Record, Rehabilitation Literature,* and the *Journal of Counseling Psychology* is still faced with the disconcerting fact that ideas and research results that he should know about are passing him by. This includes papers appearing in the journals of the American Psychological Association, the American Sociological Association, and the many medical publications. Several of the publications mentioned succeed in meeting this need in part, but none completely.

PROFESSIONAL ASSOCIATIONS RESPONSIBILITIES

The annual meetings of both professional associations make greater contributions to their members' continued education today than they have in the past. However, they too must be strengthened as media for improving the range and quality of counselors' knowledge. One possibility would be to forego the substantial amount of time invested in inspirational, "big think" talks, as well as those ten- or fifteen-minute research reports, which are so abbreviated as to be comprehensible only to their author and a few other people. We could instead use more and more symposia that present critical evaluative summaries of important areas of rehabilitation. The communication and learning objectives of conventions should become paramount.

EMPLOYER RESPONSIBILITIES

Since he determines what the counselor shall do and judges how well he is doing it, the employer is in a critical position to affect the quality of knowledge and competency associated with the rehabilitation counselor's role. If the employer subscribes to the principles and recommendations suggested in the recent VRA Guidelines for Action on the rehabilitation counselor manpower problem, he will enhance it. If he elects to meet the goals of his agency by employing individuals without specific training and asserts that these individuals can provide the full range of vocational rehabilitation counseling services, he will detract from it. If he assigns work to qualified counselors in accord with their training and experience, and employs support personnel to perform tasks that do not require the special skills and knowledge of the counselor, he supports the goals of professional competence and knowledge. If his job assignments provide the counselor little opportunity to use his special knowledge and skill, he does not support it. If he measures success primarily by the number of rehabilitation closures, without substantial consideration for the quality of the services given by the counselor, he is undermining rather than strengthening the profession's ideal. Whatever his views, the employer or supervisor's power to give or withhold improved position or economic status can be expected to shape the work patterns of rehabilitation counselors.

REHABILITATION COUNSELORS' RESPONSIBILITIES

Certainly, the most important determinants of the future of rehabilitation counseling as a profession are the counselors themselves. Although all rehabilitation counselors share this responsibility, by its very nature it will be borne most by those who have or are seeking formal training. It is the counselor himself, through his associations and work methods, who will determine whether rehabilitation counseling will fulfill its aspirations for professional status. Although the power and leverage of the state and federal agencies, the universities, and professional associations may cause him to wonder whether what he does makes a difference, it seems that he must answer this question in the affirmative.

Leaders in government, universities, and professional associations also see the counselor as the key to the future of vocational rehabilitation. Whether rehabilitation counseling can and will move from the position of a marginal profession to full professional status depends largely upon the quality of the counselor's present performance. It depends on his ability to demonstrate to clients and collaborating rehabilitation workers that he has unique skills to contribute to the rehabilitation of his clients and is worthy of their trust.

The counselor himself must assume considerable responsibility for his own continued professional growth. As suggested before, the resources for continued education today are for the most part either poorly organized or inaccessible. It is the counselor, individually and through his associations, who must press for patterns of continuing education that help him meet the professional ideal. It is the mark of a profession that its members have a commitment to their work beyond meeting the day-to-day demands of the job, a commitment that assumes that membership in the profession requires continued personal effort to keep abreast of new developments, to respond to the needs of clients in creative ways, and to assimilate new developments in ways that meet their clients' needs. Clearly, the counselor himself has the greatest responsibility for determining the value and status of his job. His stake in it is high, not primarily because he has so much to gain in prestige and income but because his clients' opportunities for enriched lives depend upon his knowledge and competency and his own feelings of worth depend upon how well he does his job.

At this time there is no simple reply to the question, "Is rehabilitation counseling a profession?" Counselors employed in the Veterans Administration programs definitely meet the major criteria suggested by Barber and others. Some of the rehabilitation facilities and agencies that have high educational and performance standards for their counseling staff and have judiciously used support personnel to strengthen their total service program, have enhanced the professional stature of the rehabilitation counselor. Unfortunately, it is still true that some counselor employers have educational standards for, and work expectations from, counselors that can result only in dissuading those with professional aspirations and competencies from joining their organization.

In summary, we could say that some rehabilitation counselors, in some places, meet the requirements of a profession very well, but that in the main, rehabilitation counseling must be classed as an emerging profession. Much remains to be done before the profession can confidently say it has emerged from the status of a marginal profession to one with wide public acceptance as a profession on a par with such groups as lawyers, psychologists, and teachers.

NOTES

1. Presented at Seton Hall University, South Orange, N.J. on May 3, 1966, as part of the Guest Lecture Series on Principles and Practices of Vocational Rehabilitation.

2. In October, 1967, NRCA had approximately 3,800 members and ARCA, 1,500.
3. Career Contingencies of the Rehabilitation Counselor Professions Project. *Professional Associations and Memberships in Rehabilitation Counseling,* Working Paper No. 2 (Cleveland: Western Reserve University, 1965).
4. Hall, J. H., and Warren, S. L., eds., *Rehabilitation Counselor Preparation* (Washington, D.C.: National Rehabilitation Association, 1956), pp. 20–22.
5. Rusalem, H., "An Analysis of the Functions of State Vocational Rehabilitation Counselors with Implications for the Development of a Training Course at Teachers College, Columbia University," unpublished doctoral dissertation (Columbia University, 1951).

DISCUSSION QUESTIONS

1. Whitehouse makes a strong case for rehabilitation counselors having a firm commitment to their profession. Does this conflict with the counselor's having a similar professional commitment to his client, his agency, and society in general?

2. Whitehouse describes both explicit and implicit criteria for a profession. The explicit criteria include degrees, certification, codes of ethics, and a body of knowledge. The implicit criteria include commitment, responsibility, and integrity. Although the implicit criteria often are even more important to a profession than the explicit, they are frequently disregarded because it is so difficult to measure them. How can these implicit variables be evaluated?

3. Strict adherence to a code of ethics might cause a counselor to behave in ways that appear injurious to a client, for example, not criticizing a colleague whose ineptness is damaging the client. Faced with such a dilemma, how would you behave? It has been stated that ethics sometimes are adopted by a profession not so much for the protection of the client as for the benefit of the professional worker or society. Would you agree? Why?

4. If college and university grades are abandoned, as has been suggested in some quarters, will we lose an important means of ascertaining professional competence? Would this be compatible with the concept of professional standards?

5. "Professional nationalism" allegedly contributes to the rehabilitation counselor's functioning level in that it delimits his activities. In view of the coordinating and team roles that most counselors are required to assume, can such "nationalism" deter professionalization as well as abet it? How?

6. The research evidence cited by Muthard indicates that rehabilitation counselors assume many functions, use the knowledge and skills of many disciplines, and operate in many different types of settings. Is it reasonable to expect that an undergraduate liberal arts program or even a two-year master's degree curriculum can prepare counselors adequately for this complex responsibility? Given the alternatives of redesigning the job so that it requires less comprehensive preparation, or extending the period of preservice training, which would you prefer? Why?
   In-service training is sometimes mentioned as a solution to this dilemma. What are the strengths and weaknesses of relying on this approach?

7. A variety of administrative and clinical reasons are offered to explain why counselors seem to devote only 40 per cent or less of their time to counseling duties. Would you agree that the major reason that this is so is the overwhelming volume of paper work and noncounseling duties assigned to counselors? Why? Some authors have hypothesized that this modest amount of counseling may be a function of the unconscious avoidant behavior of poorly trained counselors who prefer to work in more routine areas in which they feel more secure. Is there validity to this hypothesis?

8. A number of professional organizations enrol rehabilitation counselors in their ranks and presume to speak for them to some extent, for example, the American Psychological Association, the American Personnel and Guidance Association, and the National Rehabilitation Association. Which of these organizations seems best qualified to speak for rehabilitation counselors on professional matters? Why?

9. Much controversy has developed around the use of subprofessional personnel in rehabilitation. Is it possible that some of

the resistance to subprofessionals reflects the inadequate training of some counselors? That these counselors feel threatened because they do not see themselves as more skilled than the subprofessionals?

10. What is the relationship between membership in professional organizations and the development of professional criteria?

BIBLIOGRAPHY

PART I—VOCATIONAL REHABILITATION:
PAST AND PRESENT

"Action for Mental Health." Digest of Final Report of Joint Commission on Mental Illness and Health. *The Modern Hospital,* March, 1961.

Babor, Irving. "Vocational Rehabilitation and Re-Employment of Psychiatric Patients in the U.S.A.," pp. 171–74. Proceedings of Ninth International Congress, Denmark, 1963. *International Society for Rehabilitation of Disabled.*

Campbell, Ian. "Introductory Remarks by Chairman," p. 198 in "Disability, Prevention-Rehabilitation." Proceedings of Ninth World Congress, *Ibid.*

Deutsch, A. *The Mentally Ill in America.* New York: Columbia University Press, 1949.

Di Michael, S. G. "Emotional Effects of Physical Disability on Religious Attitudes," pp. 150–66. American Catholic Psychological Association, Fordham University, New York, 1960.

Kirk, Samuel. "Educating the Handicapped," pp. 100–07. *White House Conference on Education,* August, 1965. Washington, D.C.: U.S. Government Printing Office.

Mental Illness and Its Treatment: Past and Present. U.S. Department of Health, Education, and Welfare, Public Health Service Publication #1345, 1965.

National Action to Combat Mental Retardation. President's Panel on Mental Retardation, October, 1962. Washington, D.C.: Government Printing Office.

Ninth World Congress, Session 12 on "Congenital Defects," pp. 177–97, *Ibid.*

Obermann, C. Esco. *A History of Vocational Rehabilitation in America.* Minneapolis, Minn.: T. S. Denison and Co., Inc., 1965.

Ranta, Aarno. "Placement Principles," pp. 205–09, in "Disability

Prevention-Rehabilitation." Proceedings of the Ninth World Congress, *Ibid.*

U.S. Department of Health, Education, and Welfare. Public Health Service, Vital and Health Statistics, Series 10, No. 9, 1964, pp. 52 and 58.

U.S. Department of Health, Education, and Welfare. Annual Report 1964, Vocational Rehabilitation Administration, pp. 327–65. Washington, D.C.: Government Printing Office.

Vocational Rehabilitation Act Amendments of 1965. Report of Senate Committee on Labor and Public Welfare, September 30, 1965.

Wright, Beatrice A. (ed.). *Psychology and Rehabilitation.* Washington, D.C.: American Psychological Association, 1959.

PART II—PHILOSOPHICAL VIEWPOINTS

Barker, R. G., and Wright, H. F. (1955). *Midwest and Its Children: the Psychological Ecology of an American Town.* Evanston, Ill.

Becker, H. S., and Strauss, A. L. "Careers Personality and Adult Socialization," *American Journal of Sociology,* 1956, 62.

Berle, A. A., Jr. "Jobs for the Displaced: a Public Responsibility," in R. M. Hutchins and M. J. Adler (eds.), *The Great Ideas Today—Work, Wealth, and Leisure.* New York: Atheneum Publishers, 1965.

Bieri, J., Lobeck, R., and Plotnick, H. "Psychosocial Factors in Differential Social Mobility," *Journal of Social Psychology,* 58, 1962, 183–200.

Bloom, Benjamin S. *Stability and Change in Human Characteristics.* New York: John Wiley, 1964.

Breytspraak, Charlotte. *The Relationship of Parental Identification to Sex Role Acceptance in Married, Single, Career and Noncareer Women.* Ed.D. thesis for Teachers College, Columbia University, 1964.

Buehler, C. *Der menschlich lebenslauf als psychologisches problem.* Leipzig: Hirzel, 1933.

Davis, Allison. "The Motivation of the Underprivileged Worker," in W. F. Whyte (ed.), *Industry and Society.* New York: McGraw-Hill Book Co., 1946.

Dembo, T., Leviton, G. L., and Wright, B. A. (1956). "Adjustment to Misfortune—a Problem of Social Psychological Rehabilitation, *Artificial Limbs,* 3, 4–62.

Heider, F. *The Psychology of Interpersonal Relations.* New York: Wiley, 1958.

Henderson, Harold L. *The Relationships Between Interests of Fathers and Sons and Sons' Identifications with Fathers.* Ph.D. thesis for Columbia University, 1958.

Herman, Mary W. "Class Concepts, Aspirations, and Vertical Mobility," in Gladys L. Palmer, *et al., The Reluctant Job Changer.* Philadelphia: University of Pennsylvania Press, 1926.

Inkeles, A. "Social Stratification and Mobility in the Soviet Union," in R. Bendix and S. M. Lipset (eds.), *Class, Status and Power.* Glencoe, Ill.: Free Press, 1963.

Ibid. "Industrial Man: the Relation of Status to Experience, Perception, and Value," *American Journal of Sociology,* 66, 1960.

Jackson, E. F., and Crockett, H. J., Jr. "Occupational Mobility in the United States," *American Sociological Review,* 29, 1964, 5–15.

LoCascio, Ralph. "Delayed and Impaired Vocational Development," *Personnel and Guidance Journal,* 43, 1964, 885–87.

Miller, D. C., and Form, W. H. (eds.). *Industrial Sociology.* New York: Harper, 1951, revised 1964.

Mulvey, Mary C., "Psychological and Social Factors in Prediction of Career Patterns of Women," *Genetic-Psychological Monographs,* 68, 1963, 309–86.

Newman, H. H., Freeman, F. N., and Holzinger, K. J., *Twins: a Study of Heredity and Environment.* Chicago: University of Chicago Press, 1937.

Owens, W. D. "Age and Mental Abilities," *Genetic Psychological Monograph,* 48, 1953, 3–54.

Palmer, Gladys L. "Attachments to Occupation and to Company," in Gladys L. Palmer, *et al., The Reluctant Job Changer.* Philadelphia: University of Pennsylvania Press, 1926.

Roe, Anne. *The Psychology of Occupations.* New York: John Wiley and Sons, 1956.

Roe, Anne, and Baruch, Rhoda. *Factors Influencing Occupational Decisions: a Pilot Study.* Harvard Studies in Career Development, No. 32. Cambridge, Mass.: Center for Research in Careers, Graduate School of Education, Harvard University, 1964.

Rogoff, Natalie. "Recent Trends in Urban Occupational Mobility," in R. Bendix and S. M. Lipsett (eds.), *Class, Status and Power.* Glencoe, Ill.: Free Press, 1963.

Scheerer, M. (1954). "Cognitive Theory," in G. Lindzey (ed.),

Handbook of Social Psychology, pp. 91–142. Cambridge: Addison-Wesley.

Schneider, L. Ronald. *The Relationship Between Identification with Mother and Home or Career Orientation in Women.* Ph.D. thesis for Columbia University, 1962.

Skeels, H. M. "Some Iowa Studies of Mental Growth of Children in Relation to Differentials of the Environment," *Yearbook of National Social Study of Education*, 1940, 39, 281–308.

Super, D. E. *et al. Career development: Self Concept Theory.* New York: College Entrance Examination Board, 1963.

Super, D. E. "The Definition and Measurement of Early Career Behavior," *Personnel and Guidance Journal.* 41, 1963, 775–80.

Ibid. Psychology of Careers. New York: Harper, 1957.

Tilgher, Adriano. "Work Through the Ages," in S. Nosow and W. H. Form (eds.), *Man, Work, and Society.* New York: Basic Books, Inc., 1962.

Vygotsky, L. S. *Thought and Language.* Cambridge, Mass.: M.I.T. Press and New York: John Wiley & Sons, Inc., 1962.

Wright, B. A. *Physical Disability—A Psychological Approach.* New York: Harpers, 1960.

Yasuda, S. "A Methodological Inquiry into Social Mobility," *American Sociological Review*, 29, 1964, 16–23.

PART III—THE VOCATIONAL REHABILITATION PROCESS

Barshop, I. "Policy and Practices in Hiring Impaired Workers," *Journal of Rehabilitation*, 25 (6), 1959, 23–25.

Carmichael, B. "Meanings of 'readiness,' " *Vocational Guidance Quarterly*, 10, 1962, 209–13.

Committee on Education and Labor, House of Representatives. *Restoring Disabled People to Jobs and Useful Living.* Washington, D.C.: U.S. Government Printing Office, 1965.

Cooperation . . . the Key to Jobs for the Handicapped. Washington, D.C.: American Federation of Labor and Congress of Industrial Organizations, no date.

Guide to Job Placement of the Mentally Retarded. Washington, D.C.: The President's Committee on Employment of the Handicapped, 1963.

Handbook for Young Workers. Washington, D.C.: U.S. Department of Labor, 1965.

Hanman, B. *Physical Capacities and Job Placement*. Stockholm: Nordisk Rotogravyr, 1951.

Hart, W. R. "Effective Approaches to Employers," *Rehabilitation Record*, 3 (2), 1962, 34–37.

Hiring Handicapped People. New York: National Association of Manufacturers, 1965.

Hoppock, R. *Occupational Information*. New York: McGraw-Hill, 1963.

How to Get and Hold the Right Job. Washington, D.C.: U.S. Department of Labor, 1962.

Jacobs, A. T. *How to Use Handicapped Workers*. New York: National Foremen's Institute, 1946.

Lillehaugen, S. T. "District Placement Counselors Can Boost Jobs for Handicapped," *"Rehabilitation Record,* 5 (2), 1964, 29–31.

Merchandising Your Job Talents. Washington, D.C.: U.S. Department of Labor, 1964.

Odell, C. H. "The Problem of Placement," *Journal of Rehabilitation*, 21 (6), 1955, 6–8 and 16–17.

Patterson, W. E. "The Facts Behind Apprenticeships," *Vocational Guidance Quarterly*, Winter 1953, 56–58.

Pearl, A., and Riessman, F. *New Careers for the Poor*. New York: The Free Press, 1965.

Scott, T. B., *et al*. *A Definition of Work Adjustment*. Minneapolis: University of Minnesota, 1958.

Shartle, C. L. *Occupational Information*. Englewood Cliffs, N.J.: Prentice-Hall, 1959.

Sinick, D. "Placement's Place in Guidance and Counseling," *Personnel and Guidance Journal*, 34, 1955, 36–40.

Sinick, D. (ed.) *Placement Training Handbook*. Washington, D.C.: Vocational Rehabilitation Administration, 1962.

So You Are Going to Supervise a Mentally Retarded Employee. Washington, D.C.: Vocational Rehabilitation Administration, 1964.

Stein, B. "Unions and the Young Worker," *Vocational Guidance Quarterly*, 10, 1962, 196–201.

Supervising the Physically Impaired. New York: Association of Casualty and Surety Companies, 1945.

The Physically Impaired: A Guidebook to Their Employment. New York: Association of Casualty and Surety Companies, 1952.

The Youth You Supervise. Washington, D.C.: U.S. Department of Labor, 1965.

Thomason, B., and Barrett, A. M. (eds.). *The Placement Process in Vocational Rehabilitation Counseling.* Washington, D.C.: Vocational Rehabilitation Administration, 1960.

Thompson, Doris M. *The Company and the Physically Impaired Worker.* New York: National Industrial Conference Board, 1957.

Thompson, Dorothy B. *Guide to Job Placement of the Mentally Restored.* Washington, D.C.: The President's Committee on Employment of the Handicapped, 1965.

Training and Reference Manual for Job Analysis. Washington, D.C.: U.S. Department of Labor, 1965.

Wagner, T. *Selective Job Placement.* New York: Association of Casualty and Surety Companies, 1946.

Why Young People Fail to Get and Hold Jobs. Albany: New York State Employment Service, 1963.

Workers Worth Their Hire. Chicago: American Mutual Insurance Alliance, 1961.

PART IV—COUNSELING

Allport, G. W. "Psychological Models for Guidance," *Harvard Educational Review,* 1962, 32, 373–81. Reprinted in Mosher, R. R., Carle, R. F., and Kehas, C. D. (eds.). *Guidance: An examination.* New York: Harcourt, Brace and World, 1965. Pp. 13–23.

Cartwright, D. S., and Cartwright, Rosalind D. "Faith and Improvement in Psychotherapy," *Journal of Counseling Psychology,* 5, 1958, 174–77.

Ellis, A. "Requisite Conditions for Basic Personality Change," *Journal of Consulting Psychology,* 23, 1959, 538–40.

———, *Reason and Emotion in Psychotherapy.* New York: Lyle Stuart, 1962.

Fiedler, F. "The Concept of an Ideal Therapeutic Relationship," *Journal of Consulting Psychology,* 14, 1950, 235–45.

Ibid. "A Comparison of Therapeutic Relationships in Psychoanalytic, Nondirective and Adlerian Therapy," *Journal of Consulting Psychology,* 14, 1950, 436–45.

Ibid. "Factor Analyses of Psychoanalytic, Nondirective, and Adlerian Therapeutic Relationships," *Journal of Consulting Psychology,* 15, 1951, 32–38.

Ford, D. H., and Urban, H. B. *Systems of Psychotherapy*. New York: Wiley, 1963.

Frank, J. D. "The dynamics of the Psychotherapeutic Relationship," *Psychiat.*, 22, 1959, 17–39.

Ibid. Persuasion and Healing. Baltimore: Johns Hopkins Press, 1961.

Goldstein, A. P. *Therapist-Patient Expectancies in Psychotherapy*. New York: Macmillan, 1962.

Jourard, S. M. "On the Problem of Reinforcement by the Therapist of Healthy Behavior in the Patient," in Shaw, F. J. (ed.), *Behavioristic Approaches to Counseling and Psychotherapy*. Tuscaloosa, Ala.: University of Alabama Press, 1961.

Ibid. The Transparent Self. Princeton, N.J.: Van Nostrand, 1964.

Kelly, G. A. *The Psychology of Personal Constructs. (Vol. I: A Theory of Personality. Vol. II: Clinical Diagnosis and Psychotherapy)*. New York: Norton, 1955.

Krasner, L. "The Therapist as a Social Reinforcement Machine," in Strupp, H. H., and Lubersky, L. (eds.), *Research in Psychotherapy, Vol. II*. Washington: American Psychological Association, 1962.

Krasner, L., and Ullman, L. P. (eds.). *Research in Behavior Modification*. New York: Holt Rinehart and Winston, 1965.

Lindsley, O. "Free Operant Conditioning and Psychotherapy," in Masserman, J., and Moreno, J. L. (eds.), *Current Psychiatric Therapies*. New York: Grune and Stratton, 1963.

London, P. *The Modes and Morals of Psychotherapy*. New York: Holt, Rinehart and Winston, 1964.

May, R. "Contributions of Existential Psychotherapy," in May, R., Angel, E., and Ellenberger, H. F. (eds.), *Existence*. New York: Basic Books, 1958.

McNair, D. M., and Lorr, M. "An Analysis of Professed Psychotherapeutic Techniques," *Journal of Consulting Psychology*, 28, 1964, 265–71.

Mowrer, O. H. *The New Group Therapy*. Princeton, N.J.: Van Nostrand, 1964.

Murray, E. J. "Learning Theory and Psychotherapy: Biotropic Versus Sociotropic Approaches," *Journal of Counseling Psychology*, 10, 1963, 251–55.

Patterson, C. H. *Counseling and Psychotherapy: Theory and Practice*. New York: Harper and Row, 1959.

Ibid. Theories of Counseling and Psychotherapy. New York: Harper and Row.

Rogers, C. R. "The Necessary and Sufficient Conditions of Therapeutic Personality Change," *Journal of Consulting Psychology,* 21, 1957, 95–103.

Ibid. On Becoming a Person. Boston: Houghton Mifflin, 1961.

Ibid. "Divergent Trends," in May, R. (ed.), *Existential Psychology.* New York: Random House, 1961.

Ibid. "The Fully Functioning Person," *Psychotherapy: Theory, Research and Practice,* 1, 1963, 17–26.

Ibid. "Psychotherapy Today or Where Do We Go from Here?" *American Journal of Psychotherapy,* 17, 1963, 5–16.

Rosenthal, D., and Frank, J. D. "Psychotherapy and the Placebo Effect," *Psychology Bulletin,* 53, 1956, 294–302.

Salter, A. *Conditioned Reflex Therapy.* New York: Capricorn, 1961.

Schofield, W. *Psychotherapy: The Purchase of Friendship.* Englewood Cliffs, N.J.: Prentice-Hall, 1964.

Skinner, B. F. *Walden Two.* New York: Macmillan, 1948.

Ibid. "Reinforcement Today," *American Psychologist,* 1958, 14, 94–99.

Strupp, H. H. "An Objective Comparison of Rogerian and Psychoanalytic Techniques," *Journal of Consulting Psychology,* 19, 1955, 1–7.

Sundland, D. M., and Barker, E. N. "The Orientations of Psychotherapists," *Journal of Consulting Psychology,* 26, 1962, 201–12.

Truax, C. B. "Effective Ingredients in Psychotherapy: an Approach to Unraveling the Patient-Therapist Interaction," *Journal of Counseling Psychology,* 10, 1963, 256–64.

Truax, C. B., and Carkhuff, R. R. "The Old and the New: Theory and Research in Counseling and Psychotherapy," *Personnel and Guidance Journal,* 42, 1964, 860–66.

Ibid. "Client and Therapist Transparency in the Psychotherapeutic Encounter," *Journal of Counseling Psychology,* 12, 1965, 3–9.

Ullman, L. P., and Krasner, L. (eds.). *Case Studies in Behavior Modification.* New York: Holt, Rinehart and Winston, 1965.

Ungersma, A. J. *The Search for Meaning.* Philadelphia: Westminster Press 1961.

Wallach, M. S. and Strupp, H. H. "Dimensions of Psychotherapists' Activities," *Journal of Consulting Psychology,* 28, 1964, 120–25.

Wolpe, J. *Psychotherapy by Reciprocal Inhibition.* Stanford, Calif.: Stanford University Press, 1958.

PART V—PROFESSIONAL CONSIDERATIONS

American Psychological Association, Division of Counseling Psychology. *The Role of Psychology in the Preparation of Rehabilitation Counselors.* Washington, D.C.: American Psychological Association, 1963.

Anderson, R. P. "The Rehabilitation Counselor as Counselor," *Journal of Rehabilitation,* 24 (2), 1958, 4–5 and 18.

Arkansas Vocational Rehabilitation Service. *Vocational Rehabilitation: This Is One Way.* Little Rock: Arkansas Vocational Rehabilitation Service, 1961.

Balint, Michael and Enid. *Psychotherapeutic Techniques in Medicine,* Springfield, Ill.: Tavistock Publications, Chas. C Thomas, 1962.

Barber, B. "Some Problems in the Sociology of Professions," In K. S. Lynn (ed.), *The Professions in America,* pp. 15–34. Boston: Houghton, Mifflin, 1965.

Baumgarten, Franziska. "Examiner's Check List Adapted in Bingham," Walter Van Dyke, *Aptitudes and Aptitude Testing,* pp. 229–35. New York: Harper and Brothers, 1937.

Cantrell, D. "Training the Rehabilitation Counselor," *Personnel and Guidance Journal,* 36, 1958, 382–87.

Carr-Saunders, A. M., and Wilson, P. A. *The Professions,* Oxford: Clarendon Press, 1933.

Clements, S. W. "The Counselor As He Sees Himself," *Journal of Rehabilitation,* 23 (3), 1957, 6.

Gluck, Samuel, *et al.* "A Proposed Code of Ethics for Counselors," *Occupations,* 30, 1952, April, No. 7, 484–90.

Goode, William J. "Encroachment, Charlatanism and the Emerging Profession: Psychology, Sociology and Medicine," *American Sociological Review* 25, December, 1960, 902–14.

Granger, S. G. "Psychologists' Prestige Rankings of 20 Psychological Occupations, *Journal of Counseling Psychology,* 6, 1959, 183–88.

Greenwood, Ernest, "Attributes of a Profession," *Social Work* 2, July, 1957, 45–55.

Hall, J. H., and Warren, S. L. (eds.). *Rehabilitation Counselor Preparation.* Washington, D.C.: National Rehabilitation Association and National Vocational Guidance Association, 1956.

Hansen, D. A. "Functions and Effects of 'Sub-Professional' Personnel in Counseling," in J. F. McGowan (ed.), *Counselor De-*

velopment in American Society, pp. 211–33. Columbia, Mo.: University of Missouri, 1965.

Hughes, E. C. *Men and Their Work.* Glencoe, Ill.: The Free Press, 1958.

Jaques, M. E. *Critical Counseling Behavior in Rehabilitation Settings.* Iowa City, Iowa: University of Iowa, 1959.

Johnston, L. T. "The Counselor As He Really Is," *Journal of Rehabilitation,* 23 (3), 1957, 9–10.

Joint Liaison Committee of the Council of State Directors of Vocational Rehabilitation and the Rehabilitation Counselor Educators. *Studies in Rehabilitation Counselor Training: Agency-University Communication, Coordination and Cooperation in Rehabilitation Counselor Education.* Minneapolis: University of Minnesota, 1964.

Lofquist, L. H. "An Operational Definition of Rehabilitation Counseling," *Journal of Rehabilitation,* 25 (4), 1959, 7–9 and 24–25.

Martin, S. P. "The Role of the University in Professional Education," in Joint Liaison Committee of the Council of State Directors of Vocational Rehabilitation and the Rehabilitation Counselor Educators, *Studies in Rehabilitation Counsel Training: Agency-University Communication, Coordination, and Cooperation in Rehabilitation Counselor Education.* Minneapolis: University of Minnesota, 1964.

McGowan, J. F. "The Counselor As Others See Him," *Journal of Rehabilitation,* 23 (3), 1957, 7–8.

McGowan, J. F. (ed.). *Counselor Development in American Society.* Columbia, Mo.: University of Missouri, 1965.

Miller, L. A. "A Study of a Case-Review Criterion for Evaluating Rehabilitation Counselor Performance. Unpublished doctoral dissertation, University of Iowa, Iowa City, Iowa, 1963.

Miller, L. A., Muthard, J. E., and Barillas, M. G. "A Time Study of Vocational Rehabilitation Counselors," *Rehabilitation Counseling Bulletin,* 9, 1965, 53–60.

Muthard, J. E., and Miller, L. A. *The Criteria Problem in Rehabilitation Counseling.* Iowa City, Iowa: University of Iowa, 1966.

National Rehabilitation Association. "The Rehabilitation Counselor: What He Is and Does," *Journal of Rehabilitation,* 28, June No. 3, May-June 1962, 17.

National Rehabilitation Association. Symposium: "What Is the

Rehabilitation Counselor," *Journal of Rehabilitation,* 23, May-June, 1957, No. 3, 5–12.

Obermann, C. E. "The Professionalization of Rehabilitation Counseling," *National Rehabilitation Counseling Association Professional Bulletin,* 4, 1964, 1.

Office of Vocational Rehabilitation. "Utilization of Counselor's Services in State VR Agencies," in Part I, *Proceedings of the Ninth Annual Workshop on Guidance, Training, and Placement,* Rehabilitation Service Series No. 373. Washington, D.C.: Office of Vocational Rehabilitation, 1956.

Olshansky, Simon. "Why Some Counselors Won't Use Workshops—a Proposed Solution," *Journal of Rehabilitation,* 33, July-August, 1967, No. 4, 14–16.

Patterson, C. H. "Counselor or Coordinator?" *Journal of Rehabilitation,* 23 (3), 1957, 13–15.

Ibid. Counseling the Emotionally Disturbed. New York: Harper, 1958.

Ibid. "The Nature of Rehabilitation Counseling Curricula." Paper presented at the American Personnel and Guidance Association Convention, St. Louis, Missouri, 1958.

Porter, T. L., and Saxon, J. P. "Rehabilitation Counselor Qualifications, Salaries, and Benefits: 1965, *NRCA Professional Bulletin,* 6, 1966, 1–4.

Rusalem, H. "An Analysis of the Functions of State Vocational Rehabilitation Counselors with Implications for the Development of a Training Course at Teachers College." Unpublished doctoral dissertation, Columbia University, 1951.

Seidenfeld, M. S. "The Need-Oriented Profession of Rehabilitation Counseling," *Journal of Rehabilitation,* 28, July-August, 1962, No. 4, 11–13.

Smits, S. J. *Rehabilitation Counselor Recruitment Study: Final Report.* Washington, D.C.: National Rehabilitation Association, 1964.

Sussman, M. B., Haug, M. R., and Krupnick, G. A. "Professional Associations and Memberships in Rehabilitation Counseling," *Rehabilitation Literature,* 27, December, 1966, No. 12, 354–59.

Sussman, M. B. "Occupational Sociology and Rehabilitation," in *Sociological Theory, Research, and Rehabilitation.* Washington, D.C.: American Sociological Association, 1965a.

Sussman, M. B. (ed.), *Professional Associations and Memberships in Rehabilitation Counseling.* Working paper No. 2. Cleveland: Western Reserve University, 1965b.

Ibid. Professionalism and Rehabilitation Counseling: An Annotated Bibliography. Working paper No. 1. Cleveland: Western Reserve University, 1965c.

Sussman, M. B., and Haug, M. R. *The Practitioners: Rehabilitation Counselors in Three Work Settings.* Working paper No. 4. Cleveland: Western Reserve University, 1967.

Sussman, M. B., Haug, M. R., and Trela, J. E. *Profile of the 1965 Student Rehabilitation Counselor.* Working paper No. 3, Cleveland: Western Reserve University, 1966.

Truax, Charles B. "Effective Ingredients in Psychotherapy: An Approach to Unraveling the Patient-Therapist Interaction." Paper presented at American Personnel and Guidance Association Convention, April 11, 1963.

U.S. Dept. of Health, Education, and Welfare, Office of Vocational Rehabilitation, "Problems and Issues in Rehabilitation Counseling." Report of a Symposium, Annual Meeting American Psychological Association, Sept. 3, 1957, Rehabilitation Service Series No. 440.

Vocational Rehabilitation Administration. *Guidelines for Action: Increasing the Supply of Qualified Rehabilitation Counseling Personnel in State Vocational Rehabilitation Agencies.* Washington, D.C.: VRA, 1966.

Warren, S. L. "The Rehabilitation Counselor Today: What, Where, and Why," *Journal of Rehabilitation,* 25 (5), 1959, 709 and 13.

Whitehouse, F. A. "The Rehabilitation Counselor as a Professional," *Reach,* Vol. 6, No. 4, 5, 6, July-August 1958 through March-April 1959, N. Carolina Rehabilitation Service.

Ibid. "Profess and Profession," *Catholic Psychological Record,* Vol. 3, No. 2, 1965, 95–115.

Ibid. "Rehabilitation as a Concept in the Utilization of Human Resources," American Association of Medical Social Workers, Social Work Practice in Medical Care and Rehabilitation Services, in Monograph I, *The Evolving Concept of Rehabilitation,* pp. 17–37, Washington, D.C., 1955.

Ibid. "Teamwork as a Dynamic System," *Cleft Palate Journal,* Vol. 2, January, 1965, 16–27.

Ibid. "Rehabilitation and the Life Cycle." Presented at NRA Conference, Oklahoma City, Okla., Oct. 12, 1960. Shorter version in *Journal of Rehabilitation,* 27, Jan.-Feb. 1961, 30–32.

Ibid. "Humanitation II: Some Aspects of a Human Economy."

Presented as Dabelstein Memorial Lecture, National Rehabilitation Association Annual Meeting, October, 1966, Denver, Colorado. Shorter version, *Journal of Rehabilitation,* 33, Jan.-Feb., 1967, 20–24.

Ibid. "Client Evaluation in the Habilitation Process," *Journal of Rehabilitation,* Vol. 19, Nov.-Dec., 1953, No. 6, 4–5, 26, 28.

Ibid. "Vocational Training in a Rehabilitation Center, Part I, *Journal of Rehabilitation,* Vol. 17, No. 1, Jan.-Feb., 1951, 3–8.

Ibid., Part II, *Journal of Rehabilitation,* Vol. 17, No. 2, March-April, 1951, 19–23.

Whitehouse. "Communication: An Introduction to Some Basic Constructs," *Reach,* Vol. 11, No. 3, pp. 14–18, May-June, 1963. Shorter version of paper presented at NRA Convention, Oklahoma City, Okla., Oct. 12, 1960.

Ibid. "The Concept of Therapy: A Review of Some Essentials," *Rehabilitation Literature,* Vol. 28, August, 1967, No. 8, 238–47.

Ibid. "Teamwork as a Dynamic System," *Cleft Palate Journal,* Vol. 2, January, 1965, 16–27.

Ibid. "Teamwork as a Therapeutic Experience," Address at Institute for Medical Social Workers, Association of Rehabilitation Facilities of Upstate New York. Albany, New York, April 26, 1962, mimeo 25 pp.

Wrenn, C. G., and Darley, J. G. "An Appraisal of the Professional Status of Personnel Work," in E. G. Williamson (ed.), *Trends in Student Personnel Work,* pp. 264–87. Minneapolis: University of Minnesota Press, 1949.

INDEX